Girl in Flight

By Cat Buchanan

Woodbridge Publishers

276 5th Avenue Suite 704 #944

New York, NY 10001

Copyright © 2024 Cat Buchanan

ISBN (Paperback): 978-1-0685144-1-8

ISBN (Hardback): 978-1-0685144-2-5

ISBN (eBook): 978-1-0685144-0-1

All rights reserved

Cover Design by Woodbridge Publishers.

WOODBRIDGE
PUBLISHERS

For Sandy

PART 1
CLOUDS

CHAPTER 1

I'm five years old and traveling at an altitude of 35,000 feet. High above the clouds, I'm alone, but this isn't my first flight. That happened when I was three days old and ready for collection from the hospital because my parents regarded their private plane as an elegant way to bring home a new baby. I was born an orphan in Hollywood, and then, like any other unwanted script, I was adapted. My parents, George and Meyera Buchanan, had unlimited funds. Mom's first two words, "Charge and send," will have been my father's last. When his sperm and her egg refused to join in the act of conception, they opened their wallets, allowing the adoption to take its course.

The Los Angeles Times announcement of my parent's wedding read Manhattan Playboy Marries West Coast Socialite, which essentially says it all. They were a glamorous pair whose needs were met before they could identify them, and everything was theirs for the taking, occasionally punctuated by the pesky need to ask. Their blindingly bright future together began with a honeymoon that extended over six months when they set sail for Europe to collect a limited-edition Porsche direct from the factory in Germany. Driving according to the dictates of whim, they'd pull over for lunch in Austria and stay three weeks.

George and Meyera shared an insatiable appetite for luxury. Both were only children who were indulged to a spectacular, if not excruciating, degree and regarded fulfillment as a birthright. Each held on tight to the arrogant certainty that, simply by continuing to exist, everything would flow in their direction *ad infinitum*. The six-foot-five-and-a-half-inch tall husband adorned by his chic five-foot-eight-inch elegant wife were perfectly matched and once hitched, in what the society pages called the Wedding of the Decade, they gorged themselves on a dedicated diet of obscenely expensive items. Their California home featured a sparkling swimming pool and freshly renovated garage to accommodate the Aston Martin and new Gull Wing Mercedes, which was the first of five ordered for export to America. Not just fun, these fast-moving machines were considered necessary. How else to hit ski lifts in the morning and arrive down to the desert in time for cocktails? When parked outside the Racquet Club of Palm Springs, their Merc caught the attention of television legend Desi Arnez, who wasn't just admiring it but paying his respects.

As a young bride, Meyera was unaccustomed to mundane tasks and her first forays in the kitchen produced dubious meals but delicious edicts such as 'Never fry bacon in the nude.' A comprehensive collection of cookbooks enabled her to eventually gain a reputation for fabulous food, and no matter how many casual drop-ins they had for dinner, her culinary creations accommodated any number of hungry guests. Putting on a few unwanted pounds, they kept calories under control by switching from three olive vodka martinis to gin Gibson's with one pearl onion, which did the trick. Perusing the preface in her copy of Escoffier's *Ma Cuisine*, Meyera discovered she'd been preparing meals for eight to ten. Errors of this nature were a leg-up compared with the *tabula rasa* she started with, and when asked to help prepare a turkey for the oven, she turned the bird, whispering, "It's not nearly as hot in there as you think."

Elite cars served as a gateway to powerboats, and they raced at Lake Tahoe, Marina Del Ray, and Lake Arrowhead. Water-skiing to Catalina Island and back, they were dubbed the Smart Set by journalists, but Fast Set describes their pursuit of financially fueled fun. My parents and their privileged pals appeared regularly in social and sports columns. Photographers were dispatched to chronicle and applaud their every move. If Meyera sneezed on Friday morning, the evening headline read *Gesundheit.*

Whether celebrating the end of another rigorous week traversing time zones or toasting the acquisition of a new toy, the press was never far away. Rather than court attention, they tolerated reports of their antics at the Stork Club, Brown Derby, and Perino's. This crowd dressed each night for dinner and wore only silk to bed. They danced at El Morocco and greeted most days with a Bloody Mary. Jewelry was purchased at Tiffany & Co., and social discourse was conducted in accordance with the rules of Emily Post's *Etiquette,* whose strictures were observed as sanctified religious texts.

Speed continued to gain momentum when they purchased a Jaguar XK120 to race at Torrey Pines, Stockton, and Santa Clara. British racing driver, Stirling Moss, was a regular on the scene, and when he took one look at the new Jag, he said, "It's an attractive alternative to the purchase of a Beverly Hills bungalow."

The only time my parents slowed down was when driving for Ford in the Mobilgas Economy Run, testing fuel efficiency during long-distance driving in real weather and road conditions. Meyera was part of a two-woman team, among the first allowed to participate in the 1950s, competing against General Motors, Chrysler, and other big makes. The aim was to maximize gas mileage, and Meyera kept their speed low while driving in accordance with her navigators' instructions for over twenty-seven hours straight.

Stimulants both assisted and ended my parents' annual Economy Run. Meyera saw a phantom hay wagon crossing the lane, which scared her enough to call it quits, and George complained about the short temper flares accompanying the journey's end. When handing in their driving gloves, George observed, "Amphetamine, not Ampheta-nice. As in name, as in impact."

George and Meyera based their romance on mutual attraction, unbridled fun, and reflected approval. They traveled more, lived more, laughed more, and loved more than ten times ten others put together. After exploring extravagance to exhaustion, they bought accessories for their accessories and treated George's Breitling watch to something aerodynamic with the purchase of his and hers private planes.

While waiting for clearance to takeoff, Meyera sat in the cockpit (a term she felt should be revisited) and overheard the air traffic controller say, "That's the first time I've seen a broad set off shopping in her own Cessna."

Qualifying for the pilot's license proved a challenging afterthought. The long hours of study and in-flight training required a focus unfamiliar to my parents. Meyera suffered from dyslexia long before this cognitive disorder was identified, and she was ashamed of her inability to read. Each day before class, she worked with a friend, trying to memorize paragraphs that students might be called upon to read aloud so that she could mimic the act of reading.

George also lacked familiarity with academic study of any notable nature, and attending a lesser-known college in a lesser-known flyover state was the extent to which he'd advanced the ranks of higher learning. Fortunately, no formal training or permit is required for a baby.

Recreational lovemaking at Browns in London, Georges V in Paris, and Villa d'Este on the Italian Rivera failed to achieve pregnancy. So much for Europe. Increased copulation at The Pierre in Manhattan, Moana Hotel in Honolulu, and Beverly Hills Hotel delivered the same disappointment domestically. They tried to conceive in Canada and shagged like rabbits in Montreal. They tried again in Mexico, and rather than fish for blue marlin, they focused on fornication but had only a topped-up tan to show. At least Mexico provided George with an opportunity to test his prescription snorkeling and diving mask, which were rare items at the time.

Having contracted German measles when he was a boy ended any claim he'd have to twenty-twenty vision, and his pale-blue eyes were kept behind thick glasses forming a border on his classically handsome face. Far-flung exotic venues were not assisting the cause. They could lead his sperm to her ovum, but not make it sink.

They redoubled their efforts with the work of strategic home sex and ovulation charts joined grocery lists posted on the refrigerator door. These critical yet frustratingly few days a month were highlighted in red pen precedence over the crowded calendar dates earmarked for social events.

When asking the gods to deliver a baby for christening, they christened every room in the house, including the garage. On one occasion, they briefly excused themselves as dinner party hosts to nip upstairs and do the deed as swiftly and quietly as possible before rejoining guests with a conspiratorial smirk.

First, negotiating and then remonstrating with the universe achieved nothing. Month after month, the crimson messenger arrived, and they'd look at each other in dismay, feeling brokenhearted by the inconceivable evidence of their inability to conceive. Meeting friends for lunch at Bullocks Wilshire became off-limits for Meyera. The infant department was situated next to the restaurant's entrance, and one glance at the baby range would leave her dissolved in a puddle of tears. She forgot fine dining and lived without fashion models parading like panthers around the room. Her attendance at christenings, infant showers, and children's birthday parties was unthinkable when feeling so low that being boxed in represented an upgrade.

Meyera managed to keep up appearances and never left home unless smartly put together. Lingerie was a particular favorite, and she enjoyed the fact that anything lacy left visible on George's side of the bed irritated her mother-in-law to no end when visiting. George's large-scale size required his wardrobe to be made to measure, and fabric samples regularly arrived for tailored suits created in Saville Row.

From the age of twelve, his feet were encased in Church's shoes so personally crafted it takes a team of artisans fifty-eight days to create a single pair. Shirts, pajamas, and handkerchiefs (also handmade) featured his family crest gracing them all. Matters of interior design required special attention. Most emporiums didn't stock *Land of the Giants* size furniture, so they turned to custom-crafted instead.

First up for commission was a nine-foot-long green couch with room for George to stretch out with his feet or head on Meyera's lap. Master and guest beds were handmade to generous proportions so that, in the event of an argument or insomnia, a good night's rest was not lost for lack of sleeping space or comfort. Having given so much care to items they'd rest on, they took their eye off the ball when chandeliers from Venice arrived. Installation was left to their team of average height craftsmen whose work was first seen, and then felt when the glass cascade from Murano tackled George with sharp shards each time he passed underneath. Yesterday's spending can't satisfy today's whim, and once the basics were in place, they shopped for frivolous items they considered indispensable.

Content to capture family events with Kodak's 16mm camera, the cinema room needed something spectacular, and they opted for a 35mm projection on the basis there wouldn't be any better at the homes of most studio heads. An ice cream parlor stocked with Wil Wright's pistachio and banana flavors provided the finishing touch, along with the emporium's equally iconic macaroons bearing the slogan *It's Heavenly!*

Their camera collection rivaled most retail specialists,' featuring Leica, Nikon, Pentax, Mamiya Sekor, and George's favorite Swedish model, Hasselblad, which he'd been using long before NASA took their lenses into Space. Photography was a fabulous hobby until the caustic chemical smell caused them to shut down the darkroom, so they turned their attention toward the outdoor area.

George had been fascinated with radios ever since he was a boy, and the 200-foot-high antenna tower he'd always dreamed of was finally in place. This installation was one of the few pleasures he'd had to wait for, and it provided considerable gratification. A lavish kennel built for George's dog Hako included grooming, run, sun and shade areas, but architectural plans were redrawn when George said, "Shouldn't Hako have a bachelor pad section where he'd feel comfortable entertaining females at night?"

Any Doberman pinscher belonging to my father could rely upon indulgence, but as man's best friend, he wasn't entirely on board with the recently introduced matrimonial, community living, and sharing of affection regime. Hako would hackle whenever George put his arm around Meyera until she began to feed him, after which a miniature pinscher purchased from a breeder in Germany arrived. My parents would promenade with Hako on the leash held by George, and Meyera sporting her tiny bonsai version. They cut a dashing image on Rodeo and Beverly Drive where Meyera's naturally auburn hair, slender shape, and long legs were able to keep pace with my father's military gate, a lengthy stride I struggled to follow as a child when George and I strode Manhattan streets with him holding my hand.

Filling the house with books was a fun, if admittedly fast, joint venture. Meyera's taste included the classics, which George thought were best bought by the yard. They purchased a 54-volume *Great Books of the Western World* collection produced by one publisher in uniform size, and although you can't judge a book by its cover, when taken away, you miss it.

Standardization was acceptable to my parents so long as it was the highest standard, and they gave each other luggage as a wedding gift. A full set of Louis Vuitton for Mom, and Dad had Hermes. Meyera's mother disapproved and couldn't understand why so much money had been squandered on suitcases. Why would they, or indeed anyone, want to spend that much to impress a bell boy?

Entitlement often becomes a self-fulfilling prophecy, but not this time for George and Meyera, when disappointment, rather than a baby, made three. One ectopic pregnancy, two infertility teams, three exploratory surgeries, four false hopes, and five years of copulation later, they decided to adopt.

The criterion used by the Department of Social Services to determine suitability wasn't stringent, and the definition of best interests was largely banking-based. For George and Meyera, this bar was but a three-inch *cavaletti*. While I floated in the womb, submerged between conception and birth, my future placement was prepared above ground when requisite documents rattled to completion. Three days after my arrival, I was officially installed in the custody of my new mom and dad. We taxied down the runway for takeoff and headed home.

CHAPTER 2

When those blinded by avarice toss integrity to the wind, it puts a strain on a marriage. It did when bills incurred brokering my placement in the Buchanan line arrived soon after I appeared. George surprised Meyera by asking if she would pick up the tab because a speedboat for sale in San Diego Harbor caught his eye, and rather than risk someone else buying it, he did, which caused a minor cash flow issue amounting to momentary inconvenience. Everyone knew better than to question the endless line of credit at their disposal. Both George and Meyera made welcome customers, but his retail high met a reality low when Meyera shot him a low-down look.

"Come on honey, don't be disapproving," George said. "Anyone remotely possessed of taste wouldn't dare miss out on a knockout like this."

Meyera understood the attraction of a shiny object, but the timing of this extravagant purchase struck her as a bit odd. Neither had yet to discover that selfish actions rarely achieve the desired result, but she allowed George to continue with his justification.

"Anyway, it's done, and I own it," George said. "Both of us, I mean, so to hell with depreciation and inevitable write-down. The main thing is to go for gorgeous, as we've done with getting the baby. I'm a little short on immediate funds and would appreciate it if you'd take care of these bills, but I'll pick up the next set of tabs."

Meyera thought for a second or two. The idea of putting someone before her own needs was a foreign concept that hadn't appeared on the radar before. She was puzzled by his request and vaguely concerned for the future.

"Aren't we going to provide even a pretense of parental responsibility?" Meyera asked. "Set aside the toys and focus on the real live human entrusted to us?"

To her mind, George's budgetary question indicated deeper solipsism. Without either of them realizing it, this was a defining moment in their marriage, foreshadowing events to come, occasioned by an ill-conceived favor concerning comparative access to wealth. This tiny crevasse formed a small schism into which minor infractions fell, accumulating over time into a Mount Fuji of felonies.

Funding for all aspects of my adoption wouldn't be problematic. Access to payment wasn't just on tap. It flowed with the ferocity of Niagara Falls. Thankfully, Meyera was a strong swimmer, or she'd have drowned in the rushing rapids of torrential liquidity generated by her rainmaker father, Dr. Joe Zeiler. He was a Beverly Hills surgeon and the type of daddy who regarded his daughter as the center of the universe. His thriving practice created vast income, and a philanthropic streak enabled rich patients to subsidize those less fortunate, whether knowingly or not. To colleagues, patients, and friends, he was affectionately known as Dr. Joe. His Wilshire Boulevard medical office catered to the elite and was favored by politicians, journalists, and the occasional gangster.

Working late one night, his office light was on and visible to two men driving furiously toward the hospital. Dr. Joe didn't usually allow walk-ins, but on this occasion, he made an exception, and attended to an injury legally required to be reported. Inside the confidential confines of his consulting room, Dr. Joe administered medical attention in the absence of administrative action or alert, and a new demographic was added to the patient roster. Although he rarely rendered such services, Dr. Joe regularly received fully comped trips to Las Vegas, where Meyera would sit next to him at a gambling table secluded in a private room at the back.

"Hey Meyera," her father's high-stakes poker partner would say. "Skip to the kiosk and buy me a pack of gum, will you?"

In Vegas, the most mundane request can be made more interesting if sweetened with fifty-dollar bills and the injunction, "Be sure you keep the change."

One such gesture would spark similar requests and spread like wildfire, igniting interest from other players in a fresh blaze of competition.

"Yeah, I'd like a stick of gum, come to think of it," said another card hand. "Here's a couple hundred bucks to take with you and keep my change too."

Meyera wasn't old enough to gamble, but she didn't need to be when inundated with dollars and demands for toothpicks, hair combs or betting forms. The multitude of items grew more eccentric as the cast of poker players vied to outdo each other.

Vegas was where Dr. Joe took soon-to-be son-in-law George, and his entire entourage on a bachelor bash, chartering a private plane to transport their party of twenty-five to hedonism central. They returned worse for wear but in time for the wedding, and remained tight-lipped, unwilling to divulge details about George's last night of freedom.

My parents didn't go to Vegas all that often after my father was targeted and reverse-heckled by stand-up comedian Don Rickles during a dinner show. George and Meyera were seated next to the stage, and while they found Rickles funny, their Chateaubriand was getting cold. They joined in the laughter for the first barb or two lobbed in their direction and managed to smile at three jokes that followed, also at their expense. George finally grew angry and stood up, coming eye to eye to with Don Rickles, who ran to the back of the stage saying, "Is this guy on stilts or what?"

Dr. Joe was a short, rotund man with a larger-than-life personality. An exacting workaholic, he possessed equal measures of compassion and temper while always seen sporting an unlit cigar. Joe was bald, wore wire-rimmed glasses, and had a round face reminiscent of Jackie Gleason's smiling moon image from 1950s series *The Honeymooners*. He eschewed studios and would heal a gangster before having anything to do with Hollywood, which he considered unseemly.

Several surgeries a day, office consultations, and house calls kept him at the coalface of the profession. He wasn't at home all that often, but when he was, it became his show.

Meyera made an attentive audience, and, in return, Joe adored his daughter while deploying her as a weapon in that ancient war waged between husband and wife. Meyera's mother, Elsie Hicks, was glamorous but grounded despite a *penchant* for hats, furs, and gloves. She had cornflower-blue eyes, a contagious smile and an uninhibited, if not dirty, laugh.

Although athletic and social, she smoked like a chimney and drank like a fish, allowing her to remain balanced between the contradictions in her character. She was firmly of the view that spirits should be served neat and, when offered ice, politely abstained, claiming it would rust her stomach. Her long blonde hair was worn in a French twist with a slight *bouffant* on top, making her a trophy to look at while being comfortable to be with. Elsie represented the basic nightmare that plagued the mamas of good Jewish boys ever since the first one saw a *shiksa*.

Introduced by a mutual friend, Elsie, and Joe first laid eyes on each other at the Queen of Angels Hospital. He had completed an operation and stepped out wearing a smock covered in off-putting entrails, while she'd been at the beach narrowly escaping arrest for indecent exposure, having returned to shore not wearing, but carrying, her swimming tights which she'd stuffed full of mussels.

Elsie was adept at talking her way out of, or into, whatever trouble she created, but Joe took one look at her and seized the initiative, suggesting a date while proffering his fresh-from-surgery hand. Elsie declined the flesh-on-flesh press but, being age thirty, thought it prudent to consider a sensible future and agreed to meet again.

Years later, I'd gather with my girlfriends to hear my grandmother's astonishingly accurate advice. She specialized in guidance regarding romance, relationships, and love, both requited as well as its tragic opposite. We felt privileged to have these sessions and treated them as would graduate students attending a masterclass. Each time her prognostications proved right (which was all the time), we became convinced there really was something to be said for experience. She'd laugh at us and, through a thick waft of smoke, ask, "Did you think sex was invented in 1960?"

Who needs Moses on Mt. Sinai when you've got Calchas in the patio? She was fond of juxtaposing present freedom with future planning, and not at all shy about expressing her views, saying, "Why don't you girls do as I did and run a little wild while having fun? Farther on down the road, when it's time to think about security, let your head rule your heart and not the other way around. Trouble with you girls is you love to be in love."

We adored her straightforward, no-nonsense style, reducing our complicated entanglements to a bouillon cube of strategic wisdom. Infidelity occupied the top spot in our crisis hit parade, and her advice was consistent when reminding us that, "Like it or not, an erect penis has no conscience. First time, shame on him, and second time, shame on you. His fault for cheating, and yours should you take him back."

Empathetic to a point, she had little tolerance for misguided sentimentality, including dramatic laments from my friends such as, "He said sleeping with someone else meant nothing."

Comments such as those attracted her reply, "We are not talking about what it meant to him. We're discussing what it meant to you."

Certain phrases such as, "I like his style" or "He knows how to live" were her way of indicating approval and, to determine a potential flame's suitability, she'd ask if he's polite, interested, and generous. After that, the criteria increased exponentially, leading to the slaying of a dragon before laying down his life at your feet.

This was the period separating recreational fun from commitment, where most of our war stories are created when we transgress and return to boundaries still in formation. Not opposed to sex but unwilling to outright condone it, she'd encourage us elliptically by saying, "More concerns are caused by inertia than error, and omission rather than commission creates regrets."

Other injunctions were issued more directly, the strictest of which formed a golden trilogy: never be photographed holding a drink, never be photographed in the nude, and never leave for a date without having mad money to hand. Her definition of mad money wasn't about going crazy and buying everyone drinks, but referred to the sum tucked in your purse or bra that made it possible to get home via taxi should Mr. Right become Mr. Wrong.

The lady meant business when it came to her 'girls,' no two ways about it. She was aware of human nature, behavior, and all the complexities that go with it. Validating, supportive, and frank was how she dealt with us, and, in return, we lashed her as a figurehead to the prow of our generations' ship. No matter how rough or smooth the waters, she'd remain strong, confident, and invincible, which were all the things she wanted us to be. When I mentioned how popular she was with my friends, she laughed and said that was because I regarded her as okay, but okay doesn't deliver scores of young women lining up to avail themselves of her advice.

Joe and Elsie had fun but triangulated after Meyera was born, eclipsing the fracas of married life into the dense mist of raising a child. This was where Meyera came in strong, which was ironic considering how predominantly weak she was, but a role well-cast can be a role well-played. Elsie tried to raise her daughter with a modicum of restraint but met her husband's resistance every time. As Elsie said of her own experience growing up, "We didn't have much money, but we were never poor."

This informed my grandmother's attitude toward managing finances, and she enjoyed the good life tempered by reason. Squandering for the sake of it and indulging in needless waste were not behaviors she approved of. Meyera's favorite 1930s radio program, *The Shadow,* was sponsored by Silk Spanish Rice, which was a terrible-tasting tinned substance whose manufacturers must have known of its intrinsically limited appeal. To boost sales, a coupon competition was created for weekly promotion on the radio, and the first prize was a pony.

Elsie allowed Meyera as many entries as she wanted, conditional upon her consuming the product. Holding her nose while thinking about that adorable animal, Meyera ate twenty-two cans in total. Orson Welles announced the winners, and ratings soared that day when children with big hopes and small, sweaty hands adjusted radio dials coast-to-coast. Parents were also dubious because the ramifications would be challenging, win or lose, but Meyera and Elsie held their breath when waiting to hear which contestant received first prize. That much coveted pony was awarded to a girl in the Midwest, but Meyera won second prize, which was a case of Silk Spanish Rice.

After that disappointment, Elsie's mention of budgets attracted laughter rather than attention, and Joe went behind his wife's back, secretly opening charge accounts in Meyera's name. Ensuring all bills were sent to his office, he bragged about his daughter's retail activity, saying it was so vigorous a van rather than a postman was required to deliver the statements.

Joe, Elsie, and Meyera lived at 122 Fremont Place in a large home requiring staff, including a live-in gourmet chef called Marvin. He had been wooed away from his previous employment with actress June Allyson and remained with the Zeiler family for over a decade, organizing the spectacular charity and political events they hosted. Planning menus, preparing sumptuous meals, and overseeing swarms of serving teams wasn't a problem, but should someone wander unannounced into his kitchen, they'd be served and dismissed in moments.

He was tall, lanky, and able to reach over guests to place or remove plates without anyone noticing. Had he turned his talents toward dance rather than cooking, Alvin Ailey would've snapped him up. Marvin was from the South, with a secret signature recipe for cornbread no mortal could resist, and all his culinary creations were easy to identify.

When Meyera invited a *beau* over for dinner, claiming she made the meal herself, the ruse was vaguely sustainable until dessert. No one other than Marvin could make such a splendid lemon meringue pie. Also adept at silent symbolic forms of protest when displeased with Elsie, he'd paint his long fingernails purple before serving a formal dinner and flamboyantly flaunt them as a way of expressing irritation.

Exposing his perfectly manicured hands to harmful housework was out of the question. Consequently, Marvin can be credited with instigating Elsie's long-standing association with the Catholic Church in Santa Monica, which held a fundraising event requiring as much matching silver as Elsie could lay her hands on to lend. Her altruistic act created a great deal of enthusiasm, and I praised my grandmother's generosity, but she confessed that the favor was going the other way, right back to us. Her Kirk Repousse pattern was notoriously ornate and required Herculean effort to maintain, but as she'd observed over the course of decades, "When really fine attention to detail is needed, no one polishes silver better than Catholic nuns."

Elsie's involvement with correct causes was sincere, if somewhat socially driven, and during the Second World War, she came to the aid of her country by mixing martinis for friends and rolling bandages. She served on the board of numerous medically-related charities and organized many ladies' auxiliary lunches. Returning home unexpectedly early from one such occasion, she surprised Marvin, who was busy but not in the kitchen.

Discovering him in her dressing room was startling. Watching as he preened in front of the three-sided mirror wearing one of her formal gowns was admittedly more of a shock, causing an awkward moment all around. This constituted a crime against couture, and no amount of cornbread could cure it, despite Joe and Meyera's efforts to calm her down. They employed rational arguments, emotive pleas, and begged for clemency, but their words fell on deaf ears. Elsie's soft side was tempered by the strict.

For a brief time, they lived without Marvin's miracles performed in the kitchen and grew irritable until a replacement was found. Reportage helped distract them, and Joe enjoyed reading reviews of their lavish parties in the social column before turning to the sports pages to find Meyera's image at horse shows. A new cook was soon sourced who prepared adequate meals but became unfulfilled in her role. She was a young woman motivated by conscience rather than money, who intended to provide for those unable to do so for themselves.

While the Zeiler family sort of fit the bill, it wasn't what she had in mind. Elsie was empathetic and, on her departure, presented her with a bottle of L' Heure Bleue, which they both adored. A husband-and-wife team filled the breach, grateful for the work and residential quarters available. As recent refugees from Europe, they were relieved to be safe but remained worried beyond measure. The wife's recipes stretched from Austria to their plates each day, and her large German husband was able to act as Joe's *chauffeur* and bodyguard when making house calls late at night. They'd huddle in the kitchen listening to German language radio reports, trying to decipher from foreign broadcasts a more precise sense of events far from America's border. In a time of rationing and austerity, Elsie hosted events while America called it 'the glorious war.'

After Elsie's beloved brother Donny was killed in a Pensacola naval aircraft training accident, she retired to bed and stayed there a long time. It became a ritual she observed on the anniversary of Donny's death, and well into my adult years, she would say, "Leave me to my memories. I need a little time alone right now. Time that has nothing to do with you but everything to do with me. Loss hurts, and when confronted with death, you've got to walk straight through the middle. Skirting around the perimeter won't do any good."

It wasn't hard to imagine what she felt. Her photograph albums contained storytelling images in glossy black-and-white featuring the family at Christmas gathered around a grand piano, with Elsie playing songs for Donny and his friends. Handsome young men in uniform were in various stages of relaxation, singing, smiling and confident, with a twenty-foot fully decorated noble fir tree in the background. Glasses were full, empty, and full again as the photos document their joyous momentum until that dreadful time of Donny's demise.

Settling into bed, my grandmother said, "I'm better with it than I used to be... not that you get used to something like this. It's a case of learning to live without someone you love. I need to take a day and remember in my own quiet way."

Bed served as Elsie's sanctuary when Joe was in a snit and dishing out sanctions, greeting her in silence for periods extending from a week to a month. Fastidious in his attention to detail, these punitive measures were marked each day on the kitchen calendar, but Elsie trumped his silence with sleep — electing to rise at a civilized hour allowed her to enjoy breakfast in peace. Conversational embargos were frequently cut short when life's events proved too enjoyable to savor alone, and Elsie arranged these circumstances at her convenience.

An alumnus of USC Medical School, Joe's distinguished status was a contrast to his more fanciful trickster side with buzzers, whoopie cushions, and binoculars lined with boot polish never in short supply. A long-standing patient turned up early for a blood test and, while reading the paper, tipped the chair back, fracturing his arm.

"Wrong move but right place," said Dr. Joe before adding. "Would you care for a stick of gum?"

"No thanks," the patient replied. "There is only one left in the pack, and last time, it was triggered with a spring that smacked my hand. I also don't want to have my photo taken with that camera because I want to avoid being squired with water again."

Joe and Elsie lived with all the trappings of success, but despite such ferocious advantage, Meyera felt stigmatized. Born to a Gentile mother and Jewish father cast her as a half-breed, acknowledged by both camps yet accepted by neither. Denied admission to the California and Jonathan Club, waspy watering holes on both coasts were off-limits due to her Jewish parentage, and she experienced the same social snubbing by Hillcrest, where the chosen people prefer to keep their rosters pure.

I encountered this absurd divide when boasting about my grandfather's achievements, which caused George to clench his jaw and say, "Never ever mention anything to do with Judaism, casually or otherwise. Is that clear?"

His intention to eradicate Mom's heritage by amending her name from Meyera to Myra was insulting, but prior to that, she grew up in the press who used the original spelling. When confronted with a child with little or no proclivity for academic achievement, Elsie sought to provide a sense of self-esteem from other sources, hoping that the appearance of confidence would allow the real deal to follow.

The first of Meyera's three horses was a gift from one of Dr. Joe's patients, which kicked into high gear media attention featuring her as an equestrian, a debutante and, finally, a wife. Meyera felt this wasn't deserved and that she was, in truth, no more than a media falsification. When required to attend a party, she considered wearing the most expensive dress and jewelry in the room to be her only contribution.

Dr. Joe's stature in the community, combined with Meyera's early stature height, enabled her access to a driver's license at age fifteen. A navy-blue convertible fitted with magic plates allowed her to ignore gas rationing while driving at breakneck speed without incurring tickets. Wanting to do her part in the war effort, she dressed her pug dog Lynn in a sailor suit and placed him prominently in view in the passenger seat. Riding around town in naval dress uniform, Lynn became something of a sensation.

To celebrate Meyera's sixteenth birthday, a Hawaiian luau was held at their Freemont Place home, where a special pit was constructed to roast a suckling pig. Crane printed invitations were limited to 150 of their closest friends, and Lynn was booked into a luxury kennel for the night. Coconut daiquiris and mai tais were downed with alacrity, while hired hula girls entertained celebrants dancing to a live band. Limbo was played long into the night, and everything was a success, except for the themed treat, which rotated with an apple in its mouth untouched all evening.

Elsie couldn't understand her guests' reluctance. The empty platters of spicy crab legs, lomilomi salmon and bacon-wrapped scallops proved it wasn't a lack of appetite. After everyone left, she noticed the resemblance between the rotisserie roasted pig and Meyera's pet pug, which explained why people repeatedly asked in hushed tones, "Where's Lynn?"

Joe wore a flower lei atop his three-piece suit, watch fob and ever-present unlit cigar. Whether vacationing at Waikiki Beach, sitting astride a camel in Cairo or setting off for another day's work, his attire was consistent to the core. At Christmas, he received hand-rolled Cuban contraband, and rather than measure Meyera's height with a mark on the kitchen door, they charted her growth by the number of cigar boxes in the annual gift stack instead.

Making light of her long, skinny legs, Joe would say, "Meyera, lend me one of your socks, will you? I can't find the top of my fountain pen."

Joe spoiled Meyera while basking in reflected glory, more commonly observed at the racetrack owner's enclosure. She was raised for show, celebrated when on display, and expected to behave appropriately at all times. Embracing all that was glamorous, she would lift the hat from her father's bald head, depositing a kiss in Revlon's Fire & Ice lipstick, which tickled him pink.

Form over substance and appearance over content was the order of the day, but when adoration meets hero worship, it becomes a powerful exchange, especially when made between father and daughter. My grandmother found this amusing, but even more so after she and Joe obtained a formal legal separation. Irreconcilable differences served to bring them close again, and once the financial terms were in place, they had a significantly enhanced time together. Fair and square was how Elsie described the settlement, and once in place, she was ready to regain some fun. Who better to achieve this with than her husband?

She laughed about their reconciliation in the waiting room before progressing to the final dissolution of the marriage. They exchanged smiles, feeling awkward until Joe took his customary lead, saying, "Elsie, let's get out of here. With all the money and property divvied up, I think we've done enough. Why don't we have a nice lunch instead?"

It must've been a marvelous meal. Rather than return to the law office, they ventured to Egypt and Asia instead. They never divorced and enjoyed companionable circumstances until the day before my first birthday. On that day, Dr. Joe did the unthinkable while running to reach a ringing telephone. He had a cardiac arrest, and moments later, he died.

CHAPTER 3

Meyera was devastated by the loss of her father and looked to George, hoping he'd fill the void by expanding his remit from life partner to daddy substitute. With only one year of parenthood under their belt, she suggested they try living without family fiscal support and cut up the charge cards while slowing down the allowance.

Her bizarre concept was met with scandalized astonishment, and George refused to sever his financial umbilical cord made of reinforced steel, linking his Aunt Louise and her titan line of credit from Manhattan to his own. The glue of swift-paced consumerism, which initially attracted my parents, was proving insufficient to bond them together. Especially now that Meyera had lost her father and was cast adrift from former fast flows of money.

She became increasingly critical of George, projecting his shortcomings against a distorted screen of loss and, rather than come to terms with the death of her father, turned on her husband, concluding that she didn't care for him in any room she could think of. He was helpless in the kitchen, inconsiderate in bed, flirtatious in the living room, and secretive in the study.

When in transit from one location to the next, he often complained, but whatever fresh criticism he made, she let turn stale. This worked relatively well at home but less so in polite company, when she'd wince while George expressed viewpoints from the far right of Mussolini.

My father's myopia made it difficult for him to discern a trespassing sign, be it social or otherwise. Male invincibility meant freedom, and confident he'd never answer a charge of overstepping the bounds my father didn't stand on ceremony, but used it as a trampoline. Not entirely unexpected from a man who'd never met an unfavorable consequence. He'd yet to shake hands with anything that failed to please him.

Contributing only hot air and noise to a world willing to spin solely at his disposal, Meyera felt he was of little intrinsic worth and required a lot of trouble to maintain. With Dr. Joe consigned to *absentia*, George had free rein to criticize Meyera. The father-in-law figure, whom he both respected and feared, was gone forever. No more home turf advantage for Meyera, and as a result, George turned caustic.

They indulged in the relatively new vogue of couples' counseling and briefly enjoyed the process of working together, mostly confined to decisions concerning what to wear for each session. Fritz Perls had recently hit Los Angeles after he'd been the toast of the town in Manhattan, where his *Gestalt* therapy was received with resounding success. Hollywood acted in concert, as reflected in Hitchcock's *Spellbound*, *Vertigo* and *Psycho*.

Alfred and Fritz weren't the only ones on the bandwagon. *Suddenly, Last Summer* was swiftly adapted by Gore Vidal for director Joseph Mankiewicz. This chilling tale by Tennessee Williams enhanced the public's appetite for all things hidden in the psyche, ably assisted by Montgomery Clift and Katharine Hepburn, who battle over lobotomizing Elizabeth Taylor. Audiences were willing to forgive gruesome themes if only to hear the distinctive way Katharine Hepburn pronounced new vocabulary words such as *Dementia praecox*.

It was a bold and burgeoning time for psychotherapy with no shortage of choices, but despite this wide panoply, neither George nor Meyera cared to identify the particular flag attached to their therapist's consulting room door. Such was the power of a referral provided by trusted friends over dinner at Chasen's. We'll never know which theory their therapist subscribed to, only that they signed up for a course of twelve sessions and, after the first four, they decided to stop.

One of the few things they agreed upon was that, in their case, a problem shared was a problem doubled. Mystery helped create their relationship, while honesty destroyed it. The idea of listening to each other and taking responsibility for their own actions seemed like a good idea, but acting jointly rather than through unilateral will was another matter that didn't appeal to either of them, even on paper.

The sessions did provide clarity, and Meyera described living with George as analogous to Listerine mouthwash, hated but tolerated daily. Dropped socks, lowered expectations, and diminished hope for the future formed her perspective on the marriage. She felt that the house plants tried harder than her husband to please her, particularly the orchids, accustomed as they are to thriving on neglect. George pointed toward more substantive issues of selfishness and resentment, which the therapist mentioned might be manifest on both sides.

To his list of grievances, redundancy was added when made to feel marginalized and then expected to become a substitute for Meyera's father. Finding this impossible, he effectively felt castrated, which was something he wouldn't do to a dog. In matters of finding fault, they each pointed to the other for blame.

"We seem to have developed a different definition," George said.

"Of what?" the therapist asked.

"Basically, everything," Meyera explained.

All indications pointed toward the same exit sign, and they hit the turnoff early, deciding to avoid the consulting room while reuniting over what to send as a tasteful gift. The question of crystal, silver or china was not the type of question they wanted to raise with consciousness-raising friends at Scandia, and a luxury hamper was dispatched along with a check for the remaining eight unattended sessions. George grimaced at the new tie he'd bought to wear during their next appointment and threw it in the trash.

"Why jettison a perfectly fine tie?" Meyera asked.

"Who'd want a souvenir from this sojourn to suffering?" George said.

They returned to separate lives and lived in tandem by avoiding each other. Meyera was determined to weather her husband's foibles, while George made efforts to keep their relationship on the rails. Despite Dr. Joe's passing, he continued to exert influence, albeit diminishing each day he was absent. The discovery of his wealth mismanagement and protracted probate, leading to poor outcomes, proved fatal to my parent's marriage. By the time I was two years of age, their divorce was complete, although George tried to pull Meyera back from the brink at the eleventh hour.

"Honey, don't you think divorce is a bore?" George asked. "Wouldn't it be better for us to stay together?"

Meyera agreed, but she found it impossible to prize herself from the concept that he should've gotten up from the chair to where she sat on the long green couch. If only he'd put his arm around her, things might've been different, but she stuck to her guns, refusing to stand-down legal proceedings.

"I think it best we call it a day," Meyera said. "I've already got one child to raise and can't bear the thought of two. Not when you can't be bothered to embrace me."

Strange how the absence of one physical gesture can radically alter the course of events, but she felt both superior and guilty when calling it quits on the marriage, accepting settlement terms forfeiting her right to alimony. Meyera and Elsie pooled their money to purchase a forty-unit apartment building at 708 South Barrington in Brentwood. As owners/occupiers, they were firmly ensconced in separate apartments, located like shopping mall anchor stores at either end of the first floor.

A starfish-shaped swimming pool and long patio area at the back attracted my attention, while Mom stared down the demon of dyslexia by enrolling in a Landlord/Tenant Law class at UCLA. Like *Eloise at the Plaza,* I had the freedom to roam and engage with the tenants while giving Elsie the new name of Meme. Anything without the prefix 'grand' was acceptable to my grandmother, who wasn't going to be associated with a title like that, and Elsie became known to everyone as Meme.

After the divorce, George lived down the street, hoping for reconciliation. He and Meyera stayed in contact, physical and otherwise, for several years, but George found it difficult to cope on his own with a small child during custodial visits.

If I needed the restroom, what was he to do? We couldn't go into the men's or ladies' room together, nor could I visit either alone. The solution was to have another female in tow, but the first one didn't work out so well. We were traveling to Catalina Island by seaplane, which I found akin to riding in a blender, and the method of landing was far from smooth. Flying fish inhabiting that area were graceful by comparison and possessed greater airborne proficiency, despite significantly shorter periods per flight.

My father's female friend might've suffered from nerves or perhaps been trying to calm mine, but whatever her motive, I refused to share my Skipper doll, having made a deal with the universe to relinquish it, even for a second, before landing would cause untold disaster. Holding up my part of the bargain, I held onto it for dear life, inadvertently alienating the first of my father's prospective partners.

I was curious about George's dates, but regarding them as a novelty, I treated each one with casual interest. Most failed the audition, rarely appearing twice, but one stood out when George arrived to collect me accompanied by a peroxide blonde, whose hand he was holding so tightly I thought he'd mistaken her for a bouquet of helium balloons about to fly away. For my father to march his female friends right up to our front door was unusual, but Meyera invited them in for a drink. They sat down, sipped scotch, and smiled uncomfortably. George and his date occupied opposite ends of the long green couch as if separated by a disapproving parent. Meyera waited a few moments before asking the blonde, "How's Lucky, and are you still in Vegas?"

The question had a g-force on its own, and my father's friend twisted her head back in a blend of curiosity mixed with caution. Squinting at Meyera, she said, "He's fine and at home in Nevada while I'm in town for the weekend."

"I was sorry to hear that your husband passed away," Meyera said.

George grew impatient. This conversational twist was not what he'd intended, and more irritating was the fact he hadn't the foggiest notion of what was being discussed.

"Forgive me, ladies," he said, "I don't wish to interrupt, but if someone would care to let me know who we're talking about, I'd appreciate it."

The blonde looked at George and blinked. Judging by her expression, she was tetchy, and she said, "My son, Lucky. How do you know my little boy?"

"Do you recall my late father, Dr. Joe Zeiler?" Meyera asked in return.

"Why yes, of course, I remember him. We were grateful to Dr. Joe," she said.

George was mystified, but his date became anxious to leave and said, "I'd love to chin-wag all night, but we mustn't be late for our dinner reservation at La Scala, isn't that right, George?"

My father was frustrated that Meyera knew more about the blonde than he did, which cast a somber mood over dinner. Meyera hadn't recognized the blonde by sight but made the connection based on her last name. During her early twenties, she worked as a chorus girl in Vegas, where a man fifty years her senior spotted her, was smitten, and they married virtually overnight.

Was he wealthy? You bet. Was he suspicious when she became pregnant? Absolutely. Rather than subject himself to the torture of uncertain parentage, he called Dr. Joe, who could provide conclusive results in addition to support concerning any information that came to light. My grandfather promptly ordered a sperm motility test, which confirmed that the septuagenarian's semen was comprised of strong swimmers capable of impregnating a fertile female.

Once the child was born, a blood test to determine paternity followed, and they waited for the lab to return with bated breath. When this critical piece of information was to hand, everyone exhaled as the child was irrefutably traced to its legally sanctified papa, and from that day forward, everyone called the boy Lucky.

During a disastrous weekend in Palm Springs, George, and his date *du jour* settled inside the condo while I peddled my tricycle on the patio. It was perfect for riding in a figure of eight between the large swimming pool and the small circular one I assumed was for children.

I decided to complete the circuit with a spectacular *finale* seen in many a cartoon and gathered as much speed as my three-year-old legs would permit before hitting the water as would a dim sum dumpling dropped into a pan of boiling oil. Chocking, kicking, and spluttering, I rose faster than steam escaping a kettle. Storming inside the condo I was furious and demanded an explanation.

"Why is the children's pool hot like coffee?" I hollered.

"Because Jacuzzis aren't meant for three-year-olds," George answered somewhat sheepishly. "When I said you have an 'animated' character, that doesn't mean you should act like one."

To my child's mind, coffee was an incomprehensible beverage, and when grown-ups weren't knocking back scotch by the barrel, they supped this steaming brew constantly. If a mother came to collect a child with whom I wished to continue playing, I'd enticingly suggest she have a cup. Coffee was a special substance that could buy you more time with friends but wasn't something you'd wish to swim in.

I'd felt the threat of a boiling cauldron once before when I was to attend a daycare facility, allowing Meyera and Meme to manage their new property without distraction. In running the building, they were still finding their feet, and requests to repair lighting represented a change from calling an electrician. A supervised sandbox center in Santa Monica was our first port of call, and the nursery school owner invited me to sit on her lap, which I found rather forward as only a few moments had passed since we'd been introduced.

By my calculations, such fast familiarity seemed wrong, but I reluctantly agreed, and a silence followed. Someone had to break the ice, even if that meant me cracking first and taking the conversational lead.

"I like your turquoise beads," I said, looking up at the nursery owner.

"What did you say?" she asked, visibly startled.

Evidently, I was sitting squarely atop someone of limited intelligence who was unable to recall what she'd put on that morning, and I repeated my compliment at dictation speed.

"Your turquoise necklace," I said, pronouncing the five syllables slowly. "It's nice," I added, in a tone usually reserved for the deaf. "Very pretty," I stated as if talking to a mentally impaired primate.

Meyera rushed to explain that I was an only child, and we lived in an environment occupied predominately by professional residents who conversed with me as they did each other. Consequently, I had an enlarged vocabulary, regrettably accompanied by an impatient attitude. The nursery school owner thought for a moment and played with her earring. Although it matched her necklace, I doubted she knew that.

Having been given a lot of information in a short period of time, she wanted to make a considered choice, and we sat outside in the bright sun with me stranded on a stranger's lap. She agreed to admit me to her facility, and two minutes later made a different decision that placed my interests above hers by forfeiting an opportunity to attract tuition.

"There's a new educational model I'd like to suggest for your daughter," she said. "It's in its infancy but provides more than I can offer here. Custodial care is primarily what we do, and I suspect your child requires more stimulation. I appreciate this may be a disappointment, but once you have a look, I think you will agree that it is a much better match. Shall I affect the introduction?" she added, caught between contrition and candor.

Now, who's observing basic rules of etiquette? The lady who doesn't remember the necklace sitting in plain view around her neck was a strange egg, but a good one.

"Why not allow me to give them a call so you can have a tour and see for yourself?" she asked. "Make an informed choice, as this will be one of the most influential decisions impacting your daughter's life."

Meyera wasn't about to disagree and recalled a discussion on this topic during a Manhattan dinner party she and George attended early in their marriage. An intimate gathering of twelve guests was entertained in a sumptuous style, and one of the more distinguished was the Dean of Harvard, Yale or perhaps Princeton.

"What would you suggest to new parents?" the Dean was asked by a man at the end of the table. "People such as my wife and I, who may only have enough funds to provide four-years of private education."

The table fell quiet as the Dean considered his answer. Pulling himself up from the plate, he put his glass of Chateauneuf-du-Pape down, thinking it was a shame to part with the remaining bit of Béarnaise sauce he'd intended to deliver to his still salivating mouth. He'd reluctantly relinquished the salad plate with trace elements of Roquefort dressing made with sheep's milk rather than cows, but with a soup to nuts service this sublime, the Dean didn't mind fielding a question or two. It usually fell to him to make pronouncements about education, and he was gratified to know that his views had an impact.

"Your question is one I wish were posited more often," the Dean said. "Given my profession and position, you will not be surprised to know I am a firm believer in private education. However, families frequently find themselves struggling to pay steep tuition fees that, in differing degrees, are demanded by most institutions of higher learning. If access to funds is restricted, it's essential they be applied toward the period of greatest importance."

"Which particular four-year period is that?" asked the man at the end of the table.

"The first four," answered the Dean. "I believe the early years of education are crucial and lay the foundation for all development that follows."

The look of astonishment exchanged by the dinner party guests left no doubt as to what everyone was thinking, and the Dean asked, "Why the shock?"

"We anticipated a pep talk about the benefits of the big boy brigade and thought you'd name the academic all-stars," said the man who posed the question. "Although my wife thought it unlikely her alma mater Stanford would get a name check here in New York," he added, amid amused chuckles.

"I appreciate my theories concerning education are somewhat controversial, although I agree with the Jesuits," the Dean said. "Give me a child until age seven, and I will show you the man. After love, nutrition and confidence, a well-rounded education is the most valuable gift parents can provide. Are there any more questions you would like me to address?"

No one made a sound except the staff, who rushed in and busily brushed the fine linen cloth in preparation for the final course.

"Well, in that case, I'd like to ask what's for dessert?" the Dean said. "Does anyone share my fondness for crepes Suzette with lashings of Cointreau? Without wishing to hasten the end of such a delectable meal,

I must confess to the gentlemen present that I am looking forward to our traditional brandy and port in the den."

There was an agreeable mumble as the other men concurred with the Dean's statement.

A conservative banker sitting next to George and Meyera said, "At least in tonight's company, I won't need to witness any plebeian mistakes."

"Oh really, why do you say that?" asked George, relieved to move the conversation away from academia.

"Last week, I watched in dismay as a perfectly acceptable port was passed right rather than left," the banker explained, "and to make matters worse," he continued.

"Hard that it is to imagine," George interjected sarcastically.

"The bottle came to rest before a full rotation had been made!" the banker exclaimed.

Meyera had been struggling to pay polite attention to this dreary conversation and was growing anxious. The East Coast tradition of segregating the sexes after dessert struck her as absurd, and left her alone to fend for herself in a different type of den filled with aggressive Fifth Avenue felines.

These svelte, socially adept women engaged in scalding conversation that could melt Meyera faster than a chocolate teapot. Despite dressing in Dior that evening, she felt her *couture* couldn't compete with the others on display. Her emerald green sleeveless cocktail dress accentuated her auburn hair, and George loved it. Degas would've, too.

It was low-cut at the back, and as George observed, "Looks great when you're walking away."

Walk away was precisely what she wanted to do. The most elegant outfit wouldn't be sufficient to carry off the illusion of confidence she wanted to convey.

Growing nervous as the fruit and cheese platter were removed from the table, Meyera couldn't resist lobbing in a barb or two and said, "Pausing while passing port the wrong way? Sounds as if someone should have their Diners' license suspended."

George joined in on the joke, but the banker mistook Meyera's sarcasm for sympathy and said, "I couldn't agree with you more, Mrs. Buchanan. It rather ruined the meal as far as I am concerned."

"It's criminal to crucify *Le Cordon Bleu* cuisine," Meyera added.

The real crime being committed was high cholesterol blue-ribbon dinners causing code blue coronaries, requiring artery spoons to replace those monogrammed in silver. The bell rang, indicating the end of the meal and the beginning of Meyera's greatest fear of socializing all by herself.

Once the ladies gathered separately, their hostess said, "Meyera, come meet Julia Verne."

"Why not?" Meyera said, "I'm already 20,000 leagues out of my depth."

"Let's make that appointment as soon as possible, and where exactly is the school located?" Meyera asked the nursery school owner.

"Down on Colorado Avenue, about ten to fifteen minutes away," the nursery school owner confirmed.

In California, distance is measured in time. We count hours and minutes rather than miles. True to her word and willingness to allow insight rather than commerce control circumstances, she came back having secured our appointment.

CHAPTER 4

"Now we're talking" was the immediate consensus Mom and I reached after touring one of the first Montessori schools in America that became, and remained, one of the largest of its kind. *Ave Maria*, indeed.

The first owner and acting headmaster was an activist by the name of Tom Laughlin, whose public persona was perhaps more recognizable by the character he played in four feature films, all bearing the name *Billy Jack*. The title and lead role refer to a half-Navajo Vietnam war veteran who was both plagued and privileged by his counterculture ethos. The same might be said of the actor, as Tom Laughlin and *Billy Jack* both went to Washington — one looking to be elected President of the United States and the other seeking box office receipts. Turning away from Hollywood, Tom Laughlin looked toward education as a means of combatting societal ills, which was the impetus behind his radical act to run the school.

Students were encouraged to meander in whatever path struck their interest and attention. I blazed a trail to the reading corner and remained there for as long, or as little, a period as I elected. Montessori's sense of proportion mirrored mine, and I found this attractive. All I had to do was glance at a book and, in less time than it takes to say *Garson* and summon a waiter, my tutorial would begin.

Learning to decipher words preceded the mastery of individual letters, and on-demand service began with educators well before broadcasters appropriated the concept. These fine teachers understood vapor trail speed, which was refreshing but not entirely unexpected by children without siblings. An enormous section of our room was set aside exclusively for creative expression and had a magnetic lure all on its own. They called it the art table, but it was more of a banquet, allowing all you can make rather than eat. Although I made it a point never to stray near the mathematics section, I'd occasionally pass by and wave when riding fence on my way past maps, toward puppetry or French. Stepping forward to spark interest was Montessori's *Maison Special*, and stepping back when requested was their *Repas Exceptionnel*. Everything was elective, and nothing compulsory.

Naysayers claimed this unfettered approach would lead to lopsided education and, if not forced to focus on subjects across the board, they warned we would suffer the same fate as Sparky with his magic piano. Allowing us to advance toward topics of personal interest was dangerous, as they feared we'd become learned ignoramuses.

About such detractors, I've often wondered what level of 'crack the books' mentality they thought a three-year-old might possess. This permissive wave of freedom ushered in a revitalized perspective, enabling our small band to accomplish in a stroke what scores before us had tried and failed to convey. It was a simple message of solipsistic clarity that said: me first, me last, me in between, and me forever.

At Montessori, they were on board with this program and acknowledged without question that we comprised the center of the universe. If we acted as monotheistic jealous gods, it was considered the price of genius, and our demands were tolerated, but threats to smote each other were not. Civilizing the savage isn't always straightforward.

Run by progressive thinkers, this theoretical form of child development was outstanding. Even the snacks were top-rate, including that first fabulous taste of peach, pear, and apricot juice. Liberals, Democrats, and dedicated readers of Dr. Spock sent their children in droves to this educational paradigm. As did a smattering of champagne Socialists and a few conservative Republican Party members, including Meyera, which helped balance the card-carrying Communists in the crowd.

Comrades whose kids were in attendance rarely missed a meeting and, having survived the Hollywood Blacklist, they enjoyed gathering openly. Everyone wanted the best for their progeny irrespective of ideological, professional, or ethnic diversity. The demographic may have been wide, but the aperture of focus was small because everyone hoped their little blossoms would absorb inspiration like blotting paper. If pressed, many would rather extinguish a child rather than hinder his or her freedom of expression.

Marlon Brando's son Christian was enrolled at Montessori, which impressed several parents, most notably fathers, who hoped for legitimate access to this acting legend. An aspiration tempered by the more likely limited glimpse they might catch of Brando now and again. Meyera overheard a couple of dads discussing this conundrum after the Easter pageant while remnants of brightly colored eggs were cleared away.

All the photos needed to commemorate this event were safely in the canister, and these priceless images were well worth the steep price of tuition. With their official job done, they felt able to relax near the hospitality table, where they joked, plotted, and planned. Straddling the line separating sweet from savory snacks, they maintained a neutral position, much as diplomats do in Davos, Switzerland. Freshly baked carrot and zucchini bread on the right. Homemade hummus, pate, and tahina to the left. Everything was personally prepared by women who surreptitiously studied reactions to their dish while studiously pretending not to do so.

Meyera had neither the time nor inclination to bake or blend. She contributed old faithful (which was relatively new faithful, to be precise) with an easy-to-prepare mix that would sweep America, requiring only two ingredients: sour cream and instant onion soup, but despite the vast popularity of this dip, it was not a condiment to be proud of.

The men were in good spirits and riding high on the crest of another adorable evening, they engaged in good-natured competition, trying to outdo each other's comedic strategy designed to deliver their cinematic hero in person.

Meyera observed two fathers before asking, "Are you starting a starstruck coffee clutch?"

"More of a seminar," said the first dad, "on how to meet Marlon 101."

"If you've any ideas to suggest, they're bound to be better than ours," the second father added.

"Can't call his number from the school directory," the first father noted. "Not to introduce ourselves and definitely not to pitch a project."

"We've agreed it's *verboten* to trespass via telephone," the second dad explained.

"Can't purloin his address from the student roster to slip him a script in a pizza box either, although it is tempting," the first dad confirmed.

"Can't force our kids to befriend his," said the second father. "God knows I've already tried that."

"You might run into him at a fundraiser," Meyera said. "I wouldn't march directly up to the man and insist you become the best of friends. At least not right away, and I wouldn't recommend that you ask him to host a private screening either."

Although both men nodded in agreement, neither agreed at all. Any opportunity to meet Brando would qualify as an exceptional moment, and the vague mention of this distant possibility was enticing. Each man expressed complete accord with Meyera while thinking, "If only."

Invitations were issued frequently, and often formally, from Montessori. Meyera's eyes widened when she opened the mailbox and glanced at a distinctive envelope bearing the Smythson of Bond Street embossed logo. She was even more surprised to find my name, rather than hers, written in calligraphy on the front. The pleasure of my company was requested to attend a fourth birthday celebration in honor of my classmate Tyrone Power Junior. The party was held at Trader Vic's in Beverly Hills, which our parents regarded as the home of the most marvelous mai tai imaginable.

When the British Invasion hit the shores of America, they didn't confine themselves to music venues, and luminaries such as Rod Stewart and Elton John frequented this watering hole as did the Rat Pack before them. Musicians and the models who accompanied them took this tropical-themed establishment from famous to infamous, but for this event, the place was reservedly ours alone, and we were treated to a Polynesian feast.

A battalion of bright aloha shirt and skirt-attired staff descended on the grown-ups' table, dispensing drinks adorned with exotic flowers.

Crab Rangoon, miso sea bass and beef chowchow followed. Butterfly shrimp, punch served in coconut bowls, and cake worthy of a coronation were presented to the children. Hibiscus and high spirits accompanied our happy birthday wishes. Sugared up to the gills, we ran roughshod around the restaurant, and I was inadvertently bashed into.

Meyera leaped up to come rushing over, but I stopped her midway by saying, "It's okay, Mommy, that's just Ty."

"Isn't he gorgeous?" asked a woman sitting next to Meyera.

"Yes, but not surprising considering he follows a long line of handsome," Meyera said. "I loved his father's swashbuckling sword-and-sandals films."

"And I liked his work with Billy Wilder and Marlene Dietrich on *Witness for the Prosecution*," the other mother said. "It's easy to understand why he described himself as a movie star who became an actor, but passing away just nine weeks before the birth of that beautiful boy is tragic."

"Hollywood misses his talent, and on a day like today, who can help but miss the father?" Meyera added.

The conversation took a sharp twist, following a swift pat on the bottom administered to the other mother by a slightly inebriated dad.

"Loved your latest article and haven't laughed that hard in a long time," he said. "I used our new Xerox 813 desktop machine to run off two copies in just over an hour," he added, balancing his third mai tai with difficulty.

"I appreciate the support, which is a well-timed vote of confidence when I thought I was losing my mind," the other mother said. "As a freelance journalist, I'm beholden to the brief, and my commission was to write a think piece about this educational experience from a privileged perspective. Once I got behind that one-way glass to observe my child's classroom interaction, I had a crisis of conscience concerning the distinction between interested scrutiny and outright surveillance. Why not pose the same question to our readers, I asked myself. If this is the age of Aquarius, let's share some of the dilemmas of our new dawn."

"Did you write the article titled Mirror, Mirror?" Meyera asked. "How I howled when you asked the glass, 'Who was the most devoted or dreadful parent of all?'"

"What kind of adult spies on their darling?" the other mother said. "Dedicated or duplicitous, it was the reader's call."

"Hilarious," Meyera said, "I had no idea I was sitting next to the writer."

"Yes, that's me." the other mother admitted. "I don't normally stray off point, but when I started writing, it became a confession, evidencing how conflicted I felt and harnessing the article for catharsis, I delivered comedic material instead. Thankfully, our editor has a sense of humor, just like our readers if they are anything like the two of you."

All the definitions regarding education, child-rearing, and social interaction were changing, and the old rules were cast aside, except those pertaining to safety, which were the only hard-and-fast strictures at such a permissive school. I discovered this when caught in contravention of the cafeteria code when dropped-off in the morning dressed and ready for bread. Dashing toward the lunchroom table, I broke the rule forbidding running while holding a full plate of food in my hand, which constituted a breach of the crockery and cutlery laws in operation.

Are small sentries born, or do they become socialized into existence? I pondered this issue after some sniveling little shit felt it incumbent to tell on me, and as with most convicts on Parchman Farm, I professed my innocence, committing a further infraction of the rule forbidding us to volunteer fiction. Having been brought to heel by the restraint on my wrist was punishment enough. Being scolded in front of my peers was embarrassing, and without knowing the identity of my accuser, I had a hunch it was the new kid in class who had it in for me from the moment he arrived.

His mischievous nature frequently turned toward malice, and he'd been remanded to the time-out chair on so many occasions as to leave a permanent indentation on the small wooden seat. His whistleblowing was enough to send me to the headmaster, and I nervously knocked on Tom Laughlin's door before being invited in. When asked to take a seat, I sat down but saw only a desk. At the age of four, I'd yet to acquire height of any significance, but the talking wood paneling and I had a polite discussion about being more mindful of the rules.

Theoretical frameworks evolve over time, yet human nature remains the same. Montessori was a veritable paradise, and in the run-up to the holidays, I conferred with friends and compared the content of our letters to Santa. The steady diet of support we were fed each day made us supremely confident (particularly at this time of year) because we knew that in our own unique and supremely special way, each of us represented the very definition of good. As a result, hope was made redundant by cast-iron certainty that what we'd requested would be under the tree on Christmas morning.

I had my eye on a motorized toy called Tony the Pony. If augmented by a pair of riding boots or cowgirl hat, that would be great. Although accessories were largely up to the elves, it was agreed that none of us had any degree of influence or control over them. The new boy in class planned to secure the gift of his choice by asking for only one item, which would obliterate confusion by shutting the door on mistakes. Poor communication with distant relatives had caused disappointment in the past, and he didn't want to repeat the disasters of previous years.

While admittedly radical, he was determined to stick with this strategy, but a sharp intake of breath indicated our collective shock. Requesting just one thing for Christmas was drastic, and we asked what could possibly be so attractive as to supplant all other gifts. Apparently, it was a tool kit outfitted with several sized saws, hammers, and chisels. The collection he ordered contained the works that he'd need when we reconvened after the holidays.

He was the son of an ambassador, and it had recently come to his attention that his ancestors enjoyed cannibalism. Of specific interest were blonde haired little girls, widely acknowledged to be especially delicious. His intention was to bring this tool kit to Montessori and chop me up. My severed arms, legs, and whatnot would be placed in a bubbling pot so that I could be made into stew. The cauldron calls.

I said nothing. Not a word to anyone over Christmas and New Year's, but when the holidays were over, I pulled out big gun tears and tantrums while staunchly refusing to return to Montessori. Hastily assembled teachers, child psychotherapists, and Meyera met on an emergency basis to discuss how they had failed to motivate me when all indications had been so positive. Numerous theories were posited as to when this effective educational model let us down, but eventually, I disclosed the fact that to deposit me back at school was to consign me to certain death. The new boy was promptly expelled, and I wasn't sorry to see him go. Adults were relieved that the academic paradigm was safe, and that it had only been a matter of playground intimidation. Bullying didn't exist at Montessori.

Meyera's interest in the self-actualized consciousness-raising zone was at an end, and the following year, she enrolled me in a more conservative private elementary school called Bonner. After our experience at Montessori, almost any educational institution would've fit that bill.

CHAPTER 5

I'd wake up hungry most weekends and scavenge around our kitchen for food, which wasn't terribly effective unless I wanted condiments and gourmet snacks first thing in the morning. Meyera's version of staples was different from most, and she stocked jars of marinated artichoke hearts, red peppers, and pimento olives on the top shelf, leaving capers, Cardini's Caesar dressing and Maille Dijon mustard lower down. Anchovy paste, garlic puree, mint and tartar sauce were always on hand, along with a selection of jams ranging from pomegranate to apple butter. Bratwurst, baloney, and devilled ham were within reach, but bread wasn't. Neither were crackers of any description other than stale. This made it difficult to muster much enthusiasm for the camembert or brie gracing our shelves, which is good for breakfast if you're on the Continent but less attractive when you're a kid.

The vegetable bin was a no-go area with wilted lettuce, lemons turned brown, and carrots gone black, but the ever-present box of Arm & Hammer baking soda absorbed these odors. This product worked overtime, contending with garlic-laden leftover spaghetti gone stiff and Bolognese sauce turned green.

Meyera stored roll-on deodorant in the butter shelf, and our freezer was a barren tundra where Sarah Lee chocolate brownies, Stolichnaya vodka and an eye mask were kept, along with half-filled ice cube trays that broke when called upon to deliver their tiny contents. Leftover toasted pecans and almonds failed to attract my attention, and I would step away from the kitchen as you would from roadkill.

I'd wait until 9:00 a.m. before knocking on various neighbors' doors to ask tenants what they were having for breakfast. This was a bit of a ruse since I had a pretty good idea of what to expect, and I would bring the latest edition of *Dick and Jane* with me, offering to strike a barter deal involving a live reading in exchange for food. Who could fail to be enthralled by those iconic American protagonists and their supporting characters, Baby Sally, Dog Spot and Puff the Kitten?

One needs only passing acquaintance with their Radio Flyer and swing set rides to be utterly gripped by such compelling storylines. Or so I was told on numerous occasions by scores of adults inviting me in for a morning meal. I soon discovered that continuing narratives could deliver a steady stream of food, and without putting too fine a point on it, I was famished.

When Mom was passed out drunk, and Meme's not up, something's needed to prevent hunger. Cartoons can distract for brief periods, but television drew renewed attention to my stomach with all those ads for Oscar Meyer bacon and sausage links. I found Captain Birdseye and Crunch infinitely more interesting than Captain Kirk or Kangaroo. Familiar with the weekend menu available at child-friendly apartments, my decision as to whose door I would knock on was based entirely upon what I fancied that day. The building effectively became a personal version of the 'Breakfast of Champions.'

Mr. and Mrs. Newton in 207 had Kellogg's Corn Flakes. They also had a parakeet in a tall birdcage that was fun to watch while you ate.

At least Mr. Newton and I liked to look at the bird, but Mrs. Newton never sat down, flapping about more than the parakeet while asking, "How about a couple of eggs? I can cook them up any way you want. No, a piece of toast maybe? I've got Welch's Grape Jelly just for you."

Declining her offers was almost as much fun as accepting them. The woman was on a mission to feed and did not take well to rebuffs, saying, "What, again with the no? Enough refusal already. You know what that does to me."

I knew only too well, but we both knew I'd eventually acquiesce, and consumption would commence.

"Try a little poppy seed strudel," she'd suggest, cutting a slice before I had time to answer. "Is that good and was I right? Neil, look at her dimples. *Oy*, the *punim* on this one. I could just pinch those cheeks."

I was three when our breakfasts began, but Neil was 89, and his wife a spritely 84. It amused me no end that whatever I wanted was instantly accommodated, but the same couldn't be said for him.

If Mr. Newton so much as asked for another cup of coffee his wife would abruptly halt and raise her arms while saying, "Neil, how many hands do I have?"

She'd hold the position until he answered, which sometimes took a little longer than at others.

He'd smile and say, "Two hands, Mar. You've got one with which to hold the cup and one with which to pour."

Victor Holdsworth in Apartment 309 preferred poached eggs on toast served with a glass of freshly squeezed orange juice, and if you dined at his place, the latter was compulsory. He worked in banking, ascending the ranks of Wells Fargo with a meteoric rise but was recently divorced with an only child my age called Keith, who I met standing by the pool.

He was the blondest boy I'd ever seen, with masses of cherubic curls accenting pale skin and could easily have been mistaken for a water sprite, landing along with a few dragonflies. I'd read *The Littlest Angel* Christmas tale, but Keith walked right off the page, needing only a harp and a halo.

Instead, he was adorned with inflatable water wings, which made me laugh, and I said, "Why on earth are you wearing those ridiculous-looking things?"

Meme heard me and choked on her coffee before mentioning that not all children find water grounding, which struck me as absurd. Victor was allowed alternate weekend custody, which restricted visits with Keith to only four days a month, but we used our time effectively. I taught Keith to swim while he introduced me to the Catholic hymns he sang at school. His mention of mass and grace made me think of parochial education as the Masons for minors, which was confirmed when I was Keith's plus-one companion at his aunt's Roman Catholic wedding in Westwood.

Rich in theatrical pageantry and incense-swinging priests, we celebrated the glory of God on our feet and knees for what seemed an eternity. Up and down, the congregation was directed to go in a spiritual version of Simon Says. Had the priest asked us to touch our toes for the bride and groom, I would have been willing and not at all surprised. The service ran on for such a long time, a sip of wine and a wafer snack were served midway through. Sneaking in line behind Keith, I whispered how lucky he was not to be Episcopalian — we had to wait until church was over before our eggs Benedict brunch.

Keith's visits were something I looked forward to and missed when sipping the dregs from a last bottle of Mountain Dew shared on Sunday night. Shared was an important aspect of this process, considering only children would rather forfeit possession than jointly participate. We are more comfortable with the concept of exclusivity than giving. I would hum his songs while trying to keep at bay the sinking feeling of having to wait forever before my friend reappeared, and, unlike Christ's disciples, I lacked patience.

Meme took an interest in Keith's aquatic development, suggesting I invite him to play Penny Pool, which was an outstanding game from my grandmother's stable, and after she threw coins into the water, we would watch the filigree glint as they fell toward the bottom awaiting collection in a race against time.

"With a worthy rival," Meme said, "you won't need the stopwatch."

How right she was, happy to pit my competitive hankerings against a human I jumped in the water while Keith shivered next to me.

We were two tightly wound coils ready for Meme to shout, "One for the money. Two for the show. Three to get ready. Now go, go, go."

She showered the air with pennies and scattered them across the surface, where the metallic shine of different intensities was reflected when they began the descent. I'd been several times to SeaWorld in San Diego and found the pearl divers captivating. Able to hold their breath for long stretches, every move and gesture was stripped of the extraneous down to essentials before surfacing with an oyster-bearing treasure in hand.

My imagination got to work, dressing me in the white diving costume worn by Japanese ama while I dove to the deep end and back as swiftly as possible. The stack of coins on my side of the pool reached completion first, and I won the game but lost equalized pressure. Meme called it a pyrrhic victory, defining with pinpoint accuracy the piercing pain in my ear. Time and a heating pad were prescribed, but I felt sorry for myself, so I took the unusual step of laying on Meyera's bed while she slept. We were not what you would call a cuddly family. Physical contact was reserved for high holidays and formal occasions. Hugs were brief and perfunctory, while a kiss was more of a gesture than an actual smack.

Unable to sleep, I switched on Mom's TV to watch *The Million Dollar Movie*, featuring *What Ever Happened to Baby Jane?* This sounded like a film for children, but it was hard to hear over Meyera's sonic snore. Had she been an animated cartoon character, the dresser drawers would have opened and closed in synchronization with each breath. No sound was needed, however, to communicate terror during the scene in which Bette Davis serves a dead parakeet to Joan Crawford.

After Davis dished up Crawford's second helping of a dead rat, I returned to my room, and it was a long time before I donned imaginary garb, diving to the deep end again. The allure of loose change or pretend pearls was no longer effective, but Meme's reputation for concocting inventive fun remained intact. Her ability to turn an already entertaining event into something extraordinary bordered on the visionary. At least, I thought so when I was five and the circus came to town.

Ringling Brothers and Barnum & Bailey arrived in summer during a heat wave. Fly posters, full-page newspaper ads, local news and radio promotions attracted every kid in town. Excitement buzzed like a highly charged current around playgrounds, lunch tables and libraries. I was vulnerable to the temptations of this voltage. A fact that didn't escape Meme's attention.

"Any child with enough pocket money to buy a ticket can go to the circus," she said. "If you want to see something special, let's go downtown and watch the animals unload from the train. We can see them set up the big top and charm an out of character clown or two. What do you say?" she asked, temptress that she was.

We arrived at the railway station and witnessed a box of Animal Crackers come to life while each car marked Barnum's decanted its cargo of lions, lamas, camels, and kangaroos. Tigers were unloaded first, and a seemingly endless array of exotic creatures followed. To find life imitating a famous brand of snack food was a delight, but temperatures soared that day, causing animals and humans to suffer under the stultifying sun. Three tents in total were set up, each involving enough rope to rig a galleon for a sail across the far seas. Here in Hobo Junction, however, those tents would provide shade to a perspiring pubic.

"Meme, it's hot," I said. "Are you hot? Because I am," I added, proving the point by pulling off my shoes and socks.

This was the start of a total strip-down, as was my habit when coping with high temperatures, but Meme looked at me with an expression that was empathetic yet disapproving.

"You have to keep your clothes on," Meme said. "We talked about this, remember?"

I could tell she was ready to revisit well-worn ground again. We'd had this discussion innumerable times. Most recently, at the grocery store on another scorcher of a day when I made it perfectly clear I wanted to be in the nude or near the frozen food section. Either alternative was more than acceptable, but she tried to mollify me with the promise we'd be home soon, and I'd be back in the pool.

I looked at her as if she were suffering from sunstroke and said, "Seriously? Ten to fifteen minutes wait? Who's got that kind of time?"

Turning toward Meme, I brandished my sock as you would a saber while saying, "Yes, I remember, but you could take your clothes off too."

Clothing was a social convention I couldn't seem to budge, but distraction still worked wonders on my young mind, and Meme diverted our attention toward the elephants who were walking nose to tail off the train. Once unloaded, they were arranged in a semicircle and provided with water in large wooden tubs.

"Handler today might be clown tomorrow," Meme said. "When we come back to watch the show, let's see if we recognize any of these faces. I've got a funny feeling that clowns wear many hats in addition to a red nose."

Returning to see the circus as a civilian had been a certainty, and this trip was intended to peek behind-the-scenes, obtaining a before rather than backstage perspective. There's an optimism involved in setting up and being there when everything unfolds, unpacks, and unwinds. A counterbalance to the postpartum of striking the same, when what has happened overpowers hope of what might have been.

Several elephants were relieving themselves after the long train journey, and the substantial size of their emissions prompted Meme to laugh and say, "Now you know why elephants don't fly."

Meme obviously preferred the more sophisticated Babar to feather-wielding Dumbo, but the crowd of spectators was comfortably thin, allowing plenty of elbow room and a great up-front view. Without suggesting I am an elephant whisperer, one of these enormous creatures and I had a definite connection, starting with eye contact initiated and maintained by the elephant in a purposeful stare directed at me while they were cooling off.

Slurping, sloshing sounds filled the air, soothing every creature stretching with relief to no longer have the rails riding under their hooves, paws, feet, or fins. I was thinking how badly in need of suntan lotion the elephants were, wondering how many bottles of Coppertone would it take to help soothe such cracked skin when it happened, but the strange thing is, I watched it happen, having had a hunch it would. Filling its ten-liter trunk to capacity, as the others had done to drink or shower, this elephant looked me dead in the eye while turning the trunk setting from gentle to blast before aiming right at us, drenching Meme, and I from head to toe. I had no idea whether to laugh, cry or run.

Looking up at Meme to scan for clues, I found them in her doubled-over posture and laughter so intense she was batting at air while saying, "Bet you don't want to take your clothes off now."

Mr. and Mrs. Sidwell in apartment 103 were a retired couple whose first names I never did catch, but they ate Scott's Porage Oats every morning to keep their native British traditions alive. They served everything with a twist, turning toast into something transcendent by adding Frank Cooper's Original Oxford Marmalade or Marmite. Breakfast at their place felt as if dining in Europe. They preferred Colman's Mustard Powder to French's, and stocked HP Sauce rather than Heinz Tomato Ketchup.

Negotiating their kitchen table virtually required a map, and, in the land of cars, Mrs. Sidwell trundled off with her trolley to the shops each day, just as she had done in London, preserving that tradition, too. They could be counted on for either breakfast or afternoon tea. The latter was served in the library and featured crust-free cucumber sandwiches, clotted cream scones and toasted cheese on toast with one drop of Lea & Perrins Worcestershire sauce consumed with gallons of Earl Grey tea from Fortnum & Mason.

"Always keep your head in a book," Mr. Sidwell said. "To enhance life, it's essential you continue reading throughout it."

I pointed to a mysterious-looking hardback with a spooky image on the spine and said, "What's that one about?"

Mr. and Mrs. Sidwell exchanged a look of mild amusement. Considering all the books on display, I had obviously picked one less to their liking, and Mrs. Sidwell said, "That's a classic about a European salesman."

"Sounds a little dull," I said.

"Not when he wakes up as an insect, which is why it's called *The Metamorphosis*," Mr. Sidwell explained.

A transplanted trademark attorney from New York lived in apartment 409. Everyone said he was married to the law, but Len was single. He loved lox and adored bagels. On weekends, he'd hop behind the wheel of his red Mustang Convertible to purchase the best that LA had to offer. Driving along Sunset Boulevard past multimillion-dollar properties and dodging the occasional gardener's truck, he marveled at the blazing sun.

Traveling through Brentwood, Bel Air and Hollywood, he inhaled California's fruit-flavored air. Honeysuckle, gardenia, and night-blooming jasmine were a long way from his native Brooklyn. Turning right on

Fairfax, it was a straight shoot down to Canter's Deli, famous for the best bagels in town since 1931. There was an arts and crafts element to brunch with Len, which he explained in different terms.

"All the ingredients represent options," Len said. "You're under no obligation to elect components, and the red onion or capers may be excluded without penalty. Cream cheese is discretionary, as is the choice of bagel, toasted or plain. Whether to grant or withhold the sliced tomato is entirely up to you. Shall we commence building our breakfast?"

Smacking his lips after that first inaugural bite, Len pronounced his bagel, "Unimpeachable," and when asked what that meant, he said, "Unimpeachable means it can't be peached."

Len had a formidable eye for detail, which contributed to his professional success and study of the zither. His command of Patent Law was as comprehensive as his Manfred Schuler record collection, which we'd listen to while devouring our feast. Despite being a tad portly, he was an energetic man who dressed in J. Press and Chipp suits during the week with khaki shorts, polo shirts, and open-toed sandals worn with socks at the weekend. When placing his order at Canter's, Len asked for the chopped liver to be shaped like a chicken, and he allowed me the honor of slicing off its head before spreading it on rye bread.

Full-bodied food wasn't always on tap, but sustenance takes many forms, and if in the mood for interesting conversation, I'd visit Burt Taxi in apartment 502. He ran an import/export business and always kept a box of Strawberry Pop-Tarts on the premises. Given the extensive travel his work demanded, our visits weren't as frequent as I'd have liked.

His place was stacked with computers, cameras, and early video recording equipment, but one item remained safely on the shelf, which I regarded as the curio of curios. Presiding over samurai swords, silk fabrics and hand-carved furniture was a bell jar containing a shrunken head from the Amazon with eyes sewn shut and three pins holding the mouth together. I found it fascinating, making it difficult to prize myself away even when Mr. Taxi tried to divert my attention elsewhere.

"What would you like with the Pop-Tarts?" he asked from the kitchen. "There isn't any milk for this sachet of Carnation Instant Breakfast, so shall we take a look at the tea?"

"Okay, but you decide which one to have," I said.

"There are too many for me to choose from by myself," he said. "Give me some help here, will you please?"

I was staring at the bell jar and indifferent to his question about beverages. He, of course, knew this but persevered with suggestions to distract me from our glass-enclosed friend.

"Don't you think it's time to look away from the macabre and turn our attention toward more wholesome foreign finds?" he asked.

I didn't think so, but without wishing to be rude, I joined him in the kitchen, where his shelves were laden with exotic food. Tea occupied the top spot and was something of a hobby that Burt elevated to a reverential practice.

"Here's one I picked up last week," he said. "Artichoke tea is good, but more so for males. From China, we have Lapsang souchong, the first black tea in history, but the taste may be too smoky," he noted, perusing the cabinet as would a librarian searching for a specific tome.

Despite wanting to return to the living room, I remained in the kitchen because there was a certain fascination in watching someone address a topic with intense ardor.

"Oolong is nice, although neither of us needs its weight loss benefits," he said.

Burt was a slight man with dark hair accented by an immaculately trimmed beard and mustache. His blue eyes pegged him as a foreign devil when he was away on business travel. In Japan, they called him *Gaijin*, *Laowai* in China, and *Farang* in Thailand, which, roughly translated, means barbarian. It's impossible to duck immutable traits, but his respect for far-flung cultures eased the way during negotiations.

"How about Chrysanthemum tea straight from Shanghai?" he asked. "I almost had to take a blood oath before they'd allow me to import it."

"Why's that?" I asked.

"Because we don't respect their tea, by boiling it, which destroys the blend," he explained.

Burt moved a few months later, and as he was packing, I asked if he would part ways with the bell jar.

"Complete with contents," I added, to avoid a bum deal of just the jar itself.

"It's inappropriate as a gift," he said. "Especially one given to a child."

"Who said anything about a gift?" I asked, knowing the child issue was insurmountable. "I was thinking in terms of a trade."

"What did you have in mind?" he asked, obviously amused.

"My entire swizzle stick collection, which is ten times bigger than when I last showed it to you. Thanks to a new resident, Playboy Club, sticks have been added to the sea monsters and mermaids."

To his credit, he considered my proposal, or at least made the pretense, before concluding it was impossible. Instead, he presented me with an inspired parting gift that took two trips to carry from his apartment to ours.

"Behold Miss Buchanan, I bring you a true treasure," he said.

"Have you changed your mind about the head?" I asked.

"No, but I think you'll find this of greater interest for a longer period of time," he said. "Allow me to introduce you to stack number one, which contains a pristine edition of every Beatles album released to date, and stack number two provides you with every Rolling Stones record on the planet. They'll be valuable one day."

"They're valuable right now," I said.

CHAPTER 6

I was six when Malcolm knocked on our door to introduce himself. His dad, Adam, was recently divorced and lived in apartment 204, fulfilling his fatherly role on weekends but, as a part-time *pater,* Mr. Arch lacked consistency. Malcom's visits were sporadic, last-minute, and unsupervised. The absence of due care and parental attention, normally cause for concern, had no applicability to Malcolm, who was responsibility incarnate and reliability made manifest. Caring, patient and fun — that's Malcolm.

He was five years older and well-appointed in every respect, with dark hair parted on one side surrounding piercing blue eyes. A smattering of freckles joined hands during the summer, turning his complexion from a light dusting to an even tan. Only when swimming did he allow himself to go barefoot rather than wear Keds sneakers in white or black. A proponent of permanent press, his wrinkle-free trousers and undershirts stood to attention, making it difficult to determine whether his starched whites or pearly teeth were brighter.

Although I had no idea what his primary home might be like, I suspect a bevy of elder sisters whispered words of encouragement from the wings of his life, as would a Greek chorus. It had been my experience that in cases involving divorce, you rarely get a chance to meet the other half or side depending on amicability, but whatever family configuration normally housed Malcolm must've been great. How else to explain his compassionate outlook and altruistic orientation?

When swimming, Malcolm insisted I remain in the pool long enough for him to get out and have my towel ready. He was also a dab hand at tying shoelaces, which eluded me except during ballet lessons where the pink slippers were secured by a single elastic strap across the top.

Maneuvering first through fifth position was easy compared with the question of whether to put my leotard or tights on first.

Rudolf Nureyev and Dame Margot Fonteyn performed at the Dorothy Chandler Pavilion, and I left the theatre dazzled by talent but none the wiser about the order in which to dress. As memorable as the performance was, a man, seated directly behind me noticed I was having difficulty viewing the stage and suggested I sit up on my knees to watch.

Meyera politely refused, but he insisted, saying, "She should see more than the chair in front of her. The most marvelous music on earth won't make up for missing these divine dancers.'

Meyera mentioned Nureyev's defection from the Soviet Union occurred at the airport, but rather than a failure to board the aircraft, I imagined him gliding along the passenger isle in a flawless *Glissade* before a *Grand Jete* propelled him to freedom. Watching his splendid movements, I wondered if he needed to consider the order in which to dress for rehearsal or stage.

When the ties on my P.F. Flyers came undone, I'd stand in fifth position, gesturing toward the undone lace and saying, "Malcolm, look."

He'd rush to my aid so swiftly it attracted Meme's attention, who said, "If you spoil her, she'll go from prima ballerina to prima donna. The way she's waiting for you to fix that lace, you'd think she was posing for Degas with more attitude than model Marie van something."

Nestle's Push-Up orange ice cream was our favorite, and Malcolm unwrapped my cone in advance of his. He dealt deftly with dropped scoops by handing his over while saying something soothing. He had a knack for making problems disappear, but the same thing happened to Malcolm after his father went mad.

As Don Quixote tilted at windmills, Adam Arch railed with equal fervor from a window, accosting tenants in the building next door. Warnings were delivered by police officers on several occasions but had little effect. On the rare weekends I saw Malcolm, he wanted to hang around our apartment, the pool or anywhere other than at his dad's. We needed to retrieve half of my walkie-talkie set from Mr. Arch's apartment, which was worth the risk.

The two-way hand-held radio transceiver was my most popular toy, and the G.I. Joe edition George sent for my birthday proved far more powerful than the manufacturer intended. We discovered this during a trial run on the roof when Meyera inadvertently connected with a Pan Am flight approaching for landing at LAX. The pilot was furious, and Mom became flustered while rushing to end the communication, saying, "Copy that."

Still shaken, she added, "Roger. Ten Four. Over and out."

Malcolm and I were heading out the door as Adam barreled in like a demented dog kept too long before release from its kennel. His shaggy grey hair, bushy eyebrows and gruff expression were suggestive of an Irish Wolfhound.

"You've had enough of my time and attention," he hollered.

"Malcolm, let's go to my apartment where there's no such thing as enough," I said.

When we settled in the kitchen, enjoying the comfort of Meyera's exceptional peanut butter and jelly sandwiches, Malcolm indicated that our association was on shaky ground.

"My father isn't very well, and it might be a while before I stay here again," he said.

"What's wrong, Malcolm?" I asked.

"Mother thinks his profession drove him crazy and that being a physicist was one thing but the impact of his work quite another," Malcolm explained. "Dad was a patriot and felt it was his duty to invent something to beat the Nazis, but he was devastated by what happened and never forgave himself for participating in The Manhattan Project. When teaching at UCLA and USC, students started asking questions he wasn't allowed to answer, and guilt got to him."

"He went from mad scientist to outright angry?" I asked, trying to lighten the mood.

"Until my father gets better, it will be hard for me to visit," he explained, looking downcast.

"Don't worry, Malcolm, it'll be alright," I said, knowing it wouldn't.

In losing Malcolm, it was goodbye to stalwart support and farewell to my chosen child wrangler. His authority was the only one my classmates willingly recognized. Who'd blow up balloons and oversee the *piñata* at my birthday parties? What I would miss most was his ability to maintain safety without compromising fun, alchemizing chaos into neat and tidy order. Adam lost his teaching positions along with his mind, and in the nine years we owned the building, he was the only one evicted.

When you're young, friends fall from the trees like ripe fruit while new pals appear out of thin air. The building was ideal for forging associations such as the one that began with Rupert. Unlike Keith or Malcolm, he was free to come and go as he pleased, with no marital discord or dissolution in his family. The yoke of post-apocalyptic divorce never came near his neck, and there wasn't a trace of emotional shrapnel on the boy.

Rupert's two grandmothers lived in separate apartments on separate floors, but Mrs. Swift on the paternal side resided primarily in Manhattan. She rented an apartment each year to escape the sweltering heat by summering in California, and her definition of summer was generous, often extending through the Christmas holidays. She was friendly, if a trifle formal, but this was to be expected from a native New Yorker who counted The Spence School and Smith College as alma maters.

In California, her conservative leanings were constantly subject to challenge, less by traditional methods and more by her grandson Rupert. She was nervous by disposition and easily rattled by California, which struck her as out of control. Los Angeles, as she conceived it, was a mixed blessing where she could enjoy family, ideal weather, and fantastic food in a place predicated on the abandonment of social mores.

Rupert's maternal grandmother, Mrs. Wilcox, was a long-term resident who predated our reign. She had a stylish birdcage like Neil and Mar Newton's. The only two residents allowed to have pet parakeets, I assumed this had something to do with advanced age since birds don't require walks and are good company.

Meme confirmed my understanding by saying, "The birds are grandfathered in."

Rupert, Keith, and I celebrated birthdays. We visited zoos, museums, and Disneyland. Our scrapbooks are filled with faded photos of a timeline measured in leisure. It's said that one is the loneliest number, but when three are involved, the social arithmetic doesn't always add up. Each of us was an only child or had been before the sibling invasion, which should've been sufficient to achieve civilized interaction when assembled without aim. Remove the frame of structured activity, and a state of anarchy prevails when three gather and two gang up, leaving one.

This cruel calculation was one in which we were equally complicit, but Meme said, "You may be misanthropic and misguided but never murderous."

I was fascinated by the astronomical ceiling at Grand Central Station, and George sent me a telescope that Rupert suggested we take to the roof. While contemplating a constellation, I stepped on a pebble and held the injured foot up, hopping full weight on the other while continuing my dedicated gazing. We decided to take a hot chocolate break and headed to my apartment, where Meyera and Rupert's dad were having coffee. Marshmallows were uppermost in our minds, and we discussed them in detail. Were they worth sacrificing valuable cup space and, if so, large, or small size? Was it best to eat them in one big bite or incrementally, and at what stage should they be consumed to prevent gelatinous disintegration?

The big-ticket issue regarding Bosco or Swiss Miss had yet to be decided, but the cocoa powder dust or whipped cream conundrum was under discussion when our deliberations abruptly stopped. While twisting around the banister with Rupert hot on my heels, we heard a voice call, "Freeze," and saw two police officers pointing guns directly at us.

Already frozen, the only part still moving was our minds, although they too were suspended when the officer said, "Grab a piece of wall."

I had never heard such a request and wondered about the logistics. Rupert was good at this type of problem-solving and looking for wall-grabbing clues, I turned toward him, which was a mistake. The no sudden move rule applies to policemen as well as thoroughbred horses, and before we knew it, our hands were handcuffed to the handrailing. Somehow, our parents found out, and Meyera's bellowing roar was heard first.

"What in the hell do you think you're doing?" Meyera demanded to know. "How dare you handcuff my daughter and her friend? What's your badge number, who do you report to, and have you lost your mind?"

Rupert's dad had a more modulated tone when asking, "What alerted you to attend here tonight?"

Officer grab-a-wall said, "A resident on the top floor heard pounding footsteps and reported a potential burglary in progress."

Meyera stepped forward and said, "That's why you pull a gun and handcuff two harmless kids?"

The officer was defensive, but his partner looked chagrined. There was a brief pause, and everyone went silent while no one moved. Not that Rupert and I were able to do so.

Officer grab-a-wall said, "My last partner was shot and killed by a twelve-year-old."

Officer chagrin seemed startled, and I wondered if this was the first he'd heard about it. Officer grab-a-wall's comment fueled Meyera's rage. She insinuated herself between me, Rupert, and the banister to which we were still attached.

"They're children, for God's sake," Meyera hissed, "don't you understand that?"

Officer chagrin comprehended her meaning and removed our handcuffs as delicately as would a jeweler dealing with diamond bracelets.

"She lives here, I live here, and both his grandmothers live here," Meyera snorted. "I own the building, and you need to leave now."

Mrs. Swift alerted Meme to the commotion, but was too nervous to leave her apartment.

My grandmother looked at the assembled group and said, "Thank you for standing-down guns and releasing the Barrington Two. Did everyone locate what they were looking for concerning star constellations, burglars, and kids in handcuffs? Officers, thank you for your service, but let's call it a night."

The tenant who'd called the cops was a miserly old bat named Mrs. Lardon. She was an artist with a lukewarm interest when it came to working with clay. A long-ago car accident left her slightly disabled but injured enough to claim benefits.

"So long as she limps when in public," Meme said.

Mrs. Lardon was always asking for the pool temperature to be turned up beyond acceptable standards, except those pertaining to hydrotherapy, and behaved as if the world were late for a date made solely to accommodate her. The sun on her side of the building was severe, creating an ideal backdrop against which she continued to shape, but never complete, a bust in her self-portrait. The ever-evolving image lurking under the cloth and the wizened one on the other side were parched and dry with cracked creases emphasized in sharp relief.

I can never remember if art imitates life or vice versa. Rather than pin my confusion on Oscar Wilde or ascribe it to Aristotle, I blame Mrs. Lardon instead. Artistic expression was what I sought the first and only time I knocked on her door. Ceramic craft, and maybe some food, might be nice when I dropped by at what I judged to be an acceptable mid-morning hour. Offered only dry toast and black coffee I left shortly after arriving. No models were created that day. We had a wearisome lesson in wedging instead. Although familiar with the child-friendly apartments in the building, I was aware of those that weren't.

There was one final participant in the breakfast brigade by the name of Lois Bantor, but rather than eat at her place, we went to the Brentwood Country Mart and Nosh Box for weekend meals instead. Lois lived across the hallway in apartment 105 and worked in the billing department at Cedars-Sinai Medical Center. Since its inception in 1902, it's been open on a twenty-four-hour seven days a week basis, and Lois approximated the same service, dealing even-handedly with all medical tabulations crossing her desk. She fought hard for those she took to, and did the same for ungrateful patients as well.

Her work was important and proved that comprehensive medical care doesn't stop with the physician. Lois never married, despite several opportunities to do so, directing her interest toward psychoanalysis and Zionism. She became a good friend to Meme, Meyera, and me, maintaining meaningful contact without compromising integrity. Straddling two generations is a challenge, but upping it to three is a talent. Regarding her as an auxiliary family member, I knocked on her door at times other than just weekends.

"Would you mind if I came over for a little while?" I'd ask Lois from the age of three. "Mommy's out, Meme's sleeping, and it's a little lonely."

Lois was happy to have an opportunity to practice her Encyclopedia Britannica sales pitch. This part-time venture lasted less than the thirty-hour definition of part-time work, but the merchandise was made available on a sale or return basis, allowing Lois to eventually elect the latter — except for a junior edition sold to us in 1968 with the promise, "It's good for education."

Lois was convinced she'd done us a good turn, and although the set was less valuable as the years rolled on, she was right about the fact they remained educational. Twenty-plus years after purchase, all fifteen volumes surfaced in mint condition and were relegated to a garage sale. Everyone, even vaguely interested in the collection, asked the same question, "What about the Moon Landing?"

Without any mention of Apollo 11, I didn't have a ready answer but didn't want to lug the damn things back in the house.

"If it's NASA you want," I stated, with a slight huff, "you're obviously astute enough to buy a book devoted to the topic," I added, my shoulders indicating this irrefutable fact. "These are a bit earlier, but everything up to 1968 is beautifully bound in mint condition," I said, pointing to the leather binding as if it were a beloved saddle. "I'm more interested in finding the right home than the right price," I added as if parting with an even more beloved pony. "For fifty bucks, it's yours if you promise to look after it," I said, concluding a fast sale.

Neil Newton celebrated his 91st birthday with a party on our patio. He was a popular guy, and everyone turned up to toast his continued good health, including a newly married couple who'd moved in the month before. A couple who couldn't or wouldn't cook and went out for dinner every single solitary night.

Meyera was amused by this and said to Lois, "Didn't know anyone was that good in bed."

I assumed this meant they were talented when it came to matters of mattresses, pillows, and linen. This was their first social engagement in the building, and they kept to themselves at the back of the patio near my pet rabbits.

"Would you like to hold one?" I asked.

"That would be lovely," answered the wife. "How about the white one?"

I lifted Fluffer from the hutch and placed the diminutive bunny in her lap while our neighbor, Len, held the larger rabbit called Tar Baby. When asked why I chose the name, I said it matched the rabbit's coat and his surprise arrival when I returned from the La Brea Tar Pits to find his cage wrapped in newspaper by the front door.

It was an Easter gift from George, who unknowingly ordered a Belgium Hare comparable in species terms to his own ilk. Tar Baby started small but reached considerable bulk, requiring no fewer than five hutches and radically increasing in size. Meyera had her hands full on the day of Neil Newton's party with platters of cold cuts, potato salad and birthday cake. The doorbell rang repeatedly, and everyone shouted, "Out here, we're at the back come join us."

The acoustics designed to contain sound worked effectively, making it my job to open the front door ferrying in late arrivals. I was a six-year-old version of Charon taking guests across our river, Styx, while they became increasingly tipsy. Mom almost dropped the birthday cake, but Len hopped up to steady it, allowing Tar Baby to hop down.

Fluffer was also on the ground, having been placed there by our new neighbor, ostensibly only for a moment, but we hadn't had time to get acquainted, let alone allow me to explain the complex nature of my pet's relationship. She didn't know that, in rabbit terms, a moment is a long time. George advised against allowing the two pets out at once and cited a disastrous Siamese fighting fish experience he had as a boy.

These biting fish are both beautiful and aggressive, able to be made so by their own reflection (but haven't we all had days like that). Used in historic times for gambling, they fight to the end, in a custom my father averted with a custom-designed aquarium featuring frosted glass dividers. The absence of mirrors kept my father's fish safe and elegantly presented when he'd come home from school to relax while watching the weightless wending of colorful tails.

Regrettably, he returned one day to find just one fish alive with half a fin, owing to a new maid aiming to secure further work by pulling out all the stops, including the aquarium glass dividers.

"You wouldn't want something like that to happen to the rabbits, would you?" my father asked. "Best thing to do is keep them separate but equal. I believe in that and not just for pets, my policy makes more sense than that exhibited by the Supreme Court with all this integration nonsense."

Neil's party gained momentum, and so did the rabbits who were racing, dicing, and cutting across each other with Tar Baby in pursuit.

People were laughing or lifting their feet depending upon individual attitudes toward the pets while I hollered, "Help me catch Tar Baby. He wants to kill Fluffer, and it's not funny."

Mr. Sidwell tried to calm things down by saying, "It's not a fatal death Tar Baby wants but *La petite mort*."

I panicked until both bunnies were returned to their respective hutches. Keith's dad, Victor, allowed the laughter but cut short, racy comments that started to simmer.

He tempered humor with the need for decorum by saying, "Let's agree with the child it's not funny, and if anyone thinks it is, let's hear them explain why."

Everyone went silent except Neil, who said, "I think it's funny, but I'm not going to explain anything to anyone on my birthday."

Everyone laughed and raised a glass in acknowledgment of his charm. Neil died not long after that. I went to his memorial service and stood in line to sign the guest book.

Victor lifted me up to reach the podium on which it rested, and, writing my name as best I could at age six, Len said, "What nice handwriting."

It was my first funeral and last penmanship compliment. Today, my signature would be more suitable for the Bates Motel register featured in Hitchcock's film *Psycho*. Mr. and Mrs. Sidwell attended the funeral and said, "Good innings," but to my mind, there wasn't anything good about the end of Neil Newton.

Growing up in the apartment building provided a fabulous foreshadowing of what later life could, ideally would, and most definitely did deliver in terms of both the light and dark aspects of experience. Embracing literature, music, and the art of conversation not only informed but shaped the foundation on which to build core character. Residents who spared time (let alone compassion) for a neglected child inspired tremendous affection, but I'm also grateful to those who didn't, because that too is an inevitable part of the journey.

CHAPTER 7

George came out quids in on the financial aspect of the divorce, but his visitation rights excluded Christmas, and, to soften the blow, he was granted custody on New Year's Eve. I was five when I flew solo from LAX to JFK, and the first-class ticket, intended for an entirely different demographic, was wasted on me. Unlimited 7-UP soft drinks were another matter, and I ordered these as would a parched camel coming off the Sahara seeking to slake a serious thirst.

One of our residents was a TWA stewardess named Gert, and I joined her coast-to-coast flight, during which she made repeated trips to check on me from her station at the back of the craft. Did I want to color or wear a pair of plastic TWA wings pinned to my blouse? Perhaps I'd have a word with an unruly six-year-old in Economy traveling with his parents who regarded air travel as inclusive of childcare.

After boarding, they abdicated all responsibility for the boy, and Gert was furious, as were other passengers in the immediate vicinity of this hell-raiser. To satisfy the demands of many, rather than indulge a few, she corralled the brat in one of the toilets, adding an Out of Service sign. This was a different era, long before the cavalcade of legal action such a gesture would attract today. Looking out the window proved more interesting than watching the movie, but at least I had a window, unlike the bad boy at the back. When we landed, George took Gert and I to dinner.

21 was famous for fabulous food served in the chic surroundings of a former speakeasy. Cast-iron painted jockeys line the entrance, and anything smacking of horses appealed to me. The *Maître de* took us to the bootlegger's cave hidden at the back and showed us an ancient bottle of champagne kept among private stock that, when turned upside

down, caused gold filigree to drift toward the bottom, creating a contraband snow globe fit for a gangster.

The 1960s were known for the consumption of recreational drugs, but for me, it was a time of turtle soup. George laughed when I asked the chef to please make my portion light on the sherry. He also laughed at Meyera's failed security blanket subterfuge when her loving attempt to conceal my comforter by sewing it on the underside of a quilt was doomed. I had two such blankets called Bobo, and wanted one to travel with me.

Meyera's solution was ingenious, and I left the other one safely at home. George, however, favored Victorian methods of child-rearing, and when he discovered the camouflaged comforter, it was incinerated. This may be why I tend to purchase favored items in twos, although with girls, you do everything twice.

New Year's Eve in Times Square was spectacular, and midnight in Manhattan was only nine o'clock by my California time setting. I was wide awake and wide-eyed while sitting on my father's towering shoulders, which provided an unrestricted aerial view of merrymakers bidding farewell to *Auld Lang Syne*. Barely controlled frenzy below was focused on a great glowing ball above, and I watched this teeming mass with rapt fascination when the last ten seconds of the calendar year were counted down in a dramatic chorus.

A fresh year would momentarily arrive, and with it, all the resolutions to create something better. Strangers were hugging, kissing, and toasting. Everyone's attention was directed toward that great ball as it descended, and each beat elevated a collective hope for the future. A palpable wish swept through the crowd. People united in the hope that this clean slate would be the one upon which to etch a new start, and optimism exploded.

I tried to replicate this event back at school during art class, but capturing the anticipation when the clock struck twelve, accompanied by the detonation of confetti, wasn't quite as easy as it sounds. Our kindergarten teacher gave us large sheets of rough blank paper with bits of kindling embossed on the surface, and we scaled these random snags with dull edged crayons in traditional colors because Blizzard Blue, Jazzberry Jam, and Key Lime Pie had yet to be invented.

To a young palate, these *palette* additions probably taste the same, but after selecting a few shades from Crayola's box of eighteen, I set to work creating a visual memory from the Christmas holiday by filling my canvas with stick figures holding each other in spirited *bonhomie*. Flecks of multicolored snow falling all around the swift-moving scene formed my first attempt at backlighting, and to emphasize that enormous ball as it moved toward its final landing, I added a halo effect.

Granted, my depiction of George and I standing above the central figures was a function of artistic license, but the fact we were significantly taller than New York skyscrapers was appealing. Each work of art was held up on view the next day, and the most popular subject featured families around the Christmas tree. When my picture was displayed, our teacher frowned before asking which of us was responsible for such a renegade image.

I responded with the enthusiasm of a novice artist thrusting not just one arm, but two, in the air while shouting, "It's me."

I was asked to remain behind and miss recess, which both irritated and worried me. As a low-flying, high-octane child, I needed to cool my jets, and this was an unwelcome interruption.

"Didn't you have a Christmas tree, turkey dinner and presents from Santa?" our teacher asked.

"We had a beautiful tree," I said with genuine feeling, "and a delicious Christmas day dinner with all the trimmings. I got everything I wanted from Santa and everyone else."

She was neither appeased nor impressed and said, "Why didn't you draw those memories as your classmates have done?"

Although I didn't have a ready answer, I knew enough to pretend that I was giving the issue due consideration when she said, "Your picture is all out of proportion. A human being can't be as tall as a building, and what are stick figures doing all bundled together?"

I shrugged in a gesture that suggested, "Crazy world, eh."

"You know that snow is white, so why make it various colors?" she asked.

What was I to say? Not all artistic expression has a rationale behind it, so step outside the confines of limited perspective and join me.

I wasn't confident in the strength of my aesthetic argument and nodded when she said, "Next time, make something understandable that doesn't confuse people."

Confused but compliant, I agreed. Confinement to representational images was preferable to confinement in the classroom, but when released, I went outside in a dark mood. If Chagall was lauded for having figures floating in the air, why not me? Meyera had an extensive collection of *Catalogue Raisonne* featuring prominent artists whose work I was familiar with, and if called upon to debate the distinction between *Homage* and the derivative nature of my picture, I'd have been ready to roll. Julian Lennon's drawing of *Lucy in the Sky with Diamonds* went global, while mine struggled to get a foothold in LA.

Our next art class involved that same nobbily paper but clipped lengthwise on easels involving paint brushes, as difficult to navigate as the crayons. Allowed to pursue the subject of our choosing, inspiration refused to grace my canvas, and the muse forgot all about me. I was left floundering with a blank sheet staring me in the face. Time was running out, yet everyone else was happily painting away, making me envy and resent them.

Frustrated and pressured to put something down on that tyrannical paper, I started and finished with one enormous red circle. Abstract Expressionists Mark Rothko and Willem de Kooning had yet to be recognized by most kindergarten teachers, and not by mine. Rather than separate the wheat from the chaff, I was indoctrinated to distinguish a sophisticate from a philistine, but this didn't prevent me from dreading the moment when my work would be held up on display, likely to attract disapproval.

We were eager to see the art created with paint, which, to us, was a new medium of expression. The subjects dealt predominately with images of trees, pets, and that ever-popular intact nuclear family. *Boring*, I thought. *Unimaginative, pedestrian and no flair.*

My canvas made it to the top, and, as expected, our teacher fixed her narrowed eyes on mine, saying, "I know who is responsible for this. What on earth have you made this time?"

Ready to do battle, I was armed with literature and film as my weapons of choice.

"It's *Le Balloon Rouge* from the story about a little boy in Montmartre, sac de cur," I said, grateful for Montessori's screening the previous year. "Last time I drew Manhattan and this time Paris. Do you like it?"

She'd had enough of this nettled artistic issue, which was clear from the exasperated shrug of her shoulders, but nothing more was mentioned. We ran outside for recess, and I looked forward to leaving the rug rat mentality of kindergarten behind. Progressing to the more erudite realm of elementary education was bound to be better, but our first-grade teacher, Mrs. Stillwater, was fresh from England with short hair, short bangs, and a short temper.

She whipped us into submission on day one and did the same with our parents, who nodded obediently when she said, "I will tell the children something once and one time only. Is that understood?"

George was barely cognizant of school terms, frequently taking me out of class for holidays. The dictates of a regular academic schedule were of no concern to him and always subordinate to travel plans. His generous annual donations encouraged the school's administrators to turn a blind eye to these casual comings and goings following the adage 'Whenever they pay, they get to say.' I was only six and, as George was fond of saying, "Unlikely to miss a major lecture."

Show-and-tell was designed to sharpen our public speaking ability, and I rejoined classmates three weeks late from a trip to Montreal, ready to share the remarkable experience of watching our favorite cartoons in French. Mrs. Stillwater wasn't frowning exactly, but disapproval was in the air. Unlike her predecessor, she took matters of concern directly to parents, summoning Meyera to a meeting.

"Your daughter often misses school to go galivanting, and while I don't agree with that, I've been asked to remain silent on this issue," Mrs. Stillwell stated. "Truant is only technically transformed by consent, but it all adds up to absent in my book."

"Her father does like to travel, and we both feel that broadening horizons by crossing borders is a form of education," Meyera said.

"Not when journeys such as this most recent jaunt result in fanciful stories," Mrs. Stillwater said. "Are you aware of the ludicrous yarn she spun in front of the entire class? It was an absurd tale of cartoon characters speaking a foreign language, which is a classic case of an overactive imagination."

"How can this be a function of imagination when she told me all about it, too?" Meyera said. "Watching children's programming in Canada and seeing her favorite shows broadcast in French was a treat for the child."

Mrs. Stillwater was momentarily lost for words, and Meyera was momentarily empowered by the silence. The two women sat opposite each other, considering what to do next.

"I can only conclude that I must use the new passport I've been issued with greater frequency," Mrs. Stillwater said.

"Why not venture to Canada?" Meyera suggested. "I can't think of anyone from Britain who doesn't adore it," she added, relieved that the discussion was at an end.

Mrs. Stillwater's immaculate accent, clipped words, and strict demeanor appealed to me, despite being part Mary Poppins and part Cruella de Vil. My child's instinct suggested that she was suffering from adjustment problems. Negotiating a new marriage and a new career in the new world can't have been easy. Little did Mrs. Stillwater know how much we had in common while scrambling to make sense of unfamiliar circumstances confronting us both. Our respective challenges may have been borne of different difficulties, but they required similar skills with which to cope, and I hoped that she'd eventually regard America as a happy home.

Time moves in accordance with emotional gears. It flies when you are having fun, but crawls by on hands and knees when you're divorced relatively young. After four years of fruitless waiting for Meyera to return, George moved on. The inconvenience of his custodial weekends with me might have been a contributing factor, but who could blame him for seeking a permanent mate? Isn't that what the parade of womanhood was all about?

Those desirous females served as gap-fillers during his lapse in the trough between marriages, and, as with most pageants, this one came to a *grand finale*. The last one on view became a permanent fixture when my father's beautiful bride, Susan, appeared. I was instantly enamored but unable to keep hold of her name. It got lost in the shuffle of all the other names I encountered when George was dating. Addressing her in a roll call of each romantic predecessor was not a cognitive act, and I would cringe each time I made this mistake, immediately saying her name three times to make it stick.

Susan was loving, available, and inventive. She could braid my hair, make up stories, and read to me. It soon became evident that children's literature made a grave error when describing stepmothers, because mine couldn't have been further away from evil. Her reading aloud represented long overdue rain on an arid desert, and was a welcome contrast to Meyera's stammering attempts to navigate words on a page.

Not only impatient, I was also a long way from decent during book at bedtime sessions, yanking the text from Meyera's hands and saying, "Forget it. I'll read aloud to you instead."

Susan's name settled into my head and heart by the time I was seven, although at the time of the meeting, I was age six, she twenty-four and George thirty-seven. From the beginning, her relationship with my father was distinctly different, and I recognized this when we went to a five-star restaurant in Beverly Hills called Poor Richard's. This was my favorite place for dining, but it had nothing to do with the menu.

Sophisticated surroundings were crowned by a train set running along the ceiling perimeter, and a selection of toys was displayed inside the coat room. The subliminal bargain on offer was unmistakable to younger patrons who'd behave during the meal to obtain a toy. Troll dolls with plump plastic bodies adorned with bright shocks of dayglow hair were all the rage, and, however hideous in hindsight, I loved to collect them.

George and Susan were checking their coats when I spotted an enormous one with orange hair. During dinner, I observed protocol and sat with ramrod posture while chewing with my mouth closed, which wasn't easy with braces running the length and breadth of my teeth, Grand Junction style. I made sure my elbows remained off the table, and, true to form, the troll was presented to me as we left the restaurant. I came back to the apartment, hugging the doll to my chest, when Meyera snatched it from me.

"What's this, and where did it come from?" she hissed.

Stunned by her anger, I was shocked by her gesture. Removing a toy from my possession was an uncharacteristic maneuver never encountered before.

"Who gave you this?" she demanded to know.

"Daddy and Susan," I blurted out, instantly regretting my answer.

If only I had refrained from that second named reference and taken a moment to reflect, weighing the impact of my reply. Unrattled, I'd have credited the gift to just my father, but the word Susan escaped my lips, making it impossible to unring the bell. Meyera ran out of the apartment, sprinting down the long hallway leading to the building's front entrance. As she dashed to the curb, her aim was unmistakable, and my troll was flung at George's departing car. I knew not to say a word and allow events to unfold. What was a doll compared to this insanity?

Fresh trauma arrived and looked likely to remain a catastrophe for Mom, which confronted us all. The distance between our front door and George's rapidly disappearing car was enough to prevent the doll's destruction, but the same can't be said for the rest of us. An unmistakable seismic shift occurred that day, irrevocably impacting the emotional landscape. Our universe tilted on its axis, and everything changed, requiring me to tread with caution, avoiding overt references to Susan, let alone anything smacking of demonstrable love for my new stepmother.

Susan would not make the same mistake Meyera had, by suggesting she and George silence the splashy sums they swam in. Despite the downpour that drenched and finally drowned the first marriage, Susan wasn't about to go it alone. Her father, Joe Wright, had one thing in common with Dr. Joe, which was endless capital.

Joe Wright owned his own island in the Bahamas, along with homes in Chicago and Florida, where his boats were used for racing and lavish entertaining. He loved to travel, sail, and drink vodka in a cocktail of his own invention called Razorblade Soup. He was a Chicago lawyer, extremely intelligent, attractive, and confident enough to assert that he wasn't at work to be popular but to deliver results. That's what he said, and that's what he did as CEO of Zenith Electronics, moving production overseas.

Manufacturing in Korea made sense, resulting in a skyrocketing share price. A formidable figure in the boardroom, Joe's earnings were tied to company performance in a contractual calculation, which caused him to hold his breath every year, concerned about shareholder suits for excessive remuneration. He needn't have worried. A year into his retirement, the company took a nosedive, requiring Joe's immediate return to service. The Board of Directors presented his wife with a diamond bracelet as an attractive way to apologize for calling upon him one last time. It came with a card inscribed: Joe Wright is never wrong.

Joe was a visionary who frequently stepped outside the corporate mandate to confer with others of similar orientation, including Howard Hughes, who insisted they meet at 3:00 am on his Culver City airstrip, where they discussed advanced uses of television technology. Adjourning to their privately piloted planes at the crack of dawn, Joe shared his favorite joke with Mr. Hughes about two fellows who had been exemplary in their business and family lives.

Before departing this mortal coil, they promised to let the survivor know what the afterlife was like. Many happy years preceded the eventuality of one partner's death, and the other awaited contact that was eventually whispered in his ear.

"Hello, partner, is that you?" asked the surviving associate.

"Yes, and I want to let you know that everything here is fantastic," said the deceased.

"What a relief," said the survivor. "Tell me about your typical day."

"Every day is the same," the deceased said. "I wake up in the sunshine, have a lovely breakfast, and then make love to my heart's content. After that, I will go for a dip and take a nap."

"I knew heaven would be like that," said the survivor.

"I'm not in heaven," the deceased explained. "I'm a buffalo in Wyoming."

My attendance at George's second honeymoon with his second wife took him only a second to decide, and Aspen, Colorado, seemed ideal to them, but the idea of skiing on anything other than water terrified me. Summoning all pains deposited by the psyche on the soma, I developed a high fever and strep throat, making me unfit to fly. This was a brief reprieve, and to accommodate my late arrival, the honeymoon was extended. On this journey, there'd be no familiar sherpa or *loco parentis* stewardess to shepherd me there and back. In preparation for this solo sojourn, I was drilled daily with instructions to remain on the plane after the first landing.

"Do not, under any circumstances, get off the aircraft until after the second touchdown," Meyera instructed.

"Don't become curious and wander off in a strange airport," Meme added.

At the age of seven, I considered myself a seasoned traveler and had infinitely more in-flight experience than the passenger next to me, who was in her mid-twenties and anxious about her first flight. I smiled when we encountered turbulence, and explained that the sound of the landing gear was nothing to be afraid of.

When the second and final landing was secure, I noticed a flight of stairs moving manually toward the exit door. Never having seen this method of deboarding, I regarded it as a novelty and joined the line of passengers waiting to step off the plane. When it was my turn to disembark, I stood at the top of the stairway leading from the cabin to *terra firma*, grasping the handrail before making my way down. Two steps in, I stopped dead in my tracks as true cold confronted me for the first time. It was intense, unceasing, and comprehensive. I couldn't imagine how such a thing was possible, let alone desirable. Breathing in with great difficulty, I was struck numb by the fact that snowy weather hits you everywhere all at once.

Even with my new stepmother's presence, the trip was a catastrophe, but to be fair, my sense of panic started early when shopping in LA for the unfamiliar equipment required by this expedition. At the sporting goods store, a compelling poster featured US alpine ski racer Spider Sabich somersaulting midair from the peak of a great summit, and I wondered if I'd be expected to jump in such a way.

I pictured Disneyland's Matterhorn ride with me stranded at the top and no little red toboggan to spirit me safely down. Standing on a bunny slope with our ski instructor, I noticed the other students were significantly younger and shorter, which provided them with an advantage. That and the fact that they were fearless. Their low center of gravity gave them a proficiency on snow that I felt in water, but when water turns to ice, it's a dangerously different proposition: no brakes, no reins, and no mane to grab hold of in the event of an emergency. Fall, and it hurts.

When I finally managed to stand, the nightmare began all over again, and on top of that gentle hill, I pledged never again to allow a snowy mountain to threaten me. Escaping the lesson, I liberated my legs from treacherously slippery skis and hideously heavy boots. Once all the various bindings were undone, I checked my feet, half expecting to find the lotus shape popular in ancient China. Feeling light as air, I ran inside the *après-ski* area, hoping to find George and Susan. They weren't in the lounge, restaurant or at the bar, and a quick glance around the room revealed only adult strangers. I didn't have a key for our chalet and was out of choices as to where I should be.

Scanning for a responsible grown-up, I pinpointed a conservatively dressed man, which was as close as I could get to finding an adult in uniform, which was a fallback emergency tactic Meme taught me.

He was standing at the bar talking with several adults, satisfying the safety in numbers threshold, and after waiting for a break in their conversation, I looked at the conservative man and asked, "Where do you go when you're lost?"

Later, during dinner, I had more success navigating the endless cut-lery needed for endless courses. George downed several cocktails be-fore we sat at the table. He was working his way to the bottom of a sec-ond bottle of wine when I pulled out my mathematics homework book. Arithmetic was my Achilles heel, and having struck out on the slopes earlier, I was already intimidated that evening. The assignment was a math/spelling crossover involving the number eight, but numbers rep-resented danger, and I froze as my mind refused to wrap itself around those five digits. With the ferocity of the *Fuhrer,* George fixed the white light on me.

He was a towering, inebriated ogre of a man who demanded to know, "How do you spell E-I-G-H-T?"

I was scared stiff, and incapable of hazarding a guess. At seven, the number eight eluded me.

"No, that's wrong," he bellowed. "Get it right, goddamn it," he roared. "Can't you spell a simple number correctly?"

Several patrons looked over at us with eyes sympathetic to Susan and me but daggers to George. They were visibly irritated by this intru-sion, and rightly so. We effectively obliterated an otherwise peaceful dining ambiance.

The emotional temperature directed toward our table matched the frost outside when our waiter asked, "Will there be anything more you'd like this evening?"

The entire restaurant fell silent while awaiting his answer. With a dismissive wave of his hand, George said, "Most likely."

Susan gently placed her hand on my father's wrist and said, "George, we've all had a long day, and perhaps we should postpone the lesson for another time?"

My father turned his disapproving gaze toward Susan while sipping the last of his wine with an air of disdain.

"Why not head back to the hotel?" Susan suggested. "It would allow the younger diner at our table to get some sleep and provide you with an opportunity to have a brandy."

"After this exercise in abject frustration, a Hennessy XO would hit the spot," he said.

"I could do with a Remy Martin myself," Susan added.

That's when I knew she was rattled by events at our table. We walked back to the hotel in veiled silence caused by the fresh fall of powder snow and icy emotions from dinner.

Neither had yet to melt, but Susan stopped short at a snow drift and shot me a look of sheer mischief before saying, "Want to have some fun?"

I'd been so busy surviving the trip that her offer of recreation felt foreign.

"Lay flat back on the snow and wave your arms high over your head," she instructed, "that's right, now move your legs side to side. Stay perfectly still while I pick you straight up and look at the image with wings and a gown. It's called a snow angel, and if you make a wish, I promise it will come true."

Little did she know that my wish had already come to fruition. The only angel I'd need was standing in front of me, regrettably with the Prince of Darkness right behind her. The matrimonial bond that tied George and Susan served to sever Meyera's threadbare connection with stability.

Despite being a beast at times, George was now leashed and happily tethered, if not thriving, in the Manhattan home he shared with Susan. A balanced perspective wasn't something my parents could easily sustain, and homeostasis on one side led to disintegration on the other.

Moving to New York made sense for George and Susan. I became bicoastal, and everyone was separated by three hours and three thousand miles. Perhaps time and distance might skim off some of the tension. I hoped taking a foot off the emotional accelerator and coasting for a while would do us all good. That is, until Meyera fell off the track.

"Mommy, please come back inside," I said. "The hallway is a bad place for you to be. Not when you are wearing such a thin nightgown. It is cold, and I am afraid you'll hurt yourself. You've got to stop falling. I'm not strong enough to lift you, but I'll make a bridge with my back that you can use to hoist yourself up. After we get you standing, I'll lead you back to bed, but please stop banging against the walls."

Sometimes, a short distance is a long way. Once back in bed, I notice that her breathing is unsteady, and I make a small nest, placing my blanket and pillow on the floor at the entrance to her room. If she wakes up, she'll need to step over me, which I'm certain will grab my attention. If she scrambles, stumbles, or falls, I'll know it and be right here to remain in control during a lifetime of uncertainty.

PART 2
BICOASTAL

CHAPTER 8

Susan became pregnant, I was promoted to sibling, and George purchased books that informed children about babies. These sensitive works begin with benign images of tadpoles, taking the reader ever so slowly toward human reproduction, but despite Susan's superior skill in reading aloud, I flipped the frog pages over toward the ending.

With one eyebrow raised, Susan said, "Yep, we're almost at the good bit."

We howled with laughter, but George admonished us about disrespect and said, "If you're not willing to devote the dignity these books deserve, I'll remove them."

Susan and I locked eyes in shared camaraderie before resuming reading. Somewhere along the pregnancy path, Susan read about sibling rivalry and decided to nip it in the bud. When we went to Central Park Zoo, she took us to a section that admitted adults only if accompanied by a child.

A sign posted next to the petting pen was clear on this point, and she gestured toward it repeatedly, saying, "Thank goodness you're here. See how important you are? No one could ever replace you."

We stopped at the nine-foot-tall bronze statue of Hans Christian Anderson, and I grabbed hold of his nose while swinging up on his shoulders. This well-worn procedure was employed by scads of kids, making the bronze on this portion of the statue significantly brighter than the rest.

Snapping a photo for posterity, Susan said, "California has the shine, but New York's got the polish."

My stepmother was culturally astute, procuring tickets to off-Broadway productions of *Two by Two* and *No, No, Nanette,* but we finished with *The Fantasticks*. As in the name, this was our favorite, and over the course of two years, we saw it four times. The first song always chokes me up; *Try to Remember* was evocative of that period.

Susan was singing Simon & Garfunkel's *At the Zoo* when we left Central Park for the dinosaurs and dioramas at the American Museum of Natural History. Stepping into the past to escape the present was a pleasant way to spend an afternoon, although I preferred her other sanctuary, The Frick Collection.

I tend to go Frick, however, when in need of reflection and for reflection, read Fragonard-sponsored putti penance. There was nothing like high art when feeling low. We went to Radio City Music Hall to look at Art Deco design, relegating the Rockettes to a footnote.

George was disappointed and said, "What's the point of taking her to Rockefeller Center and ignoring the show?"

"The point is to show her that Rockefeller means more than money and represents a contribution to the arts," Susan said.

"What did you find of interest?" George asked, turning toward me.

"Lots of things I wasn't allowed to touch, but the banister was fun," I said.

"Don't tell me you allowed her to behave like a banshee?" George asked Susan. "You permitted her to run and slide?"

"One banister, one slide, and one time only," Susan said. "She flopped flat on her back a few times to look at the chandeliers from a different perspective — that of an eight-year-old — and were I less than the same number of months pregnant, I'd have joined her."

Although heavily pregnant, Susan felt the Statue of Liberty was a must-see monument, and she sat at the base fanning herself with a leaflet while I set off to summit 354 steps leading to Liberty's crown, followed by 354 steps back down. This took longer than anticipated, and Susan purchased a guidebook packed with facts about this illustrious gift from France.

"Did you know the Statue of Liberty was originally intended for the Suez Canal in Egypt?" Susan asked over dinner.

George and I shook our heads, indicating we didn't.

"New York had to compete with Philadelphia and Boston for the statue," she added. "Which was supposed to be a lighthouse, but engineering problems made it impossible to light. The designer suggested they gild it and take what isn't working, what won't work and just cover it in gold," she said, filling up with tears.

"Gold is what your heart is made of, my love," George said.

Rising from the dinner table, he walked over to Susan's chair, gently placing his hands on her shoulders. Smiling at her warmly, he cajoled her to stand up, which took several minutes.

"It's been a long, hot day, and everyone's tired," he said. "Time to acquiesce to a good night's rest," he whispered, walking her to their bedroom.

Days out with Susan provided convivial topics of conversation, and after visiting The Guggenheim Museum, I asked if next time they'd allow roller skates. As with most Upper East Side dwelling children, I was tantalized by the circular nautilus structure, regarding it as less of a design and more of a demand to put it to better use.

George and Susan socialized a lot. They were at large in Manhattan and sprawling houses rented in Rye, Harrison, and White Plains during what I termed sporting goods summers. Our East Coast social circle was comprised of the Stanford, Haltern, Lien, and Brebner family. Each had a smattering of children, except the Brebners, but they were trying. At least seven or eight kids contributed to parties held each weekend, along with games and athletic amusements.

As summer progressed, so did the fervor to outdo the previous event, be it barbecue fare one-upmanship or assembling outlandish equipment for the *kinder* to play with. Each family arrived with competitively fine wine, and wives paraded into the kitchen bearing homemade goods, creating a mountain of dips, salads, and pies. The adults either feigned or took a genuine interest in the array of flashy items for the kids, starting with Slip N Slides, Hula Hoops, and dancing sprinklers before progressing to badminton, croquet, and volleyball.

Football, basketball, and soccer followed, but the collective appetite hit a crescendo with wrestling and boxing. As kids, we took more than a modicum of pleasure from this Herculean home version of keeping up with the Joneses.

Rain showers were forecast for our extravaganza, making the swing set, and climbing frame George ordered redundant before we would have a chance to touch it. Inclement weather was bad luck, and the families with whom we spent time must've thanked the skies above that it was George's turn to contend with the crowd.

When it came to recreation, my father was a master, and rented a film projector, along with several children's movies, in case it poured. He certainly planned to, and ordered a case of scotch to accompany the box of Kobe steak from the butcher. He wouldn't run short on supplies, requiring a trip to the liquor store, which was a nuisance at the best of times but more so when over the limit.

For the social event at our house, George was on top of his game, creating decoy burgers intended to lull our guests into thinking he'd skimped on the menu. He laced the burgers with rubber bands that, when mixed into the mince and molded into paddies, aren't visible until that first bite. After that, it's quite a task to decorously disengage the mouth from the burger.

"We must make sure everyone bites in at exactly the same time," George said. "If one or two take a nibble while others are watching, the jigs up."

The Stanfords were the first to arrive, and I was delighted to see Lucy. We spent time together at private gatherings or the Westchester Country Club, where George introduced us to a prolific producer of children's cartoons called Paul Terry. A sudden storm cleared the pool area when hailstones the size of golf balls pounded down with tremendous force.

As we huddled under the club canopy, George said, "Paul, come and meet the girls. They're big fans of your work."

An elderly gentleman made his way through the dense crowd, but it took a while for him to reach us. We had plenty of time since the valets were leisurely under normal conditions, and with the sudden change in weather, they were overwhelmed.

"Do you like cartoons, and would you care to name your favorites?" Paul asked.

I liked the sound of this game and was quick to reference every cartoon character that popped into my head.

"Did you make Bugs Bunny, Woody Woodpecker or *Top Cat*?" I asked.

None of those characters belonged to his production studio, which he'd had for fifty years before selling to CBS for $3.5 million at a time when $3.5 million meant something.

Lucy was a stalwart team supporter who grabbed *Le baton* and said, "How about *The Jetsons*, Mr. Magoo or Yogi Bear?"

People crammed next to us could hear our conversion and kept their gaze directed downward. Had we been in an elevator, they'd have looked up.

"I'm sorry to say those fine figures are not mine,' he said, increasing discomfort all around.

This game wasn't fun; it was downright embarrassing, but before we gave up, Lucy scored a touchdown by saying, "Mighty Mouse might be one of yours?"

Thinking we probably struck out again, I followed with Heckle and Jeckle.

"I'm delighted you like my Mighty and those craze two birds," he said.

Lucy laughed and said, "I do now."

The Stanford's live-in maid was a vicious timekeeper who insisted lunch be served on the dot, and if we were late, she'd open the door to release a border collie called Growler. He executed his urge to herd efficiently, leaving a massacre of overturned bicycles with wheels rotating in the air. Skinned knees and a smattering of tears were something of a specialty for this pet, who remained in his vicinity, making us safe from canine enforcement here at our house.

Lucy's elder sister joined the party but ignored us. A gap of six years in age was too much for her to forgive. She remained a shadowy figure, frequently stationed on a lounger by the club pool, where Lucy and I dismissed her with equal abandon when surfacing from a high dive dare. This game was a watered-down version of truth or dare, and you must declare a wish and then dive off the top board to ensure it will come true. Sounds simple, but the Crow's Nest was the most treacherous of three diving boards on offer, with twenty-five feet separating the top from the deep end.

"You go first," Lucy said.

We were eyeing the board reverentially as we'd done many summers before. The Crow's Nest lorded itself over us, loomed large, and beckoned like an aquatic version of Rio de Janeiro's *Christ the Redeemer.*

"Okay, because I want my wish to become real," I said. "But if you lose heart and climb back down, that's going to be real too," I instructed, convinced these rules had a foundation in reality.

It's windy up there and a lot higher than it looks from below. For me, a pony hung in the balance, specified in detail as required by the rules governing wishes. Forfeiting this prize was out of the question, but so was an immediate leap. I was suspended between fear and adrenalin, which is a dreadful place to be. I found it so uncomfortable that this alone prompted me to dive, but hitting the water was easier than I thought and was over in the flash of a few seconds. The same length of time it took for my bikini bottom to fly off the moment I touched down on the water.

I watched it sway side to side toward the pool floor and found suiting up several feet below the surface the most challenging aspect of our game. There was no need or time to warn Lucy. She always wore a navy-blue one-piece and was halfway up the Crow's Nest stairs. Kissing a boy had been her wish, and when pressed for specifics (which I did only to assist the wish in becoming real), she mentioned a cute guy from the drama club.

Lucy entered the water hands and head first, with her near vertical body position suggesting, but not stirring, a splash. Everything about her smacked of precision, and when she completed the dive, her perfectly pointed toes went gracefully below water. Watching this flawless display, I was certain her wish would come to fruition.

Gareth Haltern Sr., his wife Jean and their kids came through the door with boxes for the kitchen. I was anxious because Gareth Jr. was my first crush, cute beyond measure, with a disarming simile adorned by adorable dimples. As with most preppy boys, Gareth Jr. gave the impression of being stratospherically successful well in advance of having to try. At twelve years of age to my eight, this ratio would work, and George suspected puppy love was in the air. It would have been hard not to notice, considering my sudden interest in personal appearance.

"Daddy, why didn't you tell me we're meeting the Halterns for dinner?" I demanded to know. "I've not had a shower or washed my hair, and you know how long it takes me to decide what to wear," I complained, hastily tending to these now-pressing matters.

Gareth Jr. grinned at me while handing Susan a Bundt cake. Uncertain of what to do, I took refuge behind our standard poodle called Charlie, distractedly playing with his ear. Next time Lucy and I played a high dive dare, I'd have to rethink my wish.

Mr. and Mrs. Lein joined us, along with Jeff Jr., who was accompanied by his sister, Trudy. She and I were both eight, which should have been enough in common for us to find ground of the same description, but to be blunt, Trudy was a snob. She'd been at their home in the Hamptons for the summer and regarded any other location with disdain. More irritating was that never having met the girl, I defended her against all aspersions cast by her brother, who criticized Trudy every chance he got.

The shock of real Trudy vs. possible Trudy needed no comment. It was evident from the get-go, so why acknowledge the accuracy of her brother's assessment? His character assassination of Trudy was spot-on in every respect, but despite being a sarcastic teenager, Jeff Jr. never once said, "I told you so."

Mr. Lien was a high-powered corporate attorney famous for his facility with the written word. He had written most recently to his eldest daughter, detailing why she should remain captive in a boarding camp not of her choosing.

Mrs. Lien tried to console her with long phone calls she placed each week, asking, "Have you seen any cute boys?"

The Brebners completed the *ensemble* of guests, and Aron had the distinction of being George's most long-standing friend. They bonded when Aron allowed my father to photograph New York's Finest in action. Tourists getting rolled, drug possession and prostitute arrests ensured there was never a dull moment on his beat, where police officers were perilously light on protection. Aron claimed to be outfitted with nothing more than 'A billy club, pepper spray and diplomacy.'

Having my father tower over his five-foot-four frame must have been a comfort, but although intrepid in the streets of New York, Aron feared the aisle leading to alter. His girlfriend Carley waited forever and finally won her man before aiming for a baby. With a cop among his friends, George's speeding and parking tickets vanished without a trace.

I've no idea what Mr. Stanford or Mr. Haltern did professionally, but whatever their work, I would be willing to bet they were top of the tree. All of them were blue bloods prominently positioned in the *Blue Book*. George and Meyera added my name to the social register well in advance of logging the birth certificate at City Hall. These were the folks my father felt comfortable with. His Brooks Brother, sear sucker, polo shirt, and tassel loafer-wearing friends.

It's not surprising, considering George was acquainted with Jacqueline Bouvier, accompanying her to numerous events on the way to her becoming Debutante of the Year 1947. Not long after my parents' divorce, George thought he saw Meyera outside a boutique in Boca Raton. It didn't make sense for Meyera to be in Florida, and when he said a tenuous "Hello," Jackie turned around.

"Hello, George," Jackie said. "What a nice surprise to run into you."

To all summer *soirees,* women wore shifts and sandals. Use of cosmetics was modest, and hairstyles were neatly trimmed. Susan had little need for makeup. She woke up over a decade younger than the rest every day. My stepmother had light-brown eyes and silky brunette hair. She was temperate even before expecting the baby, having established a moderate pace of consumption when growing up with her set of pedigree chums in Chicago. While the other adults were getting sloshed, she'd remain sober and involved with activities concerning the kids.

Mosquitos were a virulent problem requiring everyone to wear Off by Johnson, but no one minded. The men were successful, the women beautiful, and the future beyond bright for the kids. It's a shame this group didn't kick off their shoes and kick up their heels, but the music was incidental. The men spent time at the New York Athletic Club, rarely bending more than an elbow while exercising their tongues. Proximity to sport was regarded as a reasonable facsimile for physical training.

After provided with a drink, the adults settled in the patio, while cartwheels and push-ups transformed the lawn into a display of youthful energy. Rain clouds were approaching fast, which should have accelerated the outdoor portion of our party, but Jeff Jr. challenged Gareth Jr. to a wrestling match. The invitation was issued with aggression that, if mirrored in movement, might make an engaging competition.

Jeff Sr. and Gareth Sr. stood shoulder-to-shoulder to watch, presenting the appearance of unity while being poles apart. Each potentially proud papa had a freshly filled tumbler of scotch in his hand, and had it been anyone other than their sons ready to spar, they would have placed a considerable wager. The starling-like chirp of the women's chatter halted, and it was only social decorum that kept gambling at bay. Jeff Jr. had been in training for wrestling, which would enhance his applications to Choate and Andover. Gareth Jr. was already enrolled at Phillips Exeter Academy and a member of the boxing team. The boys squared off, and the conversation ended as everyone's attention was directed toward the match.

"Be careful of your face," I said, looking at Gareth Jr.

I cringed after issuing this warning. It hadn't been my intention to announce that I liked his face, and Lucy looked at me in shock. She knew I had a crush on Gareth Jr. and couldn't imagine why I blurted out something so telling. She was a good friend, but judging by her expression, you'd think I inadvertently released a nuclear warhead.

Trudy narrowed her eyes and twirled her Swiss Miss-style braids as would a Wild West gunslinger. She wouldn't hesitate to contort information into teasing, and if the face comment surfaced, I'd have to distract her by emphasizing my inability to distinguish wrestling from boxing.

Gareth Jr. took his opponent down fast, prompting his father to say, "Well done, son. I like to invest in talent, and I like it even more when it achieves results."

Jeff Jr. was worried; I could tell from ten feet away. Although rooting for Gareth Jr., I was impressed with Jeff Jr.'s tenacity and the way he bounced, rather than picked, himself back up.

"Don't worry, Dad," Jeff Jr. said. "It's only round one, and I'm getting warmed up, so nothing to worry about."

The young bucks returned to their starting positions while Mrs. Haltern and Mrs. Lien said encouraging words.

"Don't over-exert yourself," Mrs. Halton cautioned.

"Do you want a cold soda?" Mrs. Lien asked.

My father sensed the shift in mood driven by elevated levels of testosterone and grabbed the white line lawn marker intended for cricket.

"Let's make firm boundaries," George said. "How can any man be expected to turn out his best in less than ideal conditions? What about this line as a border? Something for you gentlemen to focus on when you recommence battle."

Mr. Stanford watched with interest when my father maneuvered the lawn marker. Neither of these men had sons to contribute to the contest and were pleased to add professional kit to the proceedings. Not wishing to be left out, Mr. Stafford leaped up to add his view.

"Another half centimeter should do it," Mr. Stanford said. "We don't want the result to be thrown by bad margins, do we?"

Margins and being marginalized were things Mr. Stanford knew quite a bit about. The Stanford residence was run strictly in accordance with matriarchal principles, in addition to those enforced by the maid. Mr. Stanford was always rushing to catch up but seemed to arrive late for most everything practical or theoretical. Empowering women left him alone on the sidelines. The flock of females he helped create forgot to include him. Aligned with my father, he was happy to design sports-oriented lines for a rare male activity he found validating.

Mrs. Stanford raised her girls to be fiercely independent and felt all females should contemplate higher education, an autonomous career and financial independence in advance of marriage. As a family, they represented a powerful but uncomfortable challenge to the existing social order, and Mrs. Stanford was tolerated when expressing views that shook the tectonic plates underlying our community. It wasn't just the men who were disconcerted by her enthusiasm for Women's Liberation, and it wasn't just the women who were amused by her campaign for recycling. Everyone dismissed her passion for strictly organic food as eccentric. On this day, however, the Staffords were relegated to the role of the audience as it was the boys' time to shine.

I'm probably not the only one who remembers the bump from boy to man first referenced by my father, and we all heard the promotion to gentlemen that followed. It gave an electrified impulse to the proceedings and was perhaps the very first time either Jeff Jr. or Gareth Jr. had been referred to publicly as men (at least in polite society), but they seemed to warm to it and engaged in combat with enhanced male bravado.

Rain started to drip down, gently at first. We were cold but gripped by the tournament and watched the wrestling while it continued to rain more heavily. Susan tried to encourage the party indoors, where it was dry, but no one paid attention. Defeated in this aim, she distributed throw blankets, which the women used to cover themselves up like nomadic Bedouin travelers.

Sitting outside in the pouring rain, they controlled their shivers and smiled without complaint. Susan unwound the patio awning, but the green and white striped material was of limited effectiveness and large drops of rain cascaded onto the herringbone brickwork, splashing the spectators. Our lawn started out as pristine pelt resembling the pitch at Lord's Cricket Ground but soon turned into a scrambled mud patch. The damage to the ground was but a footnote compared with the real harm done to and by the boys, ably assisted by their absurdly competitive fathers.

"This little summer shower will be over soon enough," Mr. Lien said. "The boys need to let off some steam, and I see no problem allowing fisticuffs."

"It would finish it off faster," Mr. Haltern said.

"How about it, boys?" both dads asked virtually in unison.

Wrestling gave way to boxing, and blood (surprisingly red rather than blue) poured from Gareth Jr.'s nose. Pitting a twelve-year-old against a large fellow of fourteen isn't fair, and I wanted it to be over, but for Mrs. Stanford and Susan, it already was. They excused themselves before round one, and Mrs. Stanford counseled Susan in the kitchen.

Her brown almond-shaped eyes were focused on my stepmother in a look that was at once compassionate and concerned when she said, "You've got to gain some control if only a small element to start with. Is this what you want? The Halterns and Lien family physically duking it out at your party?"

Susan looked lost, but Mrs. Stanford took the control she'd been promoting and marched out to the patio, saying, "On behalf of our esteemed hostess, dinner is ready, and you are called inside for a delicious if not entirely pesticide-free meal."

There was a pall at the party, and everyone returned to the house in a melancholy mood. It was uncomfortable at the kid's table, and I'd be surprised if the adults didn't feel it too. Competing with sons is a rich man's sport and must've made for interesting conversation when driving home. One of the best bits about going out was the drive home, and I loved listening to George and Susan's party postmortems. Divorced couples often cite this as the thing they miss most about being married. Sometimes, the after-party talk with a spouse is the only thing they miss. George brought the boys into a side room by the kitchen and administered steak along with questionable advice.

"Don't worry, fellas. I'm going to apply some Kobe, and then I'm going to cook Kobe," George said. "By wearing and consuming steak, you gentlemen will be well taken care of. When people ask what happened, if questioned about how you came to get these bruises, you report that the other guy got the worst of it. Say that the scrapes, always call them that, even if it's a good gash, are nothing. Not compared with the hell you rained down on the other fellow. Do you understand? The other guy is always and forever the loser. Not you. Never you. Not as long as you live and breathe."

My father wanted to get a jump on the Fourth of July weekend, which fell on us as hosts. He decided to take me and, after moderate level pestering, our dog Charlie on a mini road trip to Pennsylvania, the most lenient and well-stocked state in which to buy fireworks that, if lit, are illegal everywhere else.

Aerial repeaters, fire cones and exploding shells were selected to create a visually arresting start. Sparklers, Spinning Wheels, and three-tiered Roman candles with delayed action were bought by the box. To end with a bang, George wanted the loudest make on the market. He found what he was looking for, even though this behind-the-counter item was not officially offered for sale.

The Low Burn High Altitude Fountain made more noise than Gerald McBoing-Boing, and George bought five. We filled the trunk, back seat, and foot wells with enough firepower to crack a bank, which, in a way, we did, considering George was out over two thousand bucks by the time we finished. Charlie lost his seat and rode in my lap the entire way home.

Bigger, better, larger, and louder. That's how we lived it.

CHAPTER 9

To escape the sweltering heat in the city, we went to the Lake Placid Club. Our dog Charlie and I canvassed this private utopia until a brief but damaging encounter with a skunk put an end to our ramblings. The poor pet was suffering the consequences of toxic spray, which met his finely attuned olfactory sense, and the head chef provided industrial-sized vats of tomato juice to bathe him.

After that unusual rub-a-dub-dub, I rewarded Charlie's stoic patience with an enormous salami, but that, too, had unfavorable repercussions. Throughout the night, Charlie was belching and farting, which punctuated George's coma-like sleep with concerns a vet might need to be summoned. Not an easy evening for man or beast, nor child the next morning when I was sentenced to three days' confinement. During my 72-hour lakeside lockdown, we had a surprise visit from George's mother, Maude.

My East Coast grandmother was frosty, distant, and superior on a good day. I stumbled when addressing her as grandmother and would've preferred to call her Mrs. Buchanan. Her attitude matched the stiff brocade dresses and formal jewelry she wore, which comprised the only point of prominence about her — discounting the dowager's hump. My grandmother's face bore a vague resemblance to the late Queen Mother, minus a smile. Smiling was an uncomfortable demand Maude managed to avoid by presenting a weak, ambiguous smirk similar to the da Vinci *Mona Lisa*.

Charlie shared my upscale cabin confinement, and during our incarceration, Maude offered to make me a snack. This was a rare gesture that hadn't worked out well the previous summer when she prepared a sandwich made of aspic-covered pig meat placed between two slices of stale bread. I couldn't bring myself to choke down those clumsily concealed trotters or the homemade rice pudding that followed in a concoction reminiscent of cold risotto.

I agreed to have some fruit, and Maude returned with watermelon cut into isosceles-shaped triangles from which she'd painstakingly removed all the seeds. Although grateful, I was dubious when this beautifully prepared snack was placed in front of me and thanked her, as would Gretel, acknowledging a treat from her cannibalistic witch captor. After a few delicious bites, I couldn't resist asking why she'd gone to so much trouble.

"Because," Maude said abruptly, "if you eat the seeds of a watermelon, it will cause watermelons to grow inside you. Yes, it's true, so stop looking so surprised. Just one or two seeds are all it takes, and you will find them popping up everywhere. Just like Susan is with the baby, only for you, it would be considerably worse. Can you imagine it? Watermelons in your arms, legs, and even face. It would spell the death of you, and I'm not going to take responsibility for that."

I recalled the tadpole book and deduced that Maude must have been subjected to at least one seed to conceive George in an act she swiftly followed by an action for divorce. My father's father was a kilt-wearing figure remanded to a large silver frame. Sitting on the cabin porch, I examined each portion to ensure it wasn't life-threatening while thinking only the lake was placid.

I returned from the humidity of camp crisis to the dry heat in LA, where Meme served watermelon, suggesting that I go outside to spit the seeds on the ground.

I was stunned to the core and said, "How could you? I thought you loved me, but now you're trying to do me in? After Aspen, Colorado, where I almost broke my neck skiing (admittedly down a bunny hill). After the hot coffee jacuzzi in the desert, when I almost boiled down to grinds. After Mommy's drunken days and nights, you, of all people, turn on me?"

The tears flowing down my cheeks told Meme everything she needed to know about the depth of imagined betrayal I felt. She looked at me with astonishment while wondering who this short, angry little person was. Only a moment ago, she'd been supervising her grand-daughter swim, and suddenly, she was adrift in accusations concerning her supposed murderous intent.

Watermelon's safe to snack status was immediately made known to me, and with it came the realization that I truly disliked Maude.

My East Coast grandmother fed me another piece of sinister information that summer, which I sensed needed further verification, and I asked Meme, "If I continue to wear my hair behind my ears, will they stick straight out from my head, and does that mean I'll need a painful operation to have them surgically pinned back?"

Meme clarified matters and muttered something about Maude being more frightening than anything she had ever heard tell of, including The Brothers Grimm. Maude's unhappiness was a function of relative isolation, yet she liberally shared her discontent, which was the only thing she willingly distributed. The vast proportion of Maude's existence was spent in begrudging servitude to her elder spinster sister, and rather than participating in life, Maude was content to plod along as one of its low-key survivors. As in many families, I was named after the relative with the greatest wealth, which is why Maude's eldest sibling and I share the name Catherine Louise.

Louise was a remarkable woman and among the first of that breed to be called a force of nature. While Maude acquiesced to gravitational forces, Louise pursued the opposite track, and her rise was that of a female Horatio Alger. Louise grabbed circumstances by the neck, held opportunity in a half nelson, and choked out an empire. Little wonder those in her sphere of influence were supplicant. Maude became a well-compensated valet, attending to her sister's every need, while George buried his desire to work as a photographer, opting for a plummy job at a stock brokerage firm instead.

Louise was a fan of tailored clothing and leaned toward Rosslyn Russel's look in *His Girl Friday,* but rather than dress to compliment Cary Grant's double-breasted Prince of Wales suits, she needed only to please herself. The highly defined waist, prominent shoulder pads and below-knee skirts suited her. Whatever she had on included exactly three pieces of important jewelry, and her hair was worn in a style known today as The Thatcher.

Just like the former British Prime Minister, she also had a will of iron, worn like an accessory and wielded if necessary. Louise's life had a cinematic quality that starts *verité* and reaches very nice. She harbored the ambition to be an operatic singer, but this aspiration was quashed when her father met an early death. The family wasn't just broke, they were looking up at zero, and as the eldest of three children, Louise needed to earn a crust of bread.

There was talk of her running gin during Prohibition but little to substantiate it, and with no choice but to walk away from her chosen creative path, she struggled to generate sums supporting a family of four. Substituting formidable spirit for a formal education, she found employment on Wall Street, where she'd walk 32 blocks each way to and from work. Lining her thin overcoat with newspaper insulation and quickening her pace was the only way to defend against Manhattan's cruel winter winds. Compared with her commute, Abraham Lincoln's journey to school was a gentle stroll.

Louise began her career as a runner, taking buy/sell bids from the switchboard downstairs to the brokers upstairs. The work was tiring and tedious until all the runner girls were called to a meeting by the head of the firm. When they walked into his office, the Dow Jones Industrial Average was tick, tick, ticking with the pulse of the market rising and falling. Loss turned to gain and back again as fortune and failure danced with each beat.

The runners stood in a straight line in front of an enormous mahogany desk behind which sat the solid thickset Mr. Stanglea. He was a brutish man with red hair that matched the red of his eyes. Stanglea stood up and scowled while berating them one by one. Raging at their incompetence, he threatened to fire them on the spot, but Louise became incensed by his tirade. Her anger was rising faster than a kettle coming up to boil. She also had a volatile nature (making it a total of two quick-to-temper people in the room), and Louise had no tolerance for disrespectful words. If insulted, she intended to grab the ink wells from Langley's desk and smash them against the wall. She desperately needed the work but was unwilling to accept derision, and prepared to turn heel before permanently absenting herself.

Stanglea continued his lambast, and Louise's temper matched the mercury escalating in his voice. She selected a spot on the wall above his left ear as the target for her soon-to-be jettisoned rage. When it was Louise's turn to be excoriated, she steeled herself for combat, but Stanglea paused and abruptly swept a slip of paper from the desk.

"Who wrote this particular order?" he bellowed.

"I did," Louise answered. "And what of it?" she asked, with a defiant thrust of her chin.

Rather than the anticipated dressing down, Stanglea took a different tack and said, "This is the most legible handwriting I've ever seen, and I'm not wasting an asset like this in the runner's pool. From today, you'll be my personal assistant, but it's best if we call you Lou, as a man's name gives our clients confidence."

Once upgraded to Stanglea's assistant, Lou's responsibilities increased, along with a significant bump in salary. Working at the foot of the head partner was a privileged position, but she required greater familiarity with the machination of Wall Street's Bulls and Bears. Eager to learn about the market, she attended a night class at NYU, but the critical last lecture fell on an evening when her mental gas gauge was pointing well below empty. Too exhausted to take notes, she focused conceptually with a view to unpacking it later.

Walking home late that night, Lou was thinking about the market's pyramid structure and was horrified to find she'd walked to Hell's Kitchen on 135th Street. Lou frantically looked around and fixed her eyes on a church across the street. Two adrenaline-fueled leaps later, she opened the church door, and after lighting a candle, she knelt to pray. Although a businesswoman by necessity, she was pious by nature, and her *communique* with whatever god was awake at that hour proved effective.

The deal she negotiated for all things spiritual, corporeal, and financial paid off. Lou was Episcopalian socially and at work, but on this evening, she was at the mercy of St Francis of Assisi, which is how her long-standing relationship with the Catholic Church began.

A Priest dressed in a modest brown robe with a white rope belt sat down next to her and, after a respectful silence, asked, "What's brought you here at this juncture of the night?"

After Lou had told the priest about the lecture and her work, he asked if she would name a few promising stocks. Lou rattled off a list of investments, ranging from safe to risky, and they parted company. Despite never obtaining a stockbroker's license, she made money for herself and her clients on a seemingly forever basis. Private investors as well as commercial and academic institutions sought her advice.

Lou's client roster soon rivaled those belonging to the big boys, who dismissed her proficiency as prescient, but she had an uncanny feel for the market. Her blend of business acumen and intuition delivered untold profits, but to chalk this up to mysticism was a bit fanciful. The competition was both threatened and amused when Lou had a prophetic dream, which she regarded as a manifestation.

She'd been deeply asleep when a gentle shaking motion of the mattress woke her, and sitting at the foot of her bed was an apparition wearing the traditional St Francis of Assisi robe with a rope belt. This silent skeletal figure lifted a crowbar of the type used to start Model T Ford cars and placed it against her bedroom wall. Turning it slowly, the Dow Jones Industrial Average appeared with blue-chip stocks ticking past at below fire sale price.

AT&T was .64 cents a share, down from $304.00, when she left the office. General Motors was listed at .90 cents rather than $73.00 and expected to climb. Solid investments such as Union Pacific, B.F. Goodrich, Reynolds Tobacco and American Water Works all rushed past in a plummet of bizarre proportions before the figure disappeared.

Arriving at her office early the next morning, she hit the phone. Over the years, Lou amassed a considerable portfolio, and disposing of her assets, even at a frenzied pace, would take some time. Stanglea caught wind of her sudden sales activity and burst into her office with an astonished look on his face.

"What on earth's going on?" Stanglea asked. "I see you're selling virtually everything. What about the new stock offering we're underwriting? Need I remind you how hard we've worked to put this deal together. How is it going to look when it's discovered you're pulling out? Have you lost your ever-loving mind?"

Lou described her encounter with the apparition from the night before but didn't go into too much detail because she was in a hurry.

Stanglea listened with resigned curiosity and said, "Jesus, what are you telling me? Think about it, will you Lou? What's a monk doing in your bedroom at 4:00 in the morning?"

In addition to her temper, Louise had a reputation for temperance. She was teetotal and, if entertaining at home, would firmly shut the liquor cabinet after serving a maximum of two drinks. One slice of rye bread made her tipsy, and anyone who knew Lou would know her sighting wasn't alcohol induced. Stanglea knew he'd be unable to prevent her renegade and, to his mind, insane divestiture.

He shook his head before saying, "Hell, Lou, it is your stock. Go ahead and do whatever you please, but when it all goes wrong, don't come crying to me."

Two weeks after the apparition came to call, so did the Crash of 1929. Brokers, bankers, and everyday people were devastated. Lou watched as they shook their heads in dismay while some jumped from windows. Everyone struggled to understand how rock-solid sums turned from gold to sand overnight. Wishing to speak with the priest she met after that last lecture at NYU, she called the Saint Francis of Assisi Church, but he was no longer there.

As church bursar, he had taken the unprecedented act of investing heavily in stocks, which raised more than a few eyebrows until it yielded dividends. The St. Francis of Assisi coffers were swollen with so much money that only a tiny fraction was needed to open several new churches in California, and the priest in question was sent out West to oversee the process.

Lou was provided with a long-distance phone number, and when she placed the call to California, she heard news of the priest's passing. When she realized that the date of his death coincided with the date of the visitation, she went cold. Lou sold her shareholdings before the crash at top price and bought it all back for buttons, making October 1929 her most profitable month on record.

Aftershocks impacted everyone, including the affluent, and Lou shied away from investments involving bricks and mortar, preferring assets that were able to shapeshift from item to cash and back. The auction houses were aware of Lou's propensity, and they took it seriously. Christies and Sotheby's reserved a chair for her each week at the front of the bidder's gallery, where she had undisturbed access to everything under the hammer.

Her Beekman Place home was affectionately called the Midtown Museum, which was appropriate considering the sheer volume of items on display. Chippendale furniture, High Renaissance art, French Impressionist paintings, Persian rugs, jade, silver, china and ivory carvings ran the length and breadth of the place. Jewelry was secreted in hidden cabinets, and cash stashed in stacks behind locked doors.

Everything Lou owned could be liquidated fast. She believed that purchasing items provided pleasure on two occasions: acquisition delivered a lift, and divestment at the right price ushered in concomitant relief. Even after the stock market crash and the Great Depression that followed, Manhattan wasn't accommodating to those with new money. A bit of a bind if you're not born to it, but Lou conspicuously purchased important art as a means by which to graduate into society.

The first canvas she bought by Bouguereau was as much a dare as an investment, and when signing her check in front of press photographers, she said, "Let them try and ignore this."

She became adept at bending any set of rules, gaining admission to the Metropolitan and Manhattan Club by strictly observing the male-only members' policy and applying for membership in her nephew's name. George Buchanan was barely two years of age when he joined these esteemed ranks, but further ascent up the social scale was out of reach and deemed unnecessary. Why petition the Union Club for membership when J.P. Morgan's application was denied? These institutions were essential to Lou, although her interest in fraternity was admittedly fiscal. For Louise, there was no demarcation between fellowship and finance.

When asked about insider trading, Lou laughed and said, "Why do you think I own a dining room table?"

CHAPTER 10

Meyera and I went to Hawaii, where the island was infused with pikake, blended with further textures of pineapple, mango, and papaya, forming a heady mix. Sleeping so close to the sea drowned out Don Ho's hit *Tiny Bubbles,* which played constantly. Surfing lessons included a warning about how dangerous coral can be (when encountered outside a jewelry store) because abrasions against this aquatic terror could potentially cause poisoning. Each time I fell off the board, my feet were kept as close to my ears as possible, which provided an undignified but welcome sense of security.

Mom was treading water of a radically different nature after spotting a handsome man sitting by the pool with a tan the color of mahogany. Several women approached him whether he was reading, napping, or enjoying a sandwich, but Meyera was more sophisticated where this dance was concerned. The only move she made was to push her towel over, allowing him to sit at the end of her lounger after he walked over to join us. Meyera might've struggled to graduate from high school, but she earned an A+ in poolside politics. They enjoyed intelligent conversation while sharing the odd meal, and when engaging in a game of Baccarat, I sauntered *sans souci* down the surf line a safe distance from the waves.

Several adults were waving and shouting, but I was too far away to hear them. Their arms frantically moved in what appeared to be my direction, making it clear that I should run toward them as fast as possible to reach the dry sand that had become a great distance from the wet. Looking behind me, I was astonished to see a colossal wave rapidly approaching. My surf instructor taught me to dive when confronted with an oncoming breaker, and I took a deep breath in preparation to do so, but the only water available was ankle-deep.

Knowing escape was impossible, I dashed, but a force of hydro-might hit me from behind, pummeling me in a tumble dryer maneuver. The surface from the ocean floor was obscured, and I became an insignificant piece of jetsam tossed about in rapidly changing directions. A small shaft of light identified the top, and I swam toward it. Adults were in the water with arms outstretched to retrieve me, and I was safe but mortified to discover the lower portion of my bikini had been claimed by that massive wave. Swaddled in a large towel, I was checked for injury and accompanied back to the hotel.

A few days later, the tan man disappeared, and his lounger looked forlorn. Two women tentatively approached Meyera, asking if she had any idea where he might have gone, but she was as mystified and disappointed as they were. An emotional tsunami came crashing down in a tidal wave of disappointment, and with expectations extinguished, Meyera remained in the room, drinking alone in the dark. Canned laughter from the television was punctuated by the sound of bottles twisting open, pouring, and sliding along the bathroom sink. It was a dark, dank, dreadful, low-down bender of a dive.

Our vacation spiraled out of control, extending beyond the two weeks we had planned, and I was amazed at how easy it was to remain at the hotel indefinitely. Food was a rather tricky problem, but when hadn't it been? To order room service would risk Mom's exposure to adults with prying eyes, which might lead to difficult questions I wasn't in a position to answer.

Hungry and less inclined to go downstairs, I stayed close by, watching whatever children's programs I could find on television. A Christian series caught my eye, and I'd tune in to learn about Jesus from an animated dog with his sidekick little boy. Each episode was only fifteen minutes in length, which wasn't quite as much distraction as I'd have liked. Then came those cruel commercials making it impossible to seek diversion when tempted by treats.

Mom was subsisting on a liquid diet, and I dared not stray too far in case she woke up needing something. I certainly did, and that was anything approximating a full meal. I decided to play it safe and rely on self-help to conquer hunger. Considering that Meyera's presence was comprised of complete absence, this was the only viable alternative.

"Is it okay if I open your wallet?" I asked. "To get some money for groceries?"

If I'd shouted this request from the top of a mountain during a raging blizzard, it would've had the same impact, but, having asked for consent, I hid the room key plus twenty dollars in my pocket and went in search of affordably priced premade food. It was the first time I'd left the hotel grounds other than on the beach side, and I tried to connote a sense of purpose but became distracted by loud cymbals, swinging bells, and smooth samba sounds.

Advancing toward me was the slithering snake-like motion of a parade, accompanied by the strong scent of incense, smoldering smiles, and the suggestion I join them for a meal. Their orange and saffron-colored robes were cheerful, and with my stomach growling, I followed these strangers in what I hoped was a safe direction.

Rice and vegetables were served in generous proportions. Filling my bowl twice, I was provided with a plate and anticipated a burger would follow.

"No meat, I'm afraid," said a woman, distributing dessert.

"No problem," I said, holding up my plate as if it were the Heisman Trophy.

My stomach was full, and I left feeling replete for the first time in days. Years later, I heard that familiar music on Venice Pier, where I thanked the Hare Krishnas for their kindness in providing sustenance to a little girl. To return the support, I bought a generous quantity of incense they were selling.

"How about this one?" asked the vendor. "It is our most popular and is made from a flower called Night Queen. It blooms after sundown, reaches maturity by midnight, and dies before dawn."

"How appropriate," I said. "I'll take two packs. Actually, let's make it three since you guys were awfully good to me."

Meyera remained in emotional submersion, stirring, if at all, in her sleep. She moved with the faintest motion of seagrass when it reached up, like liquid smoke, from the ocean floor. After we failed to return on the appointed day, Meme became worried and contacted her sister-in-law, Betty. They talked every week, and Betty went directly to the source, calling the Royal Hawaiian Hotel manager who had attended high school with her son Rusty and daughter Sandy. One well-placed call from Los Angeles to Oahu was all it took to secure the child, check the mother, and evacuate us back home.

"Would you like some help with packing?" the manager asked.

'I can take care of that, but Mom can't make it downstairs for dinner," I said.

"Not a problem," he confirmed. "Here's the menu for you to order anything you'd like delivered to the room, but make sure you have a glass of milk. I'll be here first thing in the morning and will drive you to the airport."

As promised, the hotel manager placed us delicately but firmly on the plane, and we headed home. Dr. Lothar met us at the airport, executing the final leg of the plan Betty and Meme devised to get us back safely. George and Herb Lothar were close personal friends, making the circumstances surrounding our LAX collection somewhat risky. This aerodynamic landing wasn't going to be a hero's welcome.

Although Herb was Meyera's doctor, this didn't strike me as a situation attracting confidentiality or approval, but when you're ten, there's only so much you can do. Meyera argued with the cabin crew during the flight, demanding that they serve her a drink, but our stewardess refused while sprinkling me with winks followed by incrementally weak-willed smiles. Her firm denials concerning cocktails were uncomfortable for us all, and after landing, I thanked her by saying, "Aloha."

I admonished Meme about how close we came, yet again, to disaster, but she said, "You're back now, safe and sound."

Most adults would've added, "Nothing more to worry about," but Meme and I were too savvy for that. We'd concluded a fully executed agreement never to engage in deception, and to do otherwise would constitute a breach of epic proportion. There was little point in berating my grandmother since neither of us wanted to make a habit of disaster.

"Who courts catastrophe?" Meme would ask. "It makes a lousy companion."

We did what we always did, and moved forward the best we could. Our debrief was at an end when she suggested I take a swim, and frolicking like Flipper struck a forgiving chord. We returned to her apartment for our favorite bikini-based tradition and placed two water-filled glasses of celery on the small table between her two single beds, adding a cellar of Morton salt as the final touch. Once raw materials were in hand, we stretched out to watch *The Afternoon Movie* while dipping celery into our salt-filled belly buttons.

George never found out about our tropical trauma, but he indulged in terrorist telephone calls when belligerent and drunk. Yelling at Meyera, he demanded that I listen on the extension line. He was fond of having an audience when it came to the grand *finale*, and as commanded, I was in my LA-based auditory ringside seat, reluctantly listening while the last set of insults were hurled at Meyera with the finesse of an Olympian discus thrower.

The tinnitus of his deafening long-distance criticism would ring in our ears for hours. George's avalanche of threats to take me away was one thing, but Meyera's acquiescence to verbal abuse was quite another. A central theme was slowly but sharply coming into focus, and armed with a second wife, expecting his second child, he wanted a second chance at full-time custody. My father would do whatever it took to cut and paste his family back together.

He launched a fear offensive during my last visit and, in ominous tones, warned me of the danger associated with my continued residence in California. Describing Meyera and Meme as harmful reprobates, he felt them incapable of looking after themselves, much less me.

"Haven't you noticed how much they smoke?" George asked. "Don't you see how out of their gourds on alcohol they get? It's only a matter of time before they fall asleep while smoking in bed, and what happens if they're dead drunk? The entire apartment building could catch on fire, and everyone could burn up, including you. If you want to continue living, come to New York and live with us."

The concept of burning up in bed while wacked-out of your mind was familiar to me. Meyera's cousin Marilyn met the same fate when strung out on sedatives. She hit the wrong ratio of intoxicants one night, losing her hands, arms, and mind in the flames.

This was a cautionary example of what not to do, but my father's ostensibly sensible warning had the opposite effect, and I said, "Daddy, I should get back to California as soon as possible. You're right; they need me to keep an eye on things."

My wish to depart ahead of schedule was kiboshed, and for the remainder of that trip, I held my breath, hoping that if disaster was intent on visiting, it would wait to do so until after I got home. The images George conjured were vivid, but rather than focus on potentially fresh catastrophe, I reflected on Marilyn's past tragedy.

Meyera grew up with Marilyn and regarded her as a pest she wanted to swat like a determined mosquito. Although a constant irritant, Marilyn was Dr. Joe's niece, entitling her to privileges that occasionally disrupted Meyera's entitlement to the same, particularly when it came to matters of cosmetics and clothes, which Marilyn pinched from Meyera's room regularly and with impunity. When lodging complaints about items being taken from her closet with the price tags still attached, the litany of Marilyn's light-handed theft impressed no one. She had so little compared with Meyera; what difference did it make?

As the years progressed, so did Marilyn, who graduated from pilfering possessions to people. Following my parents' divorce, she dated George in a twisted *coup*. Meyera was terribly upset and cursed her cousin, but after Marilyn's dreadful accident, she recanted, feeling that evil intent gives rise to worse things than the imagination can create. It did in Marilyn's case and was a lesson to us all.

I flew home lugging with me, as I always did, a new habit, and this year, I became hypervigilant about the dangers associated with smoking. Starting with a selection of silent butlers, I insisted that active cigarette butts be placed in these containers until extinguished, and lighters were to become preferable to matches. Everyone's attitude toward candles was to be tightened up, so no more turning your back with one lit and burning.

Cellophane wrapping from individual cigarette packs was to go straight in the trash, and never allowed to loiter in ashtrays. Only when the contents of the silent butlers were cool did they join the rubbish, and not a moment before. The use of monogram wax seals was terminated with immediate effect. They were a fire hazard and not that attractive. The adornment of personal correspondence was made subordinate to safety in new legislation enacted for the greater good.

"Smokey the Bear would be so proud of you," Meme said.

"Not to mention the State Supreme Court," Meyera added.

My father's rants put Mom in a bad way. She was drowning in Egyptian cotton sheets, Canadian down duvets, and drinks with whatever demons decided to join her. Leaving her unsupervised was a risk, so I stayed home from school, blaming the Hong Kong flu for my absence. When supplies ran low, I'd run to the grocery store just before it shut, hoping to remain undetected. We were always running out of milk, and had two cats that needed feeding.

The first cat adopted us, and I named her Ershaw. We had her spayed but, feeling guilty, salved our conscience by finding an anemic kitten for her to raise called Netter-boo. Ershaw didn't care for our plan, and once Netter-boo was vaguely capable of remaining alive, she disappeared.

I wanted to do the same when shopping and kept a low profile, but I was rumbled by a classmate at the checkout counter. No words were exchanged, but when leaving the market, he had the look of a nemesis when gifted with one over on an adversary. I'd intended to return to school the next day, but Mom woke up searching our apartment for booze, creating a situation too unstable to withdraw my sentry-like support.

A week later, I marched up the school stairs with anxiety gnawing at my stomach. Bent and buckled, I might have been mistaken for an L. S. Lowry figure approaching the factory rather than Bonner School. Our fourth-grade teacher, Mrs. Eiger, was waiting, and her reputation as an ogre preceded her.

My friend Kit Manx transferred to Buckley because her elder brother suffered through his fourth-grade experience with Mrs. Eiger, who was a throwback to Dickensian methods of teaching. Mrs. Manx was not about to repeat the process with her daughter. Kit woke at 4:30 a.m. to practice her ice-skating routines, and on weekends, her stringent schedule was slightly relaxed, allowing Kit to sleep until 6:00 a.m. before presenting herself at the balance beam.

Mrs. Manx drove her children determinedly toward structure, believing this to be a solid route to success. She seemed surgically attached to her station wagon, and when disengaged from the vehicle, it was a surprise to discover she had legs. Kit's father was an architect who ran his family along the same precise lines used to design his homes, and they lived at the top of Mandeville Canyon in the very last house, which was intensely modern. Grounded by granite and suspended by glass, there was an angry vibe from all the sharp angles. The light that penetrated, rather than illuminated, the rooms was made harsh by the scant use of textiles. Kit would escape the rigors of an educational demon, and I had to brave fourth grade alone.

Although Mrs. Eiger was long in the tooth, fangs would be more accurate. A devotee of 'Don't Spare the Rod' old guard training, progressive changes in education interfered with her Machiavellian style and curbed but didn't entirely control her preference for cruelty. She resented this new liberal leash, forcing her to find intimidation with strict words rather than straight rulers and even when silent, her presence was imposing.

Her thick glass frames were 50s style with three rhinestones on either side, which were the only thing about her that sparkled. When I returned to class, she was ready to combust, and I sat rigid in my chair while waiting for the inevitable dressing down. Once the clock struck 9:00, Mrs. Eiger launched into action, devoting the entire morning to her caustic delivery. She enjoyed berating me and took her time to do so in front of the entire class.

"I see you've decided to grace us with your presence," Mrs. Eiger said. "Perhaps I have been misinformed about your absence, but let us see if I've got this right. You were out with the flu but well enough to go shopping. Not healthy enough to come to class but perfectly content to help mother. Are you running the household?"

If she only knew.

"Here you come, waltzing in whenever you want," Mrs. Eiger said, "with no thought as to what you should be learning or any consideration for my efforts to teach you. What a disgrace you well and truly are. I've no doubt that you will undoubtedly waste opportunities throughout the entirety of your life. Of all the children I have instructed over the years, you are the least deserving. Aren't you ashamed of yourself? Aren't you disappointed when you look in the mirror? Aren't you the least bit concerned for your future?"

Breathing in shallow gasps, I tried to take a deep breath of air. Inhaling might allow me to keep all the shame and despair in while coping with her carpet-bombing questions. She fired them at me so fast I didn't know which to address first. Had I known that hypothetical questions don't require answers, that big gulp of oxygen would've been mine. The classmate who saw me at the grocery store looked smug, resembling a victor with *schadenfreude* at the center of his spoils.

Mrs. Eiger's deadly diatribe was mercifully called to a halt by the bell announcing recess, and I escaped the school grounds through a side door heading home, where I went past Meyera, who was passed out in her room and got under the quilt in mine. It was hard to imagine that Mrs. Eiger could be so mean, even if unknowingly. There was a conspiracy of silence surrounding my home, and I understood her ignorance but wished for something bad to happen so that she would develop a sense of humility. As with Meyera and her cousin Marilyn, I came to regret making this wish.

Mrs. Eiger's son attained the highest rank in the Boy Scouts of America, and after twenty-one merit badges, plus years of dedicated survival training, he became an Eagle Scout. Only four percent of applicants survive the interview process, which begins at age eighteen, but he made the grade and was invited on a camping trip with three inductees chaperoned by two men of long-standing Scout rank.

A freak snowstorm ended the lives of all those stranded on the mountain. The blizzard was a bastard that came out of nowhere and kept coming to claim those ostensibly capable of claiming refuge. Everyone knew how to cope with demanding conditions. They were trained, equipped, and experienced. Mountain Rescue had been notified of their exact movements prior to departure, and after the ascent to death, every authority tried to retrieve them. An intense struggle was waged to save those who were tagged, logged-in, and anticipating protection. Urgent help was required, and, in an icy version of Dunkirk, every able-bodied man volunteered to search for them. Some answered the emergency radio call with only a compass, snowshoes, and flares.

Mrs. Eiger's son was left to linger in her entirely too vivid imagination, freezing and shuddering in the dark. Turning blue before turning toward the black on that evil mountain was a devastating image, and taking time off to grieve would've been prudent. To lament and rail against the universe was her due, but Mrs. Eiger sought the angry cure instead, which she mistook to be work. I'd never have wished for something so diabolical to happen. I wanted Mrs. Eiger to gain an element of compassion, but not at the cost of her treasured son's life. When this tragedy befell her, it was the beginning of fall, and I didn't envy the incoming fourth-grade class. In fact, I pitied them.

CHAPTER 11

Halloween was coming up, and I loved the costumed pageantry more than gathering treats, carving pumpkins, and bobbing for apples. Meyera was teetering on the brink of sobriety, and, as with a tightrope walker, things could go either way.

"What do you want to be this year?" Meyera asked, sounding contrite. "I was thinking of making your costume by hand if it's not too detailed. Any ideas?"

In Ancient Greece, they extended olive branches, but in Brentwood, it's costumes.

"How about a witch outfit that I can accessorize with our cat?" I suggested. "We have the *purrfect* prop, so why not make good use of him?"

Meyera agreed and sat awkwardly at the sewing machine, frightening us both to death. The pinned pattern approach was demanding, and I looked encouragingly at the proceedings from a respectful distance. During manufacturing, Mom was either hungover or still under the influence and I was repeatedly called back for endless sets of measurements.

A lot of recalibrations involving various segments were needed before the final assembly, but the process was as important as the result. Meyera's homemade costume wasn't just for Halloween; it was a symbol of hope that things would get better. Completing the costume was in itself a source of pride, and with a flourish that was worthy of the best design houses in Europe, Meyera swept the final creation from its hanger.

She delicately laid it out on the bed, and I gingerly stepped into it, barely able to contain my enthusiasm. Dashing to Meyera's full-length mirror, she followed with a huge smile, but the image confronting us was of a mangled jumpsuit suggestive of a black cat. There wasn't any time left to change my costume, so I had to tread carefully.

"Mom, I thought I was going to be a witch and Netter-boo would have a supporting role," I said. "Is this a cat costume?"

Meyera looked crestfallen. She hung her head and lit a cigarette.

"Oh no, don't tell me," Meyera said. "Shit, shit and damn. I hesitated when I bought the pattern, thinking something was amiss, and I completely forgot you wanted to be a witch. How could I get something so simple so wrong?"

Mom was teary-eyed, and it wasn't so much her work but very soul that needed to be retrieved.

Confident the situation could be salvaged, I said, "You know what Mom? I think your mistake is an advantage. The cat can be the witch and I'll be the cat. This is more likely to appeal to the pageant judges as our entry will be ironic."

Despite Meyera's arduous effort to make the costume, it was a source of amusement, with arms of radically different lengths and legs regrettably the same. A lopsided waist and halfway stuck zipper were secured with safety pins, allowing me to remain *in situ* where everything felt scratchy. The tail contained an incorrectly bent wire hanger, refusing to point in any direction other than despondently down, and with ears out of proportion, my cat cap drooped in a pose I suggested, "Provides an attractive air of reality."

This imperfect effort by a dented but determinedly loving soul deserved attention. It came from the heartland where Meyera scratched hard to regain hers. In the aftermath of divorce, she felt deactivated and battled with a descent into darkness Dylan Thomas would find challenging to rage against. We battled with traffic instead, and arrived late for the Halloween festival but in time for the contest.

"Our next entry," said a voice over the tannoy, "is a real live cat dressed as a witch, sporting a child in a cat costume."

I stepped onto the stage with enthusiasm, but I can't say the same for the cat. Netter-boo put his ears down flat, and I knew he'd punish me for this, which he did right up through adolescence, both his and mine.

Lydia was the Department of Parks and Recreation Director who led me to the wings of the stage, saying, "I've saved *Monster Mash* for your turn. Make sure the cat waves which will be a crowd pleaser."

I loved Lydia, and who didn't? She was in her early twenties, newly married and blissfully so. She viewed the world from enormous cobalt-blue bedroom eyes, and Crest toothpaste would have been proud to snap up her smile. Volleyball, basketball, and softball, she taught them all, and the gymnasium only went silent if her husband stopped by. Peals of laughter bounced off the walls the moment he was gone. We were happy for her but giddy when confronted with tangible proof of matrimony.

Lydia's husband saw my cat costume and said, "Is that kid blind or brave?"

"Bit of both," Lydia said. "When she bags the prize, that poor cat can retire."

The previous Halloween was celebrated at my best friend Gail Gordon's house above Sunset on North Rockingham Avenue. She lived in a *bona fide* mansion, exquisitely decorated with Asian art extending wing after wing. Her place was impeccable, but before playing hide-and-seek, we had to inform an adult about our exact location, similar to the vehicle check-in at Death Valley. If we failed to reappear within a specified time, the household cavalry would be discharged to retrieve us.

They had a swimming pool, tennis court, four separate gardens, and two live-in maids: one mean and one nice. We gave them nicknames reflecting their different temperaments, but chose so accurately, that it took vigilance to avoid using them when conversing with either directly. Nasty Chops controlled the kitchen, guarding the fridge more fiercely than Cerberus. Reach for something without asking, and she'd snarl ferociously while defending her version of the underworld gate. Kind Chops oversaw everything else, allowing a sense of calm to infuse the place.

We had a few hours to kill before trick-or-treating started, so Gail suggested we set up a lemonade stand. Anywhere else, and I'd have agreed, but at her place, I wasn't an enthusiastic recruit. Venturing into the enemy camp frightened me, as I wasn't prepared to breach the *Maginot Line* in the kitchen. Gail was disappointed, and I felt like a coward until suggesting we set up a flower stand instead.

Gail was the youngest child from her parent's marriage, making her the youngest from her father's first marriage before that. She had crowds of siblings who spilled out whenever I opened a bathroom or closet door, and we'd been friends since starting Bonner School at the age of five. Mr. Gordon was an active lawyer with a suitably active wife who drove carpool, planned menus, and volunteered for charity.

Gail's mother claimed gardening was an avocation but diligently devoted herself to the task. Little wonder Gail and I had such an easy time working our way through the rose, tulip, and iris sections. After that, we'd no idea what we were cutting, but this wasn't cause for concern. The large bouquets would attract customers once we set up shop at the start of her driveway, and all we had to do was assemble the twenty or so bunches, allowing commerce to begin. Kind Chops had sovereignty over the string and, in warm, accommodating tones, asked what we were doing. When told, she panicked in a way I'd not seen twice.

"Good Lord, help me," Kind Chops said. "Help me understand what you've gone and done. What kind of trouble did you cook up, and did anyone see you? Think before you answer. No? Absolutely sure? Okay, here's what we're going to do. Give me all those flowers you cut down, and I'll give you five dollars each if you promise to stay quiet about this. Quiet for the rest of your life, understand? If that's too much to ask, then you should stay quiet for the rest of mine."

Kind Chops bagged the flowers and hid the contents deep in the dumpster behind the garage, waiting until after dark before making this transfer. Trick-or-treating in Brentwood's highest valued neighborhood sounds more glamorous than it is. Mansion properties inhabit large acreage, requiring substantial effort to canvass. After several hours, we returned from all eleven houses closest to Gail's with a paltry haul of candy and a surplus of blisters.

Nasty Chops dismissed our concerns and scolded us by saying, "Don't complain about a high-class problem."

Eleanor Shamus couldn't care less about Halloween. She was four years older and extremely sophisticated. At her twelfth birthday party, there was no run-of-the-mill cake and ice cream on offer. We dined on the special treat of her choosing, which was escargot. Most children wouldn't dream of scoffing snails, but Eleanor's enthusiasm was all the encouragement I needed to pick up that strange-shaped cutlery and tuck in. She was an only child, and my regard for her made the most dedicated mentor/disciple relationship look like passing acquaintances. Hero worship was several rungs down from what I felt for Eleanor and I all but addressed her as, 'my liege.'

She was a well-adapted guide, able to lead the way up that Mount Olympus of emotion we were called upon to climb most weeks. Our mothers were friends who shared a sense of surprise at their single parent status, and they were both alcoholics, which provided everyone with quite a lot in common. Coping with the madness of our moms was as natural to us as breathing, and my loyalty to Eleanor was unquestionable, which made it difficult to discover she was capable of betrayal.

As an added insult, I experienced deceit masquerading as humor when visiting her home in Bel Air, after I noticed a Bonsai plant with tiny dayglow-colored carrots growing on miniature branches. This struck me as strange. I'd been given to understand that carrots grew underground.

"Hey, Eleanor," I said. "What's this little tree and are these baby carrots?"

My question set in motion a cruel urge to corrupt naivety, and Eleanor seized the opportunity to have a bit of fun.

"Go ahead and try one," she said with a sly smile. "It's a special carrot plant that's very rare. Make sure to bite deep into the middle or, better yet, bite all the way down to the end, and that way, you'll *really* taste it."

Within a flash of that first and only crunch, the Napalm-like substance was released, filling my eyes with tears. There wasn't a fluid on earth capable of coping with the explosion in my mouth, and while the impact of her trickery hit me like a locomotive, Eleanor was laughing so hard she had to lean against a chair. The phrase 'Say it ain't so, Joe' came to mind, but compared with this, the 1919 World Series fix was a minor misunderstanding.

"Things are often different from what you expect," she explained.

"Yeah, you're right," I said. "Why else would something so hot be called chili?"

Having a comrade with whom to bear souls, rather than arms, during the long campaign to cope was a gift, and Eleanor provided advice about how to deal with narcissistic parents making mercurial demands. While visiting a pet store in Santa Monica, we discovered that reptilian feeding time was measured by a decrease in rodent stock.

Using a sales technique inspired by Solomon, we watched each mouse being lifted from the sanctuary of its cage and suspended mid-air *en route* to the snake tank. Taking it in turns to save them, no less than six death sentences were commuted, and we set up a cottage business that Meme termed the Tim'rous Beastie trade. The cost of each mouse was negligible compared with the amount needed to purchase accessories.

A multitude of items were required to care for our new pets. During lunch in Beverly Hills, our mothers lingered over cognac and coffee while we dropped by a pet store near the restaurant. Eleanor looked at the rodent price list and nudged me with her elbow Vaudeville style while lowering her voice to a register normally used by criminals.

"They sell at six dollars per mouse, and we bought ours for two dollars each," she said. "If we breed mice for sale to this shop, it will cover the cost of feed, shavings, and cages. Let's see if they'd be interested in having us as suppliers."

The pet shop proprietor in Beverly Hills agreed on acceptable terms, and we returned to Santa Monica, where they promised to supply us with opposite, rather than same-sex, specimens this time, but despite the specificity of our order, it was unlikely to have attracted a through gender check on either occasion. We prepared for business, purchasing top-of-the-range drop water bottles, exercise wheels, and Frank Lloyd Wright-style cages.

Aiming to keep overhead expenditure low, we passed on the model featuring Googie-style lounge areas, confident that our mice wouldn't need soft lighting and music as a spur to copulation. Pet stores trade in the ephemeral, and our venture had the lifespan of a housefly. Infanticide is an unattractive concept, and our cages soon contained a massacre so comprehensive as to make Medea look like a neophyte.

Meme gave me an empty Yuban coffee can in which to place the remains and said, "We call them vermin, yet they behave like the Bourgeoisie."

Eleanor provided guidance concerning George's war waged to win full-time custody. After failing with his first fear offensive, he enlisted allies in the form of aggressive attorneys able to decipher deficiencies on the West Coast. These details would be used to create a dossier of disaster, requiring the removal of said child from the care of her mother, for placement with the father. While this second verse was different from the first, it constituted a viable line of attack.

Hostilities broke out when interrogatories arrived in the mail designed to take a strike at the environment in which we lived. Our apartment building served as an emotional balm because there was no shortage of reliable residents to whom I could turn if in trouble, but this was the swinging 60s, and after a few strokes with a Mont Blanc pen, George's lawyers transformed our home into a den of inequity.

Otherwise sedate tenants were castigated as promiscuous, and more outgoing residents described as drug-addled. Everyone except the elderly fell into the same category of alcohol-fueled heathen. Not the right place for a child to visit, let alone live.

Bonner was next up for the chopping block, and the Los Angeles location alone proved it was inferior to academic institutions in Manhattan. While manila envelopes continued to arrive out of the blue, so did George, who asked for Meyera's permission to take me out to dinner. She agreed, not knowing the meal would be served on board the 747 Pan Am flight from LAX to JFK. George's legal team hadn't sanctioned this unilateral act. They engaged in battle with depositions and damning affidavits. His lawyers were willing to draw blood but preferred to do so on an arms-length basis using A4 paper cuts instead. Meyera discovered the kidnap and boarded the next flight out. Streaming flu aside, she flew to retrieve me and relied on her lifelong friend Joan Barker for support.

Joan was more Manhattan than most, having attended The Spence School and Vassar College before joining The New York Junior League. She became a United Nations volunteer and was appointed to the New York State Department of Transportation despite barely being able to drive. Although extremely funny and socially adept, Joan was at her best when being a best friend, and Meyera flew to 1192 Park Avenue, where Joan had lived since childhood. She joked about dusting the same surfaces since she was twelve, but took things seriously when Meyera arrived and dug in for a battle.

Meme and Joan's mother had been friends for decades, starting with a stray conversation while standing in line at Jurgensen's market in Beverly Hills long before their daughters were born. A second generation down, Meyera and Joan remained close, allowing Mom to introduce her pal to Tom Barker, who was studying at Caltech. A marvelous marriage followed, and Joan returned the favor when Meyera was in Manhattan, where she suggested they meet her friend by the name of George Buchanan.

An intense and uncertain ten-day period followed the landing in New York. Demands were made by legal teams on both sides. Gail's father was in a first-line position for my California defense and insisted on my immediate return, but George refused to relinquish me, pending a psychological assessment to determine my future welfare. George's lawyers decreed this should be done in Manhattan. Only an East Coast child psychologist could accurately evaluate my state of mind.

They had a list of highly regarded professionals and brandished it in triplicate. Meyera was unwilling to be bullied but agreed to expert testing if conducted on home turf. The Fernald Child Study Centre at UCLA was just down the road, and its reputation was so spectacular that no legal team could take exception on either coast.

Joan researched this institution at the public library on her way home from Gristedes grocery store, and I was released to return home. Meyera abstained from booze on the flight, but she was impatient and complained about the length of our journey.

"How can you stand it?" Meyera asked. "All these long plane rides back and forth are so tiresome. Is there some way to escape this interminably dull wait?"

"Why don't you try reading or watching the in-flight movie?" I suggested. "It's not much longer until we land, but if things get really bad, I packed a chocolate bar for you."

The time of day during which I would attend Fernald was entirely up to me, which I found refreshing and vaguely reminiscent of Montessori. After a quick calculation, I opted to test at the exact hour math class began, employing the same numerical skills I wanted to avoid at school.

I looked forward to the diagnostic process which started with the Thematic Apperception Test involving pictures, about which I was required to create a storyline. One image featured a little boy with a violin who looked resigned to the fact his life had been mapped out with the monotony of a musical metronome, and I felt sorry for him. This test provided insights into a patient's attitudes, and I was pressed for details about the image.

"What would he rather be doing?" I said, repeating the question posed to me. "I bet he'd leap at the offer to go outside and dive in the pool."

This picture is allegedly copied from an image featuring Yehudi Menuhin as a young prodigy, and I wonder if we'll ever know how the most celebrated violinist of the twentieth century was occupied before and after the shot was taken. Rushing from the classroom to Meyera's car, I was eager to continue our important work. The diagnostic experience was fun.

Meme laughed uproariously when her sister-in-law Betty said, "Perhaps Catherine B will become to Fernald what Anna O was to Freud?"

Deconstructing inkblots featuring butterflies was preferable to math class, and in later life, I discovered the uncanny resemblance between Hermann Rorschach and Brad Pitt, making everything about this test attractive. After rounding the final Fernald chicane, it was time to run the gauntlet with a child psychiatrist called Dr. Bets.

Although eruditely educated, published, and cited frequently, there was an impediment to our session's *ab initio*. Only a few truncated phrases were needed for my friend Eleanor to obliterate everything this psychiatrist aimed to achieve.

"Do you want to remain in California?" Eleanor asked. "Do you want to continue living with your mom and Meme?"

After confirming that's exactly what I wanted, she said, "Then don't tell this psychiatrist anything."

This was a tall order. Social decorum alone would propel me toward some form of conversation, and I wondered if I had the fortitude for such a lapse in etiquette.

"I mean it, say nothing," Eleanor ordered. "Not about anyone or anything. That means family, friends, and school. You got it?"

"Got it, but what about you?" I asked.

"Definitely nothing about me," Eleanor said, "Psychiatrists won't like it. Neither would our mothers or anyone else."

It's amazing how effective a dissenting voice can be, and, given our mouse breeding venture, I regarded Eleanor's council as personal advice from a trusted business colleague. Each week, I'd sit in Dr. Bet's conservative consulting room, which was low-lit, but the bright sun managed to intrude by blasting uninvited in sharp strips through the shutter blinds. These strong lines of light created a reverse image effect causing the room to resemble a zebra in photographic negative.

Dr. Bet's questions were answered concisely, if not in haiku fashion, and on returning home, I provided Eleanor with a veritable stenographer's report concerning each session. No detail was spared as we comprehensively covered his questions, and what I might've mistaken for a mundane inquiry, Eleanor flagged as a trap. Even something seemingly innocuous, such as, 'How's school?' could spell disaster, and I'd be moved to Manhattan.

Dr. Bets had a selection of toys in his office, none of which interested me.

"Would you care to try one of the board games?" he asked.

I was already bored stiff.

It was a hot afternoon, and I fidgeted in my chair while saying, "No thanks, those games are aptly named."

This piqued his interest, and he said, "Why don't you like board games?"

"Because I'm an only child," I said, irritated at such an obvious question.

"Don't only children like to play with board games?" he asked.

This was straining all logic and reasoning.

It required effort, but I remained patient and had I been older, I probably would've cleared my throat before saying, "Board games are meant for more than one player, and to control both the red and blue isn't much fun.'

"I see," he said while scribbling on a large notepad.

"Don't suppose you've got any model horses?" I asked to show willingness. "Breyer, or an inferior brand?"

His office looked down on the Beverly Hills High School athletic track, and while we sat in stultified silence, students limbered up before dashing in various directions. They were a sharp contrast to this eerily calm man sitting shrouded in muted tones, and rather than occupying a large leather chair, Dr. Bets seemed consumed by it. Any more folded over, and he'd resemble a Rorschach inkblot that came to life.

I felt vaguely contrite about sabotaging his work. All the years of training, practice, and diagnostic techniques were up in smoke, where I was concerned, destroyed by an adolescent lurking in the wings. Our last session required Meyera's attendance. Dr. Bets needed to observe the mother/daughter interaction firsthand, or so Eleanor explained. I didn't regard Dr. Bets as an adversary *per se*, but I recognized his influential role in my parents' adversarial process and was willing to follow Eleanor's every suggestion.

She crafted my final performance in such detail I was effectively handed a full-blown shooting script with margin notes denoting camera angles and lighting cues. Meyera entered the room, and I hit my mark by waving with a gentle smile. No rush from the chair to hug her and nothing too overt. I needed to stay relaxed rather than exuberant. The offer to play with those insipid board games was renewed, and this time, I agreed, allowing Meyera to be in charge of the blue while I commanded red.

"Are you content to play Parchisi today because Mommy's here?" Dr. Bets asked.

I nodded affirmatively and mentioned how much I was looking forward to swimming later. Dr. Bets looked at Meyera, who was laughing at my attempt to win the board game and confirming that Mexican food would follow the swim.

"Great," I said. "I can hardly wait to get home."

A covert look at his Longines watch confirmed our last session was over, and Dr. Bets ushered me into the waiting room so that he could have a private word with Meyera. Standing face to face with Dr. Bets, Meyera gripped the pack of cigarettes in her pocket as if it were a vice (other than just smoking).

Confirming his report would mirror the findings of Fernald, Dr. Bets said that there was no need to uproot and create trauma. Meyera exhaled to such an extent she was tempted to sit down, but strutted outside his office like a prize peacock instead. Once we were safely ensconced in the car, she pulled out the pack of cigarettes to find all but two broken.

"Thank God that's all over," Meyera said. "From the lion's jaw, we pulled you, the building and Bonner."

Rather than swim when returning home, I called Eleanor. Relief was running in waves down my voice, and it was only then that she came clean with me.

"Wow, what a close call," Eleanor said. "I didn't want to frighten you, but that was one serious situation. Congratulations on being able to remain in California. Now's the time to ask for that pony."

CHAPTER 12

An unfortunate incident occurred at Mackenzie Ellis's house when I was six, and we were playing with her pet rabbit, Peter. She subsequently unveiled a trampoline that provided more exhilaration than I'd thought possible, and when I suggested we combine these elements, Mackenzie agreed, allowing me to accompany Peter to the first bounce. Rabbits don't sleep with their eyes open, and although I knew that, it was the best I could come up with when Peter failed to come up from the taut base alive. I felt awful. Bunny Bounce had been my initiative, and it was my place to take the blame.

Meyera bought a replacement rabbit, which we delivered to Mackenzie the next day, along with an apology worthy of Plato, but rabbits weren't the only problematic pets to join our family. The inventory of wedding gifts received by my parents included a mynah bird, which arrived with a limited number of phrases such as, "Hello gorgeous, I can talk, but can you fly?"

My parents had no idea how susceptible this bird was to other words spoken unguardedly in privacy, and their feathered friend soon developed an encyclopedic command of more colorful comments such as, "Pour me a scotch, will you?"

The bird's statements were made with ornithological confidence that impressed everyone except the adoption authorities' home visit representative. My parents tried to ignore the conversational quips made by the bird, but the register and reach of its voice followed them as they conducted a tour of the house.

"God damn it, George," was the first new phrase the bird mastered. "For Christ's sake, Meyera," soon became one of its favorite retorts.

"Maude can go to hell," it squawked on an endless loop during the follow-up visit.

"Out of curiosity," the adoption agent said. "Who is Maude?"

"My Mother," George and Meyera said simultaneously, to which Meyera added, "in law."

When the assessment was finished, George embraced Meyera and said, "Let's not kid ourselves. This might've gone better, but I think everything's fine."

"At least she left before the bird demanded a Dewar's," Meyera added.

"Never mynah," George concluded.

Lavish gifts were commonplace, and our Christmas tree was besieged by boxes from FAO Schwarz on Fifth Avenue. The signature red and white stripe paper was as alluring to children as Tiffany blue is to women, but George's presents were dispatched as reparation for parental absence.

Waking early on Christmas morning, I hoped Meyera and Meme would share my sense of urgency, but when they didn't, I opened a puppet theatre with landscapes featuring Buckingham Palace, the Taj Mahal, and a fantasy woodland grove. The marionettes proved too complicated to manipulate, and I cut off the strings when Meyera arrived.

"What on earth are you doing?" Meyera asked. "And why are you destroying those beautiful puppets?"

"These aren't the type to be played with," I explained. "Not in a fun way."

When George entered the toy store, he was confronted by a cacophony of out-of-work actors promoting the puppet theatre at a fever pitch, with characterful voices and skillful handling of intact strings. Think *Punch & Judy* as performed by professionals in a modern-day context, and it's not difficult to understand his enthusiasm.

My friends needed batteries for their gifts, but several Screen Actors Guild members were required to operate mine. Sophisticated puppetry may have failed to capture my attention, but the life-sized plush baby giraffe and remote-controlled helium dirigible were terrific. A large box arrived just in time for the holidays with a note suggesting Meyera prepare it for Christmas morning.

Intricate and manufactured in China, it was a train set with complicated diagrams and incomprehensible instructions, on top of which George scribbled the words 'good luck.' Meyera enlisted the assistance of two tenants who agreed to the task if provided with Tequila. They were Lockheed Aerospace engineers called Caleb and Scott, who lived in apartment 506.

"You fellows are absolute lifesavers for lending a hand," Meyera said.

"This shouldn't prove too difficult," Caleb stated.

"If we can't handle a train set, we've no business showing up for work," Scott added.

Even for guys well versed in making things run to order, the challenge of assembling tiny constituent pieces was greater than first imagined. They worked through the night, and at half past three, the train was on track, but their minds derailed. While my friends were fast asleep in their cozy beds at home, I had to use a pillow to silence the sound of slammers when shots of tequila were taken to celebrate or commiserate with their progress.

"Don't tell me this won't fit," Caleb said irritably.

"At least the track is going in the right direction, but these little cars are torturous," Scott noted.

The train traveled the circumference of our living room, with tiny stations and little trees sheltering teeny passengers waiting to board. Although the toy ran to order, our home resembled Margaritaville after closing time, with remnants of stale cheese that Meme later identified as Limburger.

George promised I'd ride on a float in the televised Hollywood Christmas Parade, and once I heard about this, so did everyone in my immediate vicinity. My father was in town to meet with a client who'd been invited to appear in the parade but forfeited the seat subsequently given to me. Called the Secretary of Defense, this athletic client was located near Disneyland in Anaheim.

"How would you like to join us for dinner at the Magic Kingdom?" George asked, obviously pleased with the offer.

At that particular moment, I was pleased with him too and said, "What time? I'll be ready and waiting to go."

Waiting while ready was more accurate, and we rushed to the restaurant where my father's six-foot-five client was expecting us.

Although half an inch shorter than George, this client occupied more space and commanded considerably greater attention, particularly from our waitress, who said, "Everyone knows your number, but how would you like to have mine?"

"I appreciate the offer, but I'm a married man now," the client said, smiling.

"I'll leave it with the check in case you change your mind," the waitress added.

"Change his mind about what?" I whispered to George.

"Whether he wants dessert," my father replied.

The chef came out from the kitchen to shake the client's hand while people in the restaurant tried, with limited success, not to look over. Everyone went silent when the chef and the client exchanged a few words about having a solid season. Victory was already in the bag, and the client described the games as a mere formality, which made everyone laugh, but I found the client intimidating. He formed part of the Fearsome Foursome. The business discussions stretched forever while I looked at Sleeping Beauty's castle outside the restaurant window, and by the time coffee was served, Disneyland had closed for the evening.

George felt guilty and said, "Sorry dinner ran so late, but we've got that special invitation to see the game this weekend," he offered. "We'll have a great time, even if you don't appreciate it now."

My father's enthusiasm was infectious, but nothing could have prepared me for what I witnessed that day. The warrior mentality and vaguely disguised violence on the field were beyond my conception. Tempers were flaring not only on the playing ground but all around. I was relieved when the game ended, and we were directed to the locker-room, where George went in to see his client while two security guards kept an eye on me. They were so tall I had to tilt my head back to see their faces, but looking down again, I noticed two women standing separately in a corner, obviously fed up and bored. A woman wearing red appeared to be having an irritable night, and I didn't blame her. Stuck inside this subterranean structure, she didn't have a princess castle to look at while being ignored, and both women waited for those, not just covered but smothered, in glory to emerge.

"Take a look at this," George said, returning from the locker-room. "Pretty good, wouldn't you agree?"

George was holding the game program more delicately than he would an organ for transplant. He pointed to the cover and said, "See all these?"

The program was signed by all the players and George couldn't be happier.

"Daddy, who are those two ladies standing over there?" I asked.

While he turned to look, I swiped the program and held onto it tightly with both hands.

"Those are the wives," George said. "You've met the husband of the one in red when we had dinner together, remember? At, well, near Disneyland."

"I'll be right back," I promised, marching to where the women were standing.

The woman wearing red looked at me and back to her friend before asking, "Honey, can we help you?"

"My father is your husband's stockbroker," I explained, "and he says your husband is the greatest football player ever. All the players have signed my program, but I'd like to have the wife of the greatest player sign it, too."

She melted into a smile so warm I needed Ray-Ban sunglasses and factor 15 lotion to avoid burning up. Her friend dutifully looked through her purse for a pen and, while doing so, gave me a left-handed compliment.

"Aren't you a brave little thing?" the friend said. "Walking all the way over here all by yourself. I wouldn't want to do that, not in this crowd," she said, nodding toward three groups waiting in designated areas.

A pack of journalists were jostling for position by the locker-room door, poised to receive quotes and take photos for the morning sports edition. While waiting, they chided each other about which masthead was superior. Throngs of fans were relegated farther back, angling for autographs with paper and pens at the ready. A third section was roped off for sponsors who didn't need to push or shove, knowing that time would be spared for them. Hospitality was in full swing as they guzzled cold champagne and premium beer from logo-covered Styrofoam cups.

Once a pen was in hand, the woman in red flipped to the back of the program, intending to add her signature discretely, but I said, "Wait, that's not right. You should sign the cover."

"What did you think of the game?" she asked, adding her name above her husband's.

"Do real rams hit each other so hard?" I asked.

"No, sweetheart, they don't, and that's why my man gets the big bucks," she said.

"My man too," her friend said. "Only he doesn't hit quite as hard, which is why I'm just providing the pen. And why I'm tied to a Toyota while she drives a Mercedes," she added, both laughing.

After thanking them, I returned to where my father was standing a considerable distance away. As I made my way back, they waved and smiled at George enthusiastically. This must've surprised him because he turned around to see if they were greeting someone else.

"What was that all about?" George asked.

"Our Los Angeles Rams' program is now complete," I said. "Mrs. Elizabeth Deacon Jones just signed it."

George was delighted and offered to drive me to the float upon which Deacon Jones declined to appear.

He described my responsibilities by saying, "Your job will be to gently throw candy canes down Hollywood Boulevard to Sunset and Vine, but make sure to smile for the television cameras while waving to your friends watching at home."

For a man with more luxury timepieces than most watch emporiums, you'd have thought him capable of keeping an appointment, but not so. Meyera and I joked about having three time zones in our lives:

New York time, California time, and George Buchanan time. This time, it wasn't funny. Floats depart according to a strict schedule, and the one slated for me to ride wouldn't wait.

Sitting anxiously on the long green couch, I listened as George called with last-minute changes requiring Meyera and I to meet him. Driving like a rally car competitor, Meyera's hands shook as she chain-smoked while dodging traffic snags and red lights. When our designated meeting place was cordoned off, we missed the float and we also missed George, who vaporized as swiftly as the dry ice escaping from Santa's chimney. I remembered to wave, and did so, when the last display featuring Father Christmas pulled away.

Disappointment gave way to concerns about what my classmates might say when they didn't see me in the parade, but Meme presented me with two options and said, "You can either fess up about the missed float or say you were dressed as an elf and ask how many happened to see you? The only problem with fibbing is that you're likely to be found out. Tell one lie, and it leads to an entire novel of trouble."

While my parents were sorry to let me down, missing a media event wasn't on their radar. They thought so little of the entertainment industry, it wouldn't qualify as disdain. Mellon, Morgan, and Rockefeller were famous figures, but those touted by Hollywood were disregarded to the point that they didn't exist. When George and Meyera were in full throttle racing mode, Lance Reventlow was among their friends.

His mother was the Woolworth fortune heiress who married Cary Grant when Lance was a child. Barbara Hutton's divorce from her third husband didn't dent the bond between Lance and his former stepfather, which was evident for all to see by the unseemly way Lance greeted him at road races. Jumping up from beneath the hood of his engine, Lance would run down the pit lane and leap into Cary Grant's arms. George and Meyera were aghast. Public displays of affection were far from the restrained behavior expected of Lance, but this is Cary Grant we're talking about. A star's star, and what did my parents take from the experience? Only shock.

Meyera resented spectators, and the kid assigned by a studio to hang around the stable irritated her to no end. Preparing for a role mattered not at all to Meyera, and even if the film involved a horse race in England, she wanted her privacy. Elizabeth Taylor was twelve, and Meyera was sixteen when they met. Meyera had two horses in livery and was looking to add a third, which was enough incentive for the barn to suggest that Elizabeth Taylor conduct her research for *National Velvet* research elsewhere. A decision likely revisited when Warner Brothers gave her the horse after the film wrapped.

"Who cares if her eyes really are violet?" Meyera said to her trainer. "Keep that brat away from me."

Those seeking the spotlight were not the sort George or Meyera would court, and missing the parade was a momentary blip that my parents brushed off a little too lightly for my taste. Our annual Christmas party was fun, but it was hard to hear the doorbell with so many guests talking while Anthony Newley crooned *Who Can I Turn To*? By the time Burt Bacharach hit the turntable, we had abandoned the practice of me opening the door and turned up the volume on *The Look of Love* and *This Guy's in Love with You*. Although *Raindrops Keep Fallin' on My Head* hadn't been written yet, we had plenty of Frank Sinatra and Barbara Streisand to listen to in the meantime.

Cookies were my contribution to the festivities, but when placed in the oven, they turned from Venetian mask design toward something grotesque. Meme characterized them as mysterious and provided a silver platter (perfectly polished by you know who), which made the cookies look great. As did the steady stream of sea creature-themed *Hors d'oeuvres*, passed on much larger platters throughout the night. Meyera served scallops on the half shell, presented more beautifully than Botticelli's *The Birth of Venus*.

George was invited to join us but felt awkward about attending an event at the building, so he took me to Hamburger Hamlet, promising to return before evening's end.

When we finished our Burger Number Nine with a side order of Those Potatoes, my father suggested we check the Fox Westwood Village and Bruin Theatre's film listings, but I said, "What about the party?"

"We've got plenty of time to catch a movie before we go back," George said. "You'll see the guests and have a chance to wish them a merry Christmas."

We were on opposite sides of concern. I was worried about missing the party, and George was uncomfortable about reappearance. The event was finished by the time we got back, and to underscore the point, Meyera played Peggy Lee's recording of Leiber and Stoller's *Is That All There Is?*

A stack of Polaroids on a side table contained two photos of my Christmas cookies. Stashed in a scrapbook, they're faded yet recognizable as an example of how yesterday's detritus becomes tomorrow's darling. These images are of a moment frozen in time, and over time, I've grown attached to that moment without being there. Brushing her teeth before bed that night, Meyera noticed that her tongue resembled that of a Chow dog, and it was black from so much red wine.

Looking at her reflection in the mirror, she said, "In hell, it's Christmas every day."

CHAPTER 13

Meyera was an atrocious housekeeper who made Phyllis Diller look like Howard Hughes. Neither Meme nor I were happy about Meyera's untidy nature, and we'd engage in covert cleaning when she was out to reduce filth without igniting her ire. If Meyera caught you tidying up, she'd take exception and fly into a fury.

"There's an implied criticism of our housework," Meme said.

"Nothing implied about it," I confirmed.

If someone stopped by, it was mortifying. Meyera's attachment to grime became a source of irritation bordering on homicidal impulse, barely controlled on both sides. In matters of house hygiene, Meyera was an absentee landlord, eschewing Colefax & Fowler for sloth and squalor instead.

Our neighbor, Victor, dropped in unexpectedly and was astounded by the post-hurricane state of our place.

It wasn't something you see every day, and he said, "Meyera, if there was a dead elephant in the room, you'd step over it."

Meyera's lack of concern about the appearance of our home was a complete contrast to the attention she devoted to herself. She was comfortable on both sides of the divide, and it was a dichotomy that suited her until after Thanksgiving when I was eight. An avid tennis enthusiast, she attended all the big matches and dated a celebrated player named Richard.

Regarded as one of the top ten players of all time, *Sports Illustrated* listed him among the most favorite athletes of the twentieth century, but the relationship didn't last. This may have been for the best because he married a total of six times, and I've never heard anyone say, 'Seven times lucky.'

In addition to an eight-year record as World Number One, he briefly held the mantle to Meyera, and I was watching television on the long green couch when she picked up his call.

"Hello Richard, how nice to hear it's you," she said. "What are we doing right now? Nothing special, just relaxing. You're just down the street, ten minutes away? Of course, it's a perfectly fine time to come over."

Meyera hung up the phone and surveyed the catastrophic state of our apartment in a panic. Never had I seen my mother move so fast, but it wasn't the pace that impressed me so much as her creative concealment of items that I admired.

Dirty dishes were loaded like torpedoes into the oven, where I heard them shift and come tumbling down. Clothes awaiting ironing joined the ironing board behind the curtains, while soiled linen went straight into the dishwasher. Pots and pans were tossed into the bathtub behind the shower curtain, and stacks of magazines were stashed under the couch, except for the September issue of *Life* magazine, which was a gift from Richard, who had his friend Arthur Ashe sign the cover.

Loose letters, bills, and an incomplete deck of cards were thrown inside the bread bin with the lid pulled down. My View-Master almost joined the *melee,* but I leaped up and saved it from languishing in the tumble dryer. This was better than the episode of *Bewitched* I'd been watching, and when the doorbell rang, Meyera was half dressed, half made-up, and half crazy.

"Oh God, is that Richard here already?" Meyera said. "Will you answer it? I'll be out in a matter of minutes, so please suggest he help himself to a drink while I finish getting ready."

"Okay, but you'd better make it speedy," I said. "Andale! Ariba!"

I greeted Richard, and while directing him to the liquor cabinet, we passed the kitchen, where he noticed our turkey, but there wasn't much left after Thanksgiving.

"Mind if I make myself a sandwich?" Richard asked, to my astonishment.

It wasn't his request for a snack, but the fact that he was able to discern one that surprised me. The bird was nothing more than a glorified carcass, so sparse even Georgia O'Keeffe would've given it a pass. Was this a legitimate question, a joke, or perhaps a dare?

"Sure, you're welcome to try," I said. "But do you mind if I watch?"

Richard dexterously removed minuscule flecks of flesh from the bone with the precision of a surgeon. Never wavering from his objective, he employed the concentration of a sushi chef and filled two slices of Wonder bread in no time. Handing him the Hellman's mayonnaise and Meyera's special cranberry sauce, I asked how he managed to make such a robust sandwich.

"I was the eldest of seven children," Richard said. "We didn't go hungry, but food was never wasted. It's all about seeing things from a different vantage point. Take this turkey, for example. You see a stripped bird, and I see a full meal. It takes practice, that's all. That's the trick to life: practice. You've got to hit it hard, and you've got to hit it every day."

Meyera joined us looking great but was flustered by the bills that spilled out of the bread box when Richard made that seemingly impossible snack.

"How on earth did this land in the kitchen?" she asked, knowing the answer.

"I put it there thinking that you wouldn't want the cat to read your correspondence," I said.

"Richard, may I serve you a drink?" Meyera asked.

"Allow me, mine's stronger," he said, both laughing.

It was difficult to determine whether he was referring to measures of alcohol or center court. His prowess confirming the latter was confirmed by journalists, who noted that if the fate of the world depended on one man's serve, you'd want it to be Pancho Gonzales.

Tennis is terrific, but horses have been the most consistent love of my life. Unlike the attraction between romantic partners, the devotion parents feel for their progeny, or the affection an artist finds in the visceral urge to create, it's another brand of adoration entirely. Equestrian enchantment is unique, and once encountered, it never completely goes away.

I was certain this majestic creature had been placed on earth for me to cherish, and Will Rodger's sumptuous 1920s stable was an ideal place to ride. The aroma of hay, horse manure, and well-oiled saddles created the best contact high imaginable.

When learning to jump, our trainer said, "Throw your heart over the fence, and the horse will follow."

Meyera and I attended the annual Fabulous Forum horse show, which was a week-long event that was well worth engaging in accomplice liability to patronize. I dictated the note written in Meyera's hand, excusing my absence from school. We became cavalier in selecting reasons requiring me to miss class, and this year, we cited the birth of my half-sibling.

A week away was easily ascribed to such an event, and we opted for the gender-neutral word sibling, hoping it wouldn't attract attention from the dates I'd be gone. Susan wasn't due for several weeks, and having no idea if the baby was a boy or girl, we glossed over specifics.

When Susan gave birth to Cynthia Jane Buchanan, I stopped skiving for the show and started packing to meet my baby sister. Our excuse was prophetic, and the epistle designed to deceive school administrators became accurate overnight. It felt off-kilter to be on the right side of a fraudulent note, but missing school was on the cards either way. Flying standby was something of a shock, and I was provided with a last-minute seat in economy class.

When I arrived, Susan had an Irish nanny *in situ* called Margery, who was from Kinsale. She was in her forties, and dressed in a white nanny's uniform with button-down blouses secured by a silver Celtic Knot brooch. A fan of fresh air, she'd place Cynthia in the Silver Cross pram, proud to push her around the park in the same brand used for Prince Charles.

Margery prepared Irish dishes with Guinness, but for this momentous event, she cooked corned beef and cabbage with dark beer instead. Susan's special dessert graced our table, and everything, including the baby, was ready for presentation. Before Cynthia touched down in my lap, protective pillows were needed to secure us in the way NASA had installed astronauts before blastoff. Between the bulk of the upholstery and complex blanket folds, I was finally ready to hold the baby, but locating her in all this fabric wasn't easy. When Cynthia was unwrapped, we sat in silence while each of us took the moment silently in.

"What do you think of your sister?" George asked.

Regarding the baby, as did Baloo when meeting Mowgli, I said, "Sticky, smelly and squirmy."

"That describes most of humanity," George added with a laugh.

"Take a closer look and describe what you see," Susan suggested encouragingly.

Describe was a game Susan invented to illustrate that there's more than first meets the eye, such as with bamboo plants, which are beautiful but better in shadow, or fresh linen that's as nice to the nose as it is to the touch. Once the objective was clarified, I scrutinized the infant more closely than Miriam when tending to baby Moses, but compared with the amount of cloth I had to cope with, dealing with the rushes would've been easy.

With the crazed enthusiasm of a game show contestant, I looked up and shouted, "Circles. I see a series of circles on her round face, blue eyes, and tiny fists at the end of each round arm. Everything attached to her body is round, including a round rear end."

Spinning out of control in concentric circles of my own, George laughed and said, "I knew it was a mistake taking her to see modern art last summer. After one Cubist exhibition, she's deconstructed our daughter."

Susan said, "I see a baby with two parents but only one sister, which makes that role significant."

Margery added, "One girl grew under her mother's heart while the other grew in it, making both Buchanan sisters extremely fortunate."

Fortunate circumstances were highlighted by my pal Donna Simone, who lived opposite a rickety fence separating our two LA-based apartment buildings in a small place with her grandmother, mother, and elder sister. Her home was the first in which I discovered fiscal disparity when requesting more meatloaf during Sunday dinner, but the iron-rod matriarch running the house wasn't prepared to indulge me and said I'd had enough from her table.

Returning home incensed, it didn't take long for Meyera to join me, considering that her taxes subsidized Donna's education while Mom scraped together my tuition fees. We figured this entitled me to a second helping, but Donna's grandmother obviously disagreed.

My pal laughed and said, "Tell your Mom I said thanks."

Ready to continue my description of the baby, our game was interrupted when Aunt Louise and Maude arrived. My grandmother approached me with an uncharacteristic lift to her step but lifted Cynthia from my lap, saying, "Isn't my real granddaughter beautiful? Having a blood of my blood genetic connection is simply superb."

Maude's attitude toward my transplanted status surprised me, but clarified why George was dead set against me knowing about the adoption. Meyera disagreed and pointed to the fact that in later life, I might need a kidney or other donation from a biological match.

This controversial issue was resolved on an informal *ad hoc* basis when I was three, after a heavily pregnant woman joined Meme and I by the pool, which prompted me to ask, "What on earth did she eat?"

"She's expecting a baby," Meme said. "This isn't a result of binge eating."

"Did I make Mommy's tummy so big?" I asked.

"No, you were in another lady's tummy getting ready for us to claim you from the moment you were born. No one else but you would do. We looked high and low but had to wait for talent such as you've got, and that's why we've got you forever," Meme explained.

Susan offered dessert to our fashionably late family members, but Baked Alaska's flames had subsided.

Aunt Louise's sharp squint alone would've doused the blaze when she looked at Maude and said, "How dare you insult my namesake? Tomorrow, I'm taking her to the restaurant of her choosing."

"Cadillac cheeseburger at P.J. Clarke's might be nice?" I suggested.

Aunt Louise laughed at having made such a child-friendly offer, and I was relieved to have a powerful foreign ally.

The next morning, Susan described breakfast as Cynthia's last meal, and when asked for clarification, she confirmed that an appointment with the pediatrician was scheduled, during which my sister was to receive a shot. Searching for a semantical distinction that might save Cynthia from pain, I requested a more specific definition of the word shot, hoping we'd discuss a new feeding regime or a different brand of diaper. An injection was on the cards, and I felt like a heel, knowing what Cynthia did not. Being in on a dreadful secret is an awkward place to be.

When we arrived at the waiting room, I was uncomfortable. When they called Buchanan, I became anxious, and when the hypodermic was administered, I was distraught. After a brief delay between the needle piercing her skin and the pain, Cynthia screamed while processing this unpleasant sensation for the first time. I tried to cheer her up, but she glared at me and clung to Susan like a marsupial. Feeling guilty when we put Cynthia down for the night, I apologized for participating in such a bad day, but Susan said she wouldn't understand me.

"Maybe you'd explain it to her?" I suggested.

Cynthia was wildly expressive but difficult to read, and when my ability to communicate with her hit a dead end, Susan filled in the blanks.

"How do you know when it's had enough to eat?" I'd ask.

"When she turns her head away and refuses the spoon," Susan answered.

"If babies dream, do they also have nightmares?" I questioned.

"Yes, probably about being dropped," Susan said.

"Do we have to wait, or does it love us already?" I asked.

"She loves us, but remember she's a person rather than it," Susan said.

When it came to understanding Cynthia, my stepmother was in Margaret Mead's league, able to decipher what was, to me, a strange and wild creature.

Finding things of interest to the baby was easy; finding things of interest to me required the dog, and finding things of interest to Charlie involved food. By blending these elements, we achieved a fun time for all. Using the same set of ingredients, my friend Mackenzie had great success entertaining us by covering her infant sister's feet in peanut butter before presenting them to their Great Dane. She was a consummate host and offered me the first peanut pasting, but I declined on the basis I'd cashed in my chips with the rabbit two years ago. The memory of Peter Mach 1 was still sensitive, so I opted for a ringside seat instead.

The dog set to work transferring every molecule from foot to mouth, which was impressive considering that both were in motion. The baby chirped while being tickled, and the dog wagged its tail. Charlie was marginally smaller than Mackenzie's dog, but tall enough for a reenactment. I glanced at Cynthia's feet while reaching for the peanut butter. It was a different brand from that used by Mackenzie, and I wondered if Jif Creamy would work as well as Skippy? Cynthia's nanny, Margery, was made suspicious by the silence and came in to see what we were up to. I'd filled a serving spoon to capacity and was ready to commence action, but Margery's presence put a halt to that.

"Are you having a snack?" Margery asked. "Mind you, don't spoil your appetite."

Back in the cupboard went the Jif, minus a large dollop, which Charlie cleaned better than the dishwasher standard. Bacon worked best with my father's Doberman, who obligingly stepped aside when I stepped into the family, and Farmer John is to be credited. Pork products enabled me to grease the wheels by smuggling strips of bacon from my hand to Hako's mouth. Meyera's father dropped by during feeding time and watched half a pound of bacon and several sausage links disappear.

Having noticed the source of Hako's bounty, Dr. Joe blew the whistle on us by asking, "Does the baby always consume such mammoth portions of bacon and sausage?"

His question had nothing to do with Judaism or keeping kosher but was intended to draw attention to my largesse concerning the dog.

"Well, yes," Meyera said. "Sausage patties and pigs in a blanket seem to evaporate. The baby has quite an appetite."

"So does Hako," Dr. Joe confirmed.

The intention to breed Hako came to fruition, and he sired a significant number of Doberman pups thanks to the retention of his testicles. While learning to stand, I'd grab hold of his dangly bits and shout,

'Eeep.' This lesson in cause-and-effect quickly lodged in both our minds and, in the absence of reaching, simply saying, 'Eeep' would galvanize Hako's hasty retreat. For a breed notoriously fierce, this dog was remarkably tolerant, making Peter Pan's rational rival, Newfoundland Nana, look negligent by comparison.

Hako had a clear code of conduct, allowing items to be delivered but not removed from the house, which he guarded with vigor. Incoming nappies were fine, but outgoing diapers were denied with a vengeance. He was the same concerning George's E-type Jaguar, and when riding shotgun with the top down, Hako's sleek coat caused many to double-take because he resembled a *chauffeur*-driven seal.

He loved luxuriating in the sunshine and was basking in the heat while parked outside the pharmacy when George went in with the aim of purchasing goat's milk. Regarded by my family as superior to cows or formula, it's not easy to source, but generations of women aren't to be argued with.

Hako was in full sun-worshiping mode, with his head tilted up toward a cornflower-blue sky, in a blissful moment that was shattered by a car buff who disturbed the dog's reverie. Faster than the Jag's zero to sixty mph ratio in 6.9 seconds, Hako placed his jaws firmly around the unfortunate admirer's wrist with no bite down but no let-up either. After an hour of shopping, George returned to find a nervous Jaguar aficionado detained, but not damaged, by the dog.

Hako's observational skills sometimes surpassed that of my parents, even when in proximity. I'd been bouncing in the crib, with George and Meyera standing on either side when a particularly energized spring powered me over the top. Airborne without a shoot, Hako was first to notice and sprinted across the room in time to cushion my fall. Rin Tin Tin, Lassie, and Toto have nothing on Hako's heroism. This unlikely *guter hund* and I shared an odd history characterized by bacon, gonads, and flight from a crib.

At the other end of the age spectrum, Hako contracted diabetes and became disabled. After his hind legs were removed, he was fitted with a wagon hitch prosthesis, which is medieval by today's standard but was state-of-the-art back then. Birds consumed what was left of the dog's spirit. Vicious crows were aware of his inability to move with any degree of finesse or speed and swooped down to peck at him. Compassion overcame the wish to delay inevitable loss, and sitting alone on the long green couch, George wept uncontrollably when Hako was put to sleep.

CHAPTER 14

On the East Coast, everyone was secure, and George wanted to embellish this foundation by stitching his family together as a matter of urgency. It became his *cause célèbre* as he sought to find a third strategy for a final custody battle solution. Stepping inside the war rooms of his mind, George discarded ethics and integrity with as much ceremony as depositing an overcoat in a public cloakroom.

It was after Christmas, and everything was frozen. The racing season had yet to start, except in California, where Santa Anita was open, as was Del Mar, where the turf meets the surf. At Hollywood Park, they were off and running, but here on the East Coast, it would be some time before the starting bell rang and the magnetic gate opened to release dreams and disappointments.

For my father and me, there were no seasons where Belmont Park was concerned, although the absence of people would indicate otherwise. No elegantly attired audience, no bright jockey silks, or flags on display. There was no color at all other than a frost-covered track and stadium.

A selection of high-octane thoroughbreds was paraded before us, each sculpted to perfection, their bloodlines designed to test speed barriers. Even at the walk, they appeared to have fire flaring from their chiseled nostrils, bringing the work of George Stubbs to mind. These elegant creatures were crafted from rarefied breeding stock, genetically designed to the point that their blood virtually ran blue. Thoroughbreds of this status occupied an exclusive sphere of the universe, far from that of kids' hunters and jumpers.

We stood in the stadium where Sea Biscuit, Secretariat, Man o' War, and War Admiral won fame to a degree few sports figures achieved. Our presence at the track on a cold December morning remained a mystery until George played his trump card. If fear and smear tactics failed to deliver me full-time to New York, perhaps he'd purchase his way out of the problem. Confident that everyone at any age has their price, my father's opening bid was strong.

"If you'll agree to live with Susan, Cynthia and me, I'll buy one of these horses for you right now," he offered. "Look at these beauties and pick the one you like best. By tomorrow, you'll have it in the stable ten-minutes' drive away. Hey, what about that one with the gorgeous bay color? I bet you'd look great showing him."

I was in shock but needed to say something. Remaining silent wasn't an option, yet I found it impossible to speak. We stood quietly for a few moments and watched the cavalcade.

"Aren't these horses a little expensive?" I asked tentatively.

"Never mind about the money," he said without missing a beat. "With a horse like that, you won't need to send away for those damn equestrian catalogs. I've told you that collecting pictures won't provide you with every horse in the world. Our mailbox is stuffed with brochures that might make people think we're White Plains farmers, and it's embarrassing. All you must do is make up your mind and select one that will be exclusively yours. Just yours to love forever. What do you say?"

He might as well have whispered, "Go on, Eve, be a good girl and take a bite."

I languished without a word in reply while struggling not to suffocate or choke on these choices. Although not a negotiating tactic, my silence was misconstrued as rejection, but George had come here to do a deal today, and he wasn't about to leave empty-handed without upping the ante.

"You drive a hard bargain," he said, "But if you agree to live with us, I'll buy not just one but any two horses you want."

Want was the word that repeated in my head. I wanted a horse desperately. Watching the display of high-level horseflesh was mesmerizing, and I was made dizzy by this cruel carousel. My father's real-life merry-go-round spun in circles of bribery, greed, and temptation.

"What about Mommy and Meme?" I asked. "Who will look after my pet rabbits and the cat?"

"I'll make sure all the animals are shipped safely," George said. "Lots of carriers specialize in transporting pets, so leave that to daddy."

All this grandeur was getting to me. At school, we were shown a film about an Irish boy who overcame debilitating shyness thanks to a confidence-generating Connemara pony. When asked what I wanted for my birthday, this film informed my wish.

"Let's fly to Ireland and buy one of those Connemaras," I suggested. "We can return home via sedate ship passage."

"From Ireland to Los Angeles?" Meme asked, with one eyebrow raised.

"How else to transport the new pony?" I countered.

I'd not said anything about George's two-horse bribe, but it came to light during one of his transatlantic shout-a-thons. The concept of brokering one offer against another wasn't something I'd engage in. Contorting George's inducement into California bounty would've been wrong. Meyera was already on a knife-edge, barely able to cope, let alone compete.

Keeping George's offer a secret served as an unwitting heartbreak, but leveraging his enticement against her guilt might've done Meyera in.

"Ireland is an interesting idea but costly," Meyera said. "What would you say instead to having your request for a dog fulfilled? How about an English springer spaniel?"

The word interesting meant highly unlikely to happen, and was the West Coast equivalent of Aunt Louise's phrase, 'It's better this way.' I took the offer on the table and tabled the pony issue, but remained ready to raise it again.

George and Susan's marriage started to show signs of strain. It was the little things that alerted me to trouble when innocuous questions attracted irritable answers.

"Any idea what you'd like for dinner?" Susan asked.

"Why consult me when you're the one who knows what's best," George said. "Isn't everything up to you? Go ahead and decide, but bear in mind I can't stomach venison again."

Every night, we'd sit awkwardly at the table, struggling to make conversation. Susan served a thick cut of sirloin, requiring more than average effort to chew, which limited my contribution to otherwise absent chat. Drops of condensation slithered down the Lalique pitcher, and I resisted adding a design that might give us something to talk about.

Susan noticed I'd stopped eating and said, "Anything wrong?"

"Nothing wrong," I said. "I'm just taking a break from chewing."

That should have been sufficient to resume continued silence, but George verbally pounced on Susan.

"Haven't you ever tired of chewing?" he asked. "Don't you remember what it was to be a child? Can't you see she's momentarily fatigued?"

The mood was escalating, and to prevent things from blowing up, I did what all kids living on a fault line do; electing to distract them.

"Let's take the baby and dog out for ice cream," I suggested. "Dinner is delicious but hard to eat with my braces."

The idea appealed to everyone. A ride in the car and a change of scenery would do us good. Forsaking Friendly's, we drove to Carvel in search of their famous Flying Saucer ice cream sandwich and on the way back, George completed four revolutions of a traffic circle rather than the one required to get home. I laughed, Susan scoffed, and Cynthia experienced centrifugal force for the first time.

When we pulled into the garage, Susan had trouble opening the heavy Cadillac door. The electric mechanism controlling the lock was stuck, and after my father fixed it, Susan collected Cynthia but was obviously angry and slammed the door shut.

"I mean it, George," Susan said. "You can bring in all the ice cream you like, but I still want out."

Companionship was a promised land located on the far side of a comfortable marriage. Susan struggled to discern its coordinates but found emotional latitude and longitude were lost. George felt the marriage was becoming a mirage but didn't want a second divorce, and they did what people on the precipice of separation do, which is try to keep it together.

My clothing for this summer included a pair of shorts featuring a peace sign on the back pocket. It was a little large in the waist, but the blue jean fabric made them trendy. Once I was in Manhattan, Susan set to work on alteration and, after breakfast, asked me to try them on. It was a perfect fit, and I returned to the kitchen as if strutting down a Parisian walkway.

I was in my mid-twirl when George said, "What in God's name are you wearing?"

"In Ireland, we call them dungarees," Margery said.

"It's not the cloth but the back pocket that concerns me," George said. "Can any of us fail to notice the symbol?"

It would've been hard for anyone to miss it. George placed one hand on my head while pointing indecorously at my bottom with the other.

"It's a bit of decoration, and all the kids are wearing them," Susan said.

"Nothing wrong with peace," Margery noted. "It's not offensive where I come from."

My Father turned me back around facing front and said, "I want you to march up those stairs, change out of that monstrosity, and throw it in the trash."

Susan tried to intervene and said, "Those shorts are perfectly fine. A peace sign isn't a Black Panther Party salute."

"I'm not allowing my daughter to dress as a hippy," George stated. "She looks like a beatnik, for Christ's sake, and I intend to burn those shorts. If necessary, with her still in them."

Susan shrugged her shoulders before saying, "I'll purchase some new shorts."

Shopping was tedious, and stuck indoors trying things on before lining up to pay, the very definition of dull. My tolerance for the retail experience has decreased since that time, and I suspect uniforms are primarily to blame.

First through sixth grade required a light-blue or yellow dress worn with white knee socks and saddle shoes. Seventh grade involved the same footwear in addition to a grey flannel skirt, white blouse, and navy-blue sweater. At the stable, we wore boots, britches, and velvet-covered riding hats. Adolescence had separate rules governing acceptable garb comprised of well-worn patchwork jeans and a gauze top, with a bra optional.

In the professional arena, the strictures are simplest by far, and blessedly so. A tailored suit, silk blouse, and heels with pearls are compulsory. Step away from these safe standards, and a wide-open sea of misguided choices awaits. I've often left a store marveling at the miracle I had clothes on my back, and today, I resemble a graduate of the Peter Falk as *Colombo* School of Fashion and Design.

Breathing space was urgently required. Susan and George needed to take time for themselves away from each other. Plans were hastily prepared for my father and I to travel from New York to Georgia via intercostal waterways on board George's luxury motor yacht. Our mission was to collect a specially conditioned engine for his new speedboat, which was an, at times, airborne craft awaiting our return in Manhattan's dry dock.

Malcolm Forbes was right; the only difference between men and boys is the price of their toys. George's passion for boats was at full tilt, as was my unbridled interest in horses. While my father perused maps and boating manuals, I read *Misty of Chincoteague* and *Stormy Misty's Foal*. Based on historically accurate accounts of a Spanish galleon's shipwreck off the coast of Virginia, the cargo of ponies swam to safety and became wild on a small island not far from Georgia. Susan mentioned that our maritime destination might potentially include this site, but I had to select the right time to suggest that we add Chincoteague to the itinerary.

Two days before departure, George mentioned over breakfast that Maude would be joining us, and everything froze in that moment. Susan was feeding the baby and went still, while Cynthia pursed her lips shut, looking from the spoon to George. My father focused on the dregs of his coffee while Margery directed her gaze toward the floor.

A seasoned nanny, she was experienced in the way of fractious family relations and knew when to retreat. Sensing a power vacuum, I offered to endure Maude's presence in exchange for a chance to witness Chincoteague's famous wild pony swim. I wanted to join the tens of thousands who watch penning day, and for that opportunity, I'd suffer proximity with Satan.

Last year's Staten Island Ferry ride with Maude served as a trial run. I'd already been to Hades and back with my grandmother. George was on board with the 'Misty detour,' as he called it, and Susan was pleased but concerned about placing me in close cabin quarters with our version of Evelyn Draper.

"Distance is what this family needs," Margery observed. "A well-deserved holiday from each other is long overdue. Contact reduced is contact enhanced, and will refresh everyone."

Margery hit the nail on the head. Hallmark's slogan 'When you care enough to send the very best' is misleading. A more honest tagline might read, 'Hallmark is here when human contact is too damn much.'

My father was unburdened now the bad news had been broken, and he readily agreed to allow our dog Charlie to join us.

"I suppose you're right to suggest we see some horses and bring the dog," George said. "Even standard poodles need a rest now and then."

Had this been an arm's-length business negotiation, I'd have left money on the table. Charlie's attendance was already secured by Maude's. This wasn't an additional bargaining point but a done deal, and I wondered what we'd do when at sea or waterway. Maybe Maude would hold the stopwatch while I practiced synchronized swimming? Meme recently whipped up a few new routines, and keeping good time was essential.

"How can one person all alone in the water practice timed sequences?" George asked, laughing.

"I train as Ester Williams does," I said. "The *Million Dollar Mermaid* practices by herself while being timed by a watchful coach."

Issues confronting only children were never an impediment to Meme, synchronized swimming included, which she seemed to take as seriously as I did.

"You're doing exceptionally well. Keep it up," she'd say convincingly.

To perform in the pool with my grandmother watching was to swim in yin, and she used an enormous pink towel to dry me off.

Smothering me in terrycloth and praise, she'd say, "Look out, Ester, there's a new guppy in town."

We gathered nervously at the dock, where George began barking orders before we left. Meeting Misty would be worth it, and I eagerly boarded before pretending to help Maude totter across the gangway. My looks of mock concern and feigned reaches in her direction created a show of support rather than actual assistance. I extended and retrieved my hand in the same motion. When it came to Charlie, there was no fake greeting, and I welcomed the dog to our floating home with open arms.

Learning to tie landing lines when we docked was easier than adjusting to the rocking motion that caused me to sway side to side like unsettled mercury. Each port of call contained kids sharing a similar slice of liberty, and we'd exchange contact information on small snippets of paper that I stashed in an empty Chock full o'Nuts coffee can, hoping today's adventurous associate would become tomorrow's correspondent. We'd yet to discover how tenuous the bond of an ephemeral encounter is, so we didn't keep in touch. Land-based communication would've tainted the experience by dragging it through the rigors of reality, distorting the purpose of being in transit.

George made a navigational error, taking us down a long, narrow, straight marked with *Do Not Enter/No Trespassing* signs. Turning around wasn't an option, and committed to this direction, we crept along quietly. Our hushed silence met an abrupt end when three Air Force jets flew astonishingly close to our boat at low altitude, whizzing past in quick succession. It was only after we had sight of them that we heard the deafening sound. The stealth approach caught us unawares.

When George's frantic search of the map revealed our exact location, he was furious and said, "You've got to be kidding. How in the hell did we enter a US Naval Auxiliary Air Station?"

The buzzing of jets and our Federal Trespass frightened Maude, but George asserted control, demanding we remain in our seats. Staging a personal mutiny, Maude ran to the stern, where she grabbed the Stars and Stripes. Flailing that flag for all she was worth demonstrated a level of emotion, I'd not thought her capable of. Rather than nautically trained semaphore signals, she approximated a whirling dervish.

"Mother, what in Christ's name are you doing?" George hollered. "Can't you see I've got enough on my hands? For God's sake, please stop whatever it is you're trying to accomplish."

My father's comments were delivered through gritted teeth, and a vein on the side of his head started to throb. Maude's jaw was also clenched.

She wasn't about to be distracted from her objective and said, "What does it look like I'm doing? I'm waving the flag to show them we're Americans. We don't want them to shoot, do we?"

Maude's fear struck me as both funny and refreshing. It was a reminder that perhaps a drop of humanity might still be afloat in the old gal, and I tried to muster concern for my grandmother but was distracted by her modified rendition of the Lambada. Winded and exhausted, she collapsed, rather than reclined, in a waiting chair.

"Remember, George," Maude said between labored breaths. "If arrested, tell them about the scores of officers you entertained during the war. Night after night until three or four o'clock in the morning. All that hard work at the Stork Club must count for something."

Tour of duty at Manhattan's hot spots? This made perfect sense while making a mockery of my father's story about his slight loss of hearing having been caused by gun battles aboard a naval ship. The rat-a-tat-tat responsible for his auditory impairment didn't come from enemy artillery, but was caused by the blaring decibel of a big band. George's version of reload was to signal the waiter for another round.

We passed through forbidden territory unscathed, and mooring at the marina was a relief. Over dinner, I dominated the conversation by drowning George and Maude in details about Misty.

"The copyright dates indicate that these aren't the original ponies," I said. "But what we'll see instead are actual descendants, which means a lot. Tomorrow's probably going to be the best day of my life."

A late departure and lack of slip reservation caused us to miss the pony swim, but determined to see the wild herd, I ran toward the teeming mass of tourists. George designated a *rendezvous* point that provided me freedom to wend at will. By employing the single-minded focus of a dedicated Misty fan, I jockeyed for position, repelling regiments of girls right out of my way. Although not proud of my guerrilla tactics, I made it to the front, where it was a shock to find Misty.

Emaciated and ungroomed, this wasn't the pony of publicity fame but an imposter, creating a painful gap between literary description and manifest reality. Stunned by the contrast between fantasy and observational shortfall, I reflected on Santa Claus, who had strict guidelines for his representatives, all of whom were smartly dressed in crisp red and white. Local agents from the North Pole accepting requests for toys looked great while doing so.

There's a magic to these characters that an only child is particularly susceptible to. We lack siblings disabusing us of these concepts. When it came to the Easter Bunny, two tiny foil wrapped eggs at the base of our apartment door confirmed my belief. They were left anonymously, providing evidence sustaining credibility. Quite a lot of children in the world equates to a lot of ground to cover, and two eggs made sense as a personal quotient.

Years later, our neighbor, Lois admitted to providing the eggs in question, which dented but did not destroy my belief in that great rabbit. Mermaids lingered as a faint but possible incarnation. I spent a lot of time at the beach and regarded Hans Christian Anderson's tale as a maritime report. The ending of that tragic story struck me on a visceral level when a foamy tide hit my legs, and I screamed, "Dead Mermaid."

Childminders heard my scream, but the wind distorted the message, morphing the three syllables from dead mermaid to jellyfish. While everyone ran to retrieve their charges, Meme tried to calm the hysteria I'd created by loudly explaining that the Pacific Ocean is vastly different from Denmark's, and sea-foam on our side of the world is one hundred percent deceased mermaid-free. Not one scale from a tail would be found in Santa Monica. Our mermaids were healthy. I considered the distinction between European vs American rules for these magnificent creatures, and concluded it a possibility.

This delightfully deceitful fraud is designed to foster hope that the non-believers got it wrong, and these characters exist, even at a stretch, as with the Tooth Fairy. In the absence of any assistance from the Sandman, this fictional sprite has an incredibly tough time carrying coins of significant weight and cumbersome bills to the more fortunate. Calcium value must be a high incentive for this macabre pixie to run bed to bed collecting milk teeth, which is an unattractive proposition, making this nymph the hardest working of all. It's also a purist, and when Meme noticed me looking covetously at her dentures, she confirmed that only real teeth are acceptable for under the pillow placement.

When I accidentally swallowed a baby tooth, Meyera panicked, and threatened to have my stomach pumped, which is an even less attractive proposition. Dodging Meyera's attempt at capture, I ran to Meme, who settled the mayhem by suggesting that Meyera call UCLA's emergency clinic. Seems the Tooth Fairy isn't the only one to benefit from calcium, and I wondered why I hadn't consumed the others. Meme gave me a five-dollar bill and said swallowing a tooth is a common occurrence for which the Tooth Fairy has a contingency fund.

Children are willing conspirators ready to invest in this benign fictional exchange, and Meme's certainty about the nocturnal activity of my toys was so convincing, I placed scotch tape on the hooves of my model horses to see if they moved during the night. I never caught them out, but Meme said they were crafty.

Adults need to get on board with this program, which means more than leaving eggnog out for Santa or a carrot for Rudolph. It's about making these dreams palatable if not actually possible. Misty was a disappointment, and although dreams die hard, I wasn't about to allow mine to crumble without moving on to look for Stormy.

A large concrete building featured a faithful reproduction of the book's cover blazoned across one side. More than just a mural, it was compelling art. The image of Stormy galloping along a windswept beach was etched into the minds of countless kids. The scale of the picture was impressive, and I couldn't wait to see the real thing confined behind a hotwire corral at the base, but angling my way forward revealed an anemic pony trying to coax nonexistent grass from a dirt patch.

This Stormy wasn't the right color, and looked like a last-minute miscast extra. Resolved to salvage something from this heinous distortion, I headed toward the concession stands and stumbled across a sign bearing the words: Ponee 4 Sale $25.00 Dollars. Twenty-five dollars was the precise sum in my pocket that might rescue me from the devastation of the day.

"Sorry, kid," the vendor said. "That twenty-five-dollar pony? He was sold hours ago, and these run for $100.00 apiece. See any you like?"

Over dinner, I showed George and Maude the keyring I bought, bearing the words Misty/Stormy/Chincoteague.

"I'm sorry we missed the Pony Swim," George said. "I hope it didn't mar the day, and you managed to have fun."

"Fun?" I said, "Today was amazing, and I had a chance to pat five wild ponies. And guess what? Two were still damp."

The evening meal extended interminably. George cozied up with a special bottle of Pouilly-Fuisse, and Maude remained indifferent to the presence of a child. While my father paid the bill, Maude indicated to a couple at the next table.

"What do their sweatshirts stand for?" Maude asked.

"It's a husband-and-wife team from the sailboat race today," George said. "They've obviously competed together before."

"Why do you say that?" Maude asked.

"Because," George said, "her's reads 'Stop Shouting at Me,' and his reads 'I'm Not Shouting.'"

CHAPTER 15

Heading home from the grocery store, an index card on the bulletin board caught my eye, advertising a pony for sale, and during dinner, I placed it on the table as would a seasoned blackjack dealer. Meyera agreed to look, and the instant I laid eyes on this adorable animal, I was besotted.

When a motivated seller and willing buyer meet, it's usually on good terms, but purchasing a pony requires a third-party veterinarian to perform a thorough check before the deal can be done. The pressure is immense, the pony is oblivious, and the joy, if pronounced fit for purchase, is a *raison d'etre* fulfilled. For dedicated equestrians, horses are less of a sport and more of a calling that follows us from cradle to grave. As with lapsed Catholics, one tug is all it takes, and we're back.

April was a half-Arab, half-Shetland Bay pony. The first half contributed an intelligent dish face with a white blaze, while the second half limited her growth to 13.2 hands and ensured her attitude was always irascible. Shetlands are notoriously cunning and as mischievous as Arabs are bright, which made April eligible for Mensa.

She'd bite, kick and, God, how I loved her. April was the antidote to an alcoholic mother, a demon of a father, or a hard day of Algebra.

This four-year-old mare more than compensated for a myriad of sins, including having to endure arcane forms of educational torture, and after school, I'd approach her corral calling, "Aaaa-Pril."

She, too, had a ritual greeting and wheeled her enormous apple bottom toward me in a deliberate motion, similar to calibrating a Second World War coastal gun emplacement. Once in position, she'd stand with a leg cocked, ready to strike, and, in hoof terms, April was ambidextrous.

Rather than *April in Paris,* I stabled mine in Malibu, where I became adept at trespass. The public footpath underneath the Pacific Coast Highway only reaches so far, and I needed to gain entry to the less populated stretch along the Malibu Colony. This isn't easy as a menacing chain link fence sloped out to sea, requiring ingress and egress to coincide with low tide. Riding bareback along the water's edge is euphoric, and if you add glorious sunshine with a sea as calm as glass, you get transformative.

Trotting along the wet sand, I remembered having stashed a spare pair of jeans in my tack box and decided to take a chance. April and I cantered down the coast, but not far, as Malibu only extends twenty-seven miles, of which the Colony represents a small fraction. Residents in this rarefied community wave to us and smile. Some salute while others raise a freshly squeezed mimosa and, rather than prosecute us for traversing their private length of the beach, they seem happy to share another perfect day in their portion of paradise.

Sitting astride, April, I direct us toward the water, past small waves to where the deep ocean starts. We are buoyant and start to swim. April's nostrils flare and her eyes are as wide as mine in a moment of ineffable joy.

Returning home effusive, I recounted the experience and said to Meyera, "For this exquisite day, I forgive everything to date."

It wasn't riding but parking horses in Malibu that led to a run-in with the Sheriff's Department. After a Colony crossing, I decided to grab a pizza in the newly constructed Malibu Shopping Center and tethered April to the parking lot hitching post intended for that purpose. A police officer disagreed and threatened to write a ticket, attracting the attention of a young woman shopper who asked what was going on. I explained that the post was primarily functional and the decorative aspect just a bonus, so I shouldn't be given a ticket any more than would the driver of a car.

While she listened attentively, the officer tried to look away from her barely concealed, well-endowed breasts, but her bikini was so minuscule that two bandage plasters would've provided greater modesty.

The officer's eyes waged war with his head during an internal dialogue conducted as follows: *I mustn't look at her breasts. Just keep my eyeline level with hers, nod and pretend I'm paying attention. If I maintain the professional stance of an officer, everything's going to be fine. What a shame I'm not off-duty and able to ask her out. Bet she's got a great ass too. Okay, she's talking, and I must concentrate. Shit. She caught me looking at those fabulous tits. Can't have that happen again. No second time. Get a grip. Nothing, repeat, nothing south of her chin is allowed. Oh God, no. What's wrong with me? Must focus and not on her chest, damn it. This has got to stop.*

While the young woman advanced an argument on my behalf, her cleavage effectively operated as a magnetic wire fence. It drew the officer's attention, then shocked and repelled his gaze straight behind the line of social acceptability.

Etiquette provided a more effective barrier than Malibu Colony's chain-link deterrent when this scantily clad Clarence Darrow asserted that parking horses were preferable to emission-polluting cars. She delivered a passionate summation to the already defeated, and the encounter ended as abruptly as it began. No tickets were issued after a warning was delivered to the officer by a beautiful riparian representative.

That sensual struggle was reminiscent of a similar encounter I witnessed before walking to school, which was a short distance, interrupted every morning by heavy traffic running along Barrington between Sunset and San Vincente. Over fifteen minutes would pass before a break in the rush hour dash allowed me to cross, and Meme suggested we contact City Hall, asking for a stoplight to be installed at the earliest convenience.

I wanted to describe the situation as urgent, but Meme said, "You catch more flies with one drop of honey than a gallon of vinegar."

A fully-fledged traffic signal soon appeared, and never have I pressed an automated button with more pride. Meme was able to spin municipal magic, but had it been erected earlier, I'd have missed a scintillating scene while standing outside the building waiting for traffic to slow.

A car from our subterranean garage pulled up, and the driver smiled before turning her attention to the matter of turning right. She was a new resident and new to Los Angeles, having moved from Corpus Christi, Texas, aiming to work as an actress. Her ambition struck me as well-founded. She was the most stunning person I'd ever seen.

Children aren't necessarily aware of these distinctions unless extreme, but this tenant blinded me with beauty. She blinded everybody else, too, and as she edged her car forward, I watched carefully, knowing her turn into traffic would clear the way for me. Misjudging the distance between her car and one approaching, she accelerated, collided, and made a loud noise accompanied by a little dent.

Visibly shaken, she pulled over, and the other driver did the same. When getting out of her car, she was crying but looked amazing, and the fellow behind the other wheel came to the same conclusion. Initially, he said nothing but blinked rapidly while straightening his tie, sleeves, and jacket. Had he a comb handy, I bet he'd have made good use of it in the wing mirror. No doubt grateful for the hit of mouthwash and deodorant he applied that morning, he extended his hand in a gesture indicating more confidence than he felt, and she did the same as they said the same thing to each other.

"I'm so sorry," each stated in unison. "This is all my fault," they added simultaneously.

"I'm twenty minutes late for an audition," she explained. 'I left the apartment feeling nervous, and now, look at what I've done. I can't tell you how awful I feel."

He'd had a minute to process and was astonished that the gods had seen fit to deposit a flawless creature in his way. What did he care if her manner of appearing was a little bumpy? She walked into his outstretched arms, and they cradled for what seemed to me rather longer than necessary, but at age eight, I wasn't best placed to evaluate such things.

"Everything's going to be fine," he said. "I've got excellent insurance. The comprehensive cover was recently renewed, and I'll say this was entirely my fault. It's only my car that's ever so slightly damaged, and yours appears unscratched. Unless, of course, you see a scratch on your car, in which case I'll be happy to take care of it. Suppose now the only responsible thing for us to do is exchange contact information. Probably a good idea to include phone numbers, primarily for reporting purposes. Since you're upset, perhaps I should drive you to the audition?"

I liked this tenant despite her beauty, and I wonder how many others can make the same claim. She loved to cook and was good at it. Most of the art decorating her apartment was made by her own hand, and there was an ethereal quality to her.

Knocking on our door wearing a robe with her hair wrapped up in a towel, she looked sensational and said, "I was taking a shower and remembered the rent is due. Sorry, I forgot to give it to you earlier, but next time it will be on time."

Meyera might've been impervious to celebrities, but she wasn't immune to charm at this level.

She said, "Never a problem. Pay whenever it suits you, and be sure to let me know if your apartment needs anything. Absolutely anything at all."

This glorious tenant and I shared one thing in common, which was that we ran late for everything. Unlike me, she was always forgiven, but when you look that great, what difference does dilatory make? She dashed last-minute for a photo shoot, racing from the beach to her car wearing a red swimsuit. When she landed breathlessly at the studio door, they told her not to change a thing. Not her windswept hair, and definitely not that fantastic one-piece featured in a poster that became the largest selling pin-up in world history.

Her now culturally significant swimsuit is at the Smithsonian. She married famously, did her hair famously, and even died famously.

Prior to that, she became more vigilant about paying the rent on time, and when I answered the door, she said, "Would you mind giving this check to your mother for me? It's on time, and next month, I'll aim to do the same."

Handing the check to Meyera, I said, "Miss Fountain was here to pay the rent."

"It's Fawcett, not Fountain," Meyera said, "Farrah Fawcett. Can't you remember that?"

I did remember and still do. When passing that traffic signal on Barrington, I toot the car horn twice to acknowledge Meme and that six-million-dollar angel.

Swimming and spending sun-drenched days at the barn were luxuriant LA freedoms I loathed to part with. Feeling reluctance verging on dread, I boarded the flight, removing myself from that precarious bubble, and when the pilot announced, "We're beginning our descent," I turned to the passenger next to me and said, "No kidding."

Yin and Yang share a sense of balance, but divorce doesn't deliver anything approaching that. Reeled in like a rainbow trout, I was hooked and headed for a hot, humid atmosphere of now familiar territory I'd learned to track. Emotional camouflage was easy to identify, and I wasn't just confident but cocky concerning my ability to discern trouble, but overconfidence is a trickster. Meyera put a brave face on my absence and woke early each morning to switch on the living room television. After finding the children's channel, she'd return to bed in a somnolent state, soothed by the sound of animated walla.

George and I departed for the suburbs, which was a welcome distance from Manhattan's scorching heat, moving us closer to the warmth of Susan's welcome. Catapulting across the threshold, I raced around the house, checking for Susan in the kitchen, den and bar, but found them empty. Living room, library and study were the same, so I ran upstairs to the bedrooms.

This year, we had five in total, yet no one was to be seen. Ascending the uppermost section, as Tenzing Norgay and Edmund Hillary must've felt summiting Mount Everest, I flew to the master bedroom expecting to find her with the baby, yet found nothing. Returning downstairs, I looked in the garden, but the only family member at home was Charlie, and while our seventy-five-pound dog gave me a ten-ton greeting, I wondered where everyone was.

Cynthia required a lot of paraphernalia, and I was stumped by the absence of such items. Leaving for lunch last summer, we packed the car to the brim with diapers, bottles, wipes, and toys.

George laughed at the increasing bulk and said, "Is all this really necessary? The Donner Party departed with marginally less, and I believe they made better time."

"Knowing I wanted to breastfeed, you're not in a position to complain about formula," Susan said.

"Oh please, after that display we witnessed during dinner in the Village?" George said. "I'm all about motherhood, but not in public. Not when it involves breastfeeding a child capable of asking for a cappuccino instead."

Normally on display and also missing were Susan's *accoutrements* of lotions, potions, and perfumes. Elixirs of infinite variety have distracted, if not defined, the women in my family since ancestral charts began. Should I have a stubbed toe or skinned knee, Meme had a homeopathic cream to soothe it. Females in my clan regard skin hydration as a serious business, tempting us to list moistening under hobbies and interests on our *resume*.

George appreciated indulgent ablution sourced from Jermyn Street and favored Floris cinnamon-scented soap before applying Eau Sauvage by Christian Dior. For formal occasions, he opted for Paco Rabanne's Pour Homme and wouldn't have cared for the Old Spice my friends gave their fathers each Christmas. Unless it came from Belgravia, Bond Street or Knightsbridge, it lacked a certain *panache* where he was concerned.

After a thorough search of the place revealed nothing in the way of extended relatives, I found George sitting in front of a large screen TV, sipping a generous measure of scotch. A tall standing fan in front of him added to the air-con blast, but even with these cooling devices, he was perspiring.

"Daddy, where are Susan and Cynthia?" I asked. "I thought they'd be here to greet me. I wonder when you expect they'll be back?'

George took a sip from the Baccarat tumbler. It was beaded with sweat, matching the drips snaking down his temple in an awkward line of liquid suggestive of sideways tears.

My father placed his hands firmly on my shoulders and said, "They're gone. Gone for good, do you understand? We never mention their names again. Am I making myself clear?"

I nodded while real tears cascaded in straight lines down my face. Niagara Falls was under my chin, so why ask questions when *Res ipsa loquitur* speaks for itself? Susan and Cynthia formed a separate continent created by emotional drift, causing our family topography to change. The San Andreas Fault only threatened to yawn and devour Southern California, but on the East Coast, the damage had been done.

Susan was banished from photograph albums, conversational references, and my life in a process of deletion that was conducted with astonishing efficiency. Disengaging a railway car from its train would've occasioned more ceremony, but somewhere along the track, my father acquired a terrible type of Teflon, allowing him to attract and alienate with equal finesse. When Susan fled to the Dominican Republic for a quickie divorce, it was the second time he'd lost something important. I read nothing but Edgar Allen Poe all summer and realized my father would need support.

On the opposite coast, Meyera was required to support her friend Barbara, whom she met in kindergarten. It was Barbara who helped Meyera memorize pages to mask the disability of Dyslexia after her mother, Janet Slade, forged a close friendship with Meme spanning over forty years. The two *maters* liked to smoke, drink, and set the world straight, which they did regularly through the art of conversation. Janet was every inch the Brit abroad, who regarded most events as either marvelous or ghastly.

She retained The Queen's English better than the received pronunciation featured on the BBC, with an accent that became further refined after a stroke. Her full recovery contained something of a surprise when she exhibited a previously unknown fluent command of Spanish. Janet was a fighter who coped with colossal challenges, including early widowhood, which forced her to find alternative arrangements for just about everything, especially Barbara's education. Converting from the Anglican Church to Catholicism as a matter of urgency allowed Barbara to attend Marymount High School on full scholarship, and Janet was understandably proud of this achievement but, in her cups, confided a different motivation more candidly to Meme.

"I'm not the first or only parent to claim a Road to Damascus moment," Janet said.

"Not when the path leads to a prestigious private school," Meme noted.

"Posing on Sunday as a devout Christian is something I'm prepared to do for my daughter," Janet continued.

"No day of rest for you?" Meme asked.

"Not on the observed day," Janet confirmed.

"You mean when the parochial headmaster observes you?" Meme asked, both laughing.

Meyera remained close to Barbara throughout their lives, and they acted as bridesmaids at each other's wedding. Disadvantaged circumstances didn't make a difference to Barbara, who was bright and beautiful just like her mother, but unlike Janet, she was a devout believer in faith. Religious instruction enhanced the grace with which she greeted the world, and this was the quality that struck most people when they first met her, including Bob Haydon.

Affiliated with Marymount was an all-boys Roman Catholic school called Loyola High, and a carefully chaperoned mixer brought them together senior year. When Barbara walked in, Bob watched her every move through soft-focus halation-affected eyes. There was a serenity about her suggestive of Olivia de Havilland's portrayal of Melanie in *Gone with the Wind.*

They dated exclusively from that first glance, and after graduation, Bob was to attend UCLA while Barbara secured an apprentice position with a prominent florist of considerable renown. Their courtship was contained to budget restaurants and home-cooked meals. Observing restraint characterized them as individuals and a couple. Before taking matrimonial vows, Barbara assumed their commitment to parsimony would continue, and her assumption was partially correct.

Bob's ambition was to remain at UCLA and attend the graduate program in architecture. If that meant cost-cutting, Barbara was accustomed to and prepared for the task. A month before their wedding day, Bob asked Barbara to sit down for a serious chat. He felt honor-bound to explain something important he'd neglected to share previously.

While he harbored tremendous creative and commercial ambition, the latter was a *fait accompli*. His family's finances were secured by a brand-name kitchen cupboard ingredient, so basic it joined salt and sugar on the shelf. Foundation managers devoted entire careers to keeping track of all the sums generated, but Bob preferred to be the primogenitor of his own success. Having withheld his status, Bob wasn't seeking to deceive but trying to understand the terms upon which he was prepared to acknowledge his fortune without being consumed by it. Barbara regarded this as a delightful surprise, and their fairy-tale wedding followed. After having four kids, they were ready for more. Barbara said she felt best when pregnant, and they both liked to please the Pope.

On our way home from San Juan Capistrano, Meyera and I went to see them in Laguna Niguel. It was October when the swallows departed in a dramatic cast of thousands, but more striking than the birds was the distinctive home Bob designed as a blueprint for California living.

Constructed above the beach on the bluff, it provided a staggering wow factor in every direction and was designed around a central courtyard with four separate stairways leading to elevated spaces, resembling a mathematically inspired M.C. Escher graphic. Rooms on varying heights achieved privacy and contained reading nooks, sewing snugs, and a glass art studio. Even if you didn't go all the way up from sand to ceiling level, the distance was considerable but kept everyone in shape. Immaculate herringbone brickwork in the driveway served as a visual starter to the sumptuous chevron-patterned tiles in the kitchen and bathrooms, prompting me to ask why they didn't use these materials to construct the entire house. Bob explained that, although brick, slate and marble are durable, he leaned toward a liberal use of textiles and wood to provide a feeling of warmth.

"Did the third little pig overdo it when creating his home?" I asked.

"Not necessarily," Bob said. "But the second little pig's place was a darn sight more stylish."

An enormous oak tree was marked for pre-construction removal until Bob's ingenuity saved it by building an annex around the trunk, sealed top, and base with heavy rubber. The texture of the tree was impressive, let alone the fact it was growing straight through the middle of a playroom lined with chalk, cork, and magnetic boards.

When the two elder kids discovered the hot tub, Bob claimed they used it so continuously as to constitute a prescriptive easement. Barbara and Bob never let the sun set on an argument and greeted each day with the same routine. Rise early, prepare a glass of freshly squeezed orange juice and gourmet roast coffee before walking down the beach with Rack and Ruin (their two Labrador retrievers). Routine is something many people tend to avoid, but not them, not with that ideal lifestyle.

It was Thursday, and Barbara collected ripe tomatoes, along with a few herbs from the garden, for an omelet. She asked Bob to grab the eggs, but while reaching into the fridge, he looked at her as if wanting to ask something. Then he collapsed.

An aneurysm ended his life before he reached the floor. Cruel blows of inhuman proportion manifest in many ways and sometimes more than one at a time. Witnessing her husband's death was, of course, traumatic, but the shock was so great she had a psychosomatic response, becoming paralyzed from the waist down. Confined to a wheelchair, the home of her dreams became inaccessible, representing imprisonment instead.

When Meyera arrived to comfort her friend, Barbara said, "I've lost my husband, my health, and my home. Why is God punishing me?"

CHAPTER 16

George reluctantly returned from matrimonial status to find that old 'single dad' chestnut waiting for him. He needed to crack it and solve the problem of my summertime supervision, but this time, he wouldn't marry his way out. Not for the sake of childcare. I asked if he had plans to search for another wife.

"Second-time losers don't bat thrice," George said. "I've had a belly-ful of wives, and two are too many to add to. The way I see it, you're you before marriage, and afterward, you're you plus one. Return to just you again and find yourself less than half of what you were before marriage. In my experience, matrimony subtracted more than added in personal, as well as bank balance, terms, and I think it's best I remain single."

This conversational calculation caused George to place a call to his LA-based accountant, who was a long-standing friend. The account-ant's daughter, Laurel, recently turned sixteen and obtained a Califor-nia driver's license, making her eligible for nanny status. Laurel was vi-vacious and a member of the Beverly Hills High cheerleading team. Suitably responsible, attentive, and fun, she represented something of a steal. Even after factoring in the cost of round-trip flights, she made sense on every front. My father and I divvied up duties for the day of her arrival. He drove to JFK to collect her, and I ran like a lunatic throughout the house.

Airports had come to represent sadness for me. The excitement of embarkation was diminished by the down of departing, but I came to terms with the fact that wherever I was, it involved missing someone somewhere else. Susan was singing *Leaving on a Jet Plane* when we drove to JFK last summer, and I'd no idea that would be the last time I'd see her.

We were standing in a crowd of people near the boarding gate, and I was putting on a brave face, trying not to cry. *Ring of Bright Water* was playing that summer, and Susan tried desperately to get us in to see it, but sold-out showings conspired against us. Before allowing passengers on the aircraft, a welcome announcement mentioned that this was the in-flight movie. Susan and I jumped with so much excitement we resembled partners in a winning lottery ticket.

Earmarked for Laurel was what I considered the best bedroom, as it looked out onto the garden. When they walked through the door, I was sold on sight. She was exactly what I'd hoped for. Athletic, with long dark hair and beautiful eyes, Laurel was ready for adventure, not afraid to get her hair wet and light on makeup when dry.

I liked her instinctively, and my instinct proved right. Having a teenager in *loco parentis* is a jackpot win. There isn't an eleven-year-old alive who wouldn't rush toward the custodial care of a sweet-sixteen. Laurel taught me many things — starting with a popular cheer to support her home team, the Normans. Her catalog was comprehensive, and she had spirit-generating moves accompanied by words such as, 'Ashes to ashes dust to dust, we hate to beat you now, but we must we must.'

Critical moments required shorter cheers such as, 'Hold that line,' which had the power to save a game if deployed correctly. I had no idea what line we were referring to, but wherever it was, I wanted to hold it. Getting the movements down was fun, but memorizing the cheers was even more so. Laurel cherished cheerleading but was modest about the squad.

"We're good but not the best," Laurel said. "Dallas has that distinction. The Buffalo Jills, Minnesota Vi-Queens and Seattle SeaGals are worth watching to see how they raise pep."

"What's pep?" I asked, eager to learn.

"Enthusiasm and motivation," Laurel said as if it were obvious. "It's what gives players and fans a feeling of..." she said before I interrupted her.

"Indomitability?" I asked.

"You know indomitable, but you've never heard of pep?" Laurel said.

"I didn't see any pep at Deacon Jones' game," I said.

"That's because the Rams didn't have the Embraceable Ewes back then," she explained.

In cheerleading terms, we live in interesting times. Laurel fell head over heels in love with a guy called Alex. Electricity reverberated off them in waves so intense I'm surprised telephone lines didn't melt during conversations to secure dates. I accidentally accompanied them on one such assignation after my riding lesson was canceled at the last minute, making it impossible to deposit me at the stable while Laurel met Alex for lunch.

I'd heard the phrase third wheel and, as we sat down, immediately understood why no one wanted to play this part. Normally talkative, I went mute and looked anywhere other than across the table, which was Alex's territory. It was a relief when the waitress came to take our order.

"Cheeseburgers and fries all around," the waitress said. "Two chocolate shakes and one vanilla phosphate heavy on the fizz. Do you want onions?"

"No, thank you," Alex said, laughing.

Laurel was laughing, too. They were in on a joke that I wasn't. Later, during Laurel's deposition, I raised the subject of onions and asked what was so funny about a vegetable.

"Kissing is why we laughed," Laurel said. "Would you want to kiss someone with bad breath? Dates and onions don't mix."

Good intel was coming in fast, and Laurel's lessons were so valuable I was tempted to buy a notebook in which to write it all down. Coming close to the Alex/Laurel perimeter a second time, I made myself scarce when he assembled a swing set at our house. This isn't to suggest that light surveillance wasn't in operation; it was. I'd also been present during Laurel's preparation phase, remaining patient while she tried on more clothes than I had in a lifetime. Her retail flight of fancy created confidence well worth the effort, so who could begrudge her?

I suggested that Laurel model the new outfits for my father to obtain an opinion in advance of Alex's arrival. Anticipating approval, I provided a resounding round of applause when she executed a flawless stride down an imaginary catwalk before completing a perfect turn and hold of the pose.

George, however, wasn't smiling and said, "Do you really want to know what I think?"

At this point I wasn't so sure that we did, but Laurel looked crestfallen and asked, "Does this midiskirt make me look fat?"

My father shook his head and said, "You must weigh the equivalent of three elegant feathers put together, so put the notion of fat right out of your head. My concern is that when Omar Sharif arrives, he's not going to want his Julie Christie dressed as if she walked out of the Middle Ages. Did you buy anything modern? If so, let's look at that."

While Laurel went upstairs to change, George put *Lara's Theme* from *Doctor Zhivago* on the turntable, which was his way of apologizing for having made such an offhand observation.

When she returned wearing a new pair of jeans and a crisp white tee shirt, he smiled and said, "Now you look sensational."

Alex arrived ten minutes early, practically giving Laurel and I cardiac arrest, but he set to work, and the swings were put together much faster than I'd imagined possible. Excited to try this new garden toy, I loitered by the back door, ready to be summoned at any moment, but the moment lingered on, and I wondered what could be keeping them.

Running upstairs to obtain an unrestricted view of the garden, I watched Alex gently push Laurel on the swing, and each time she swung toward him, he kissed her on the back of the neck. Puffing up the pillows and pulling down the blind, I picked up a book.

With Laurel around I barely noticed that Lucy Stanford was off limits, as were several friends who became casualties of my father's divorce. A toxin spread across our social life more comprehensively than an oil spill. Only intact families were considered acceptable, even if desperately unhappy. I was reluctant to believe we'd been ostracized and suggested we drop by to see if the Stanford's really meant to dismiss us. They did, and we didn't make it past the kitchen door. No coffee for my father, no cornflakes for me, and no more Lucy either.

George joined Laurel and I for lunch by the club pool, where the scent of burgers wafted enticingly in our direction. It's said that we eat first with the eyes, savoring aesthetic flavors, but at the club, our olfactory dined in advance of the stomach. An announcement on the tannoy drew our attention to a diving competition at the lower board level, and Lucy's name was broadcast as next up. I jumped up, ready to race over, but George whirled around fast.

"Don't you dare move," George said. "Stay seated and say nothing. I know Lucy was a friend, but now I hope she drowns."

Laurel sat quietly while the significance of what was said sunk in and asked, "Who's hungry? Are those Dolores burgers over there? Don't suppose Suzy Q fries are on offer?"

The club filled the gap of our social erosion, and we attended several events, including a performance by Up with People. While this ultra-conservative group staged a star-spangled show inside, parking attendants outside wrenched radio dials from *Up, Up and Away* to *War*. Members preferred Grace Kelly to Grace Slick and would listen to *True Love* any day, but *Somebody to Love* never.

The Halterns followed the Stanfords and kicked us to the curb, calling my crush on Gareth Jr. to an abrupt halt, but the Lien family remained loyal, as did the Brebner's. Aron and George drank scotch while listening to Johnny Cash at a decibel level preferred by concert promoters, and *A Boy Named Sue* played constantly. It would be years before I'd hear the same song played repeatedly, but that would be for medicinal purposes rather than reasons of recreation. The curative effects of continuous loop belong to phase four of a bad breakup, but when confronted with a romance gone wrong, there are only two tracks worth playing: *I Will Survive* and *No More Tears (Enough Is Enough)*. If Gloria Gaynor, Donna Summer, and Barbra Streisand can't help, no one can.

When we weren't entertaining, George enjoyed lounging around the house in his boxer shorts, but Laurel's presence put a damper on that, requiring my father to suppress his Oscar Madison-type tendencies. Deep down, he must've resented this unintended consequence of childcare because even on the surface, he was irritated. Whenever Laurel and I went out, George spent precious time in the company of his briefs. As she prepared for a date with Adam, I asked what they'd talk about over dinner.

"I imagine we'll discuss the selection of our song. Every time it plays, we'll think of each other," Laurel explained.

"Want some help?" I offered.

"Sure, why not," Laurel said. "Jot down the tracks you like, and I'll check your list later."

I could hardly wait for her to leave so that I could get started. Music flowed from every corner of my life in cars, at the stable and by the pool, but a singular song selection is serious business. Anyone in the music industry knows it's not quite as straightforward as you'd imagine, and to find the right track, I flipped through our stack of 45s purchased at Sam Goody.

Happy Together and *(Your Love Keeps Lifting Me) Higher and Higher* topped the list, followed by *You're All I Need to Get By*. *Go All the Way* and *Bang a Gong (Get It On)* were reminders of what they wanted to do but wouldn't, and *If I Were Your Woman* was redundant since Laurel already was Adam's. *Treat Her Like a Lady* was too instructive, so *No Matter What* might be a better choice. *You Made Me So Very Happy* was terrific but the name Blood, Sweat & Tears was unattractive. *Can't Take My Eyes Off You* and *I Love You More Today Than Yesterday* ended the list.

Later that night, Laurel floated in as if walking on air. She had the same expression worn by Elizabeth Taylor after meeting Rock Hudson in the film *Giant*.

Laurel looked at the short list of songs and said, "Good first attempt, but we'll need to keep thinking."

No summer could be called complete without a ride on the Dragon Coaster, which was the most exhilarating feature at Playland. When not astride a horse, I was content to captain a car on this magnificent carriage. Capturing that one minute forty-three seconds of fun wasn't to be missed. Laurel preferred a romantic date for dinner and a movie with Alex, so my forced friend Trudy Lein joined us instead.

I tried to conceal my dislike for Trudy, who shared this sentiment, but we took care of matters quietly in our own way. She wanted to remain with her mother, who'd been a teacher for three reasons: June, July, and August, but after acquiring the letters Mrs. on her wedding day, Mrs. Lien retired. Her husband spent weekdays at their Manhattan apartment before joining the family in the Hamptons for weekends. He and George alternated as chaperones, pressing Trudy and I together. This allowed our dads a break, but for Miss Lien and me, it was battle as acrimony was in the air from the moment we arrived.

The arcade by the front entrance attracted my father's attention, and we started with a water pistol game. First to fill a balloon on top of a ceramic clown's head won, and my father's fascination with firearms served him well. George achieved several tickets in no time, mirroring the period needed to redeem them. Securing a teddy bear, or a more substantial item, required a ludicrous quantity, and we struggled to identify a worthwhile item.

"Hurry up," George said. "The Dragon Coaster awaits."

We knew that, but we also knew only one toy would be forthcoming, and the nettled issue of ownership had yet to be determined. This slowed the decision-making process and alchemized excitement into anxiety. Welcome to the funhouse.

"What about that puppet?" George asked. "The clown head might make a nice memento. Okay, if we take that?"

"Oh, goodie," Trudy squealed, grabbing the puppet out of the vendor's hand.

Once tucked inside her jacket pocket, she said, "My little clown is adorable."

If possession is nine-tenths of the law, how much more comprehensive with Trudy? I'd have to use reasoning and every principle of equity to get it back. We headed for the rollercoaster but were distracted by a few rides on the way.

"Girls, isn't this great?" George asked. "Let's start with The Laff in the Dark. I see two places available in the next car, and you can be seat companions."

"Seat companions?" Trudy asked excitedly.

"I'd rather ride with the Grim Reaper," she added in a register too low for George to hear.

Snippy comments wouldn't deflect me from my aim, and when we boarded the ride, I brought the conversation back around to restitution.

To touch her heart, I tried a line of succession theory by saying, "If your dad filled the balloon, it would belong to you, but it was won by my father."

Pretending to be frightened by the threadbare monsters moving toward us, Trudy ignored me, but it was an act. The goblins shuddering in our direction weren't remotely scary. A Wild West ride followed, and we boarded a stagecoach while waving at George. The mechanical screeching of our coach competed with the sound of a shoot-out at the Okay Corral as cowboys discharged weapons out of sync with the sound of their guns, but the tinny noise was easy to talk above.

"Try to understand, Trudy," I said. "I don't live with my father as you do yours, so it's important I take the puppet to California."

Trudy took the puppet from her pocket, kissed it on the head and stashed it back inside her jacket. Even though we were on the shore, it was a balmy night, with thick air blasting in waves of humidity.

"Want to take off your jacket?" I asked Trudy. "It's so hot waiting in line, and I want you to be comfortable."

George extended his arm to receive the garment, but Trudy gave me a sideways glance and said, "No thanks, it might be windy when the ride starts."

George was impressed with my considerate behavior, and Trudy's sensible thinking. He hadn't understood that relinquishing her jacket might place the puppet at risk, and she wasn't about to provide an opportunity for me to pilfer it from her pocket.

"How about a photo?" George asked.

Trudy and I leaned in together. We smiled and posed before resuming our enmity.

"Mr. Buchanan, will you take a picture of us showing our snacks?" Trudy suggested.

Sounds innocuous, but this wasn't the syrupy gratitude of a simpering girl, and my father failed to register the significance of her request. Unencumbered by sinister thoughts, he didn't recognize her intent to reference treats forbidden to me by a team of orthodontists.

The list detailing banned consumables was so comprehensive that Meyera said, "What's left, snacks made of shag carpeting?"

Cuddling up, we giggled for the camera as would a couple of children's catalog cuties, and I suggested Trudy pose with a peace sign, but the camera's shutter moved too fast, taking the moment with it. She beheld the bounty of junk food in her lap with a sanctimonious smile, looking adoringly at her toffee apple, popcorn, and Coca-Cola.

Sneering at Abbott's custard and Martinelli's sparkling apple juice in my hand, Trudy said, "Shame you can't eat my treats."

"Shame you want to," I said. "When my braces are off, I'll have straight teeth, but what are you planning to do about yours?"

"I wear everything naturally, and my teeth have character," Trudy stated.

"Crooked does match the rest of you," I noted.

Auto World made me nervous. Being in control of the car was a responsibility I took seriously. Left to ignorance, I'd have focused on the track, allowing Trudy to enjoy a respite from my arguments launched in favor of puppet repatriation, but, having sensed I took this ride to be real, she couldn't resist a bit of bubble bursting. Trudy didn't know that I surreptitiously checked the water beneath us for signs of mermaids, and on the East Coast, I imagined these finely finned creatures summoned ships as land dwellers did taxis with the sound of a sharp whistle.

"You don't really believe you're driving this thing?" Trudy asked. "You're aware it's remotely controlled, right?"

I wasn't, having assumed the Leave the Driving to Us slogan was confined to Greyhound bus lines but, unwilling to let Trudy have that satisfaction, I lied and said, "Yeah, I know, but a quiet ride gives us a chance to talk about the puppet. Winning that prize is the only thing I've seen my dad do with a result you can see, and it's important I have it. Next time, your dad can get one for you, but the clown buried in your jacket belongs to me."

Trudy wrinkled her button nose, and seemed to consider my line of reasoning while flipping her Dippity-Do blonde ponytail.

"Who knows when I'll have a chance to come back?" she said. "The more I think about it, the more certain I am that the puppet should stay with me."

George was waiting to take us to the rollercoaster and said, "Are you girls having a marvelous time? Why not let loose with a few more smiles?"

My father had no comprehension of what was actually going on, and couldn't appreciate the complexities characterizing negotiations conducted between two eleven-year-old girls. Rather than *Babes in Toyland*, we were bitches at Playland, and Trudy's arm trespassed my side of the rollercoaster car as it climbed 85 feet in the air. Although physically crammed together, mentally we occupied opposing council tables.

Adrenaline-laced anticipation rippled through our fellow passengers. Some were cheering while others looked frightened, but only the brave raised their arms above their heads as we inched to the top. None of them could know that real fear was sitting right next to me. Trudy was fearfully unmoved by persuasion. Perhaps passion would succeed where fairness failed, and to take advantage of the fact no one could hear us, I'd have to act fast, as only a few minutes separated us from the Dragon Coasters' summit. Once we hit the top, our descent would be deeper than the climb, and I'd need to state my case before we fell 128 feet down.

"Trudy, I want that puppet," I said. "Hand it over. If you insist on stealing it from me, then you can go to hell."

Trudy said nothing, and neither did I, but to be fair, the next one minute forty-three seconds were rather distracting.

The aftereffects were potent as well, and we didn't speak until inside the Hall of Mirrors, where Trudy said, "If you win the arcade game, I'll return the puppet."

Catching sight of our reflections, I noticed that mine was upside down while Trudy's was twisted into a grotesque contortion. The way these mirrors projected the subjective really was magic. Returning to the arcade, I lined up, waiting for the water gun to go off, but aiming into the clown's mouth required a proficiency lacking in my skill set. Looking for a friendlier game, I spotted Skee-Ball, which was a shining symbol of the Santa Monica Pier and countless afternoons with Meme.

Her endless supply of dimes distracted us from Meyera's alcoholic absence, and over the years, I played so much Skee-Ball it could've passed for training.

"Water pistols be damned," I said to Trudy. "Let me show you how it's done in Santa Monica."

In a short period of time, I bagged more tickets than anyone expected, including George, who asked, "When did you get so good at Skee-Ball?"

I could hardly answer, "I owe it all to Seagram's Canadian whisky and the Santa Monica Pier."

Something less controversial was needed to explain my proficiency, so I shrugged my shoulders and said, "Meme calls it natural aptitude."

Ready to receive the puppet, I looked at Trudy, who said, "Are you expecting something? Did you really think I was going to give it back? The deal was to win the water balloon game, so who cares if you can play something else?"

The fistful of tickets in my hand was rendered meaningless. I wanted the puppet procured by George, and there wasn't a reasonable facsimile where this was concerned. Heading for the exit, I was furious but noticed a sad little boy standing at the prize counter who'd obviously added up the fact that his small stack of tickets didn't add up too much.

"Put these with yours," I said, handing my tickets to the little boy. "You'll get a better prize."

George noticed the handover and said, "Such generous and polite girls. I'm proud of your behavior tonight. I know it's hard to leave Playland, but you'll be back next year right here together."

George called Meyera to confirm the details for my return flight and handed me the phone.

"Have you told your father about the new pony?" Mom asked.

I hadn't and was waiting for the right time to break it to him. In the meantime, Meyera and our cousin Sandy collected April from Valley Farms stable in Pacific Palisades, where the owner's daughter Erika looked after my pony for the three months I was gone. Valley Farms wasn't easy to reach, requiring a hair-raising drive along a dirt road on the edge of a steep cliff. Add a two-horse trailer, three oncoming cars and countless potholes to get the gist of what was braved on moving day.

Sandy's recent return from Ethiopia was well-timed, and she went from Peace Corps to apple core, riding shotgun the whole way. Apparently, the roads in Liberia are better for trailering horses, and while listening to Meyera describe the journey, I watched George and Laurel discuss where to go for her last New York dinner.

While they debated Lutece or Delmonico's restaurant, Mom asked, "How's the weather?"

"Mostly calm with patches of panic, insecurity and temper," I said.

Laurel and I discussed what I'd say to George about April. Her presence would boost my confidence, but I'd have to raise the topic soon. Only a few days remained before she flew home, leaving me with George for the last week of summer. There were one or two abortive attempts to raise the subject, but the words failed to flow. Finally, I approached the bench on the night before my departure. Actually, it was an Eames lounge chair and ottoman.

I advanced to where my father was sitting in his boxers, drinking Jameson Black Barrell and smoking Marlboro Red. George was watching television and the thinking man's gameshow *Jeopardy!* blared in the background. Alex Trebek had yet to hit television screens, and it was against Art Fleming's questions that I dared pose my own.

"Daddy, as your starter for ten, tell me what scores of girls desperately want to call their very own?" I asked. "Studio audience, please remain silent while our contestant considers the question," I added in a hushed tone.

George was irritated by my attempt at humor and looked up with a scowl. Television was important to my parents, and they resented interruption when using it as a shield against actual interaction. Why risk the rigors of intelligent exchange when one-way simulated communication is on tap?

Programming relieved them from conversation by substituting an offensive range of bells, clangs, and gongs instead. Their attachment to sound as a weapon bordered on desperation, and they grasped the re-mote as if it were a life preserver. Most people tune in to view, but George and Meyera watched as a way of tuning out. Mainlining television as a form of electronic anesthesia made it difficult to rouse them, but George answered my ill-conceived game show question with one of his own.

"Are you trying to tell me about the flea-bitten nag you bought?" he asked. "If so, don't come running to me when you want a decent horse."

Laurel called after I got back to LA and said, "Did you tell Daddy about your high-level pet?"

"Yes, but he didn't exactly share my joy," I said. "It's more a case of him being informed and now officially appraised of April."

"Too bad," Laurel said. "I tried to pave the way by giving him a heads-up, as you call it, but we knew it was going to be a tough sale. At least it's done, and you can relax until next summer, which is going to be great. I'm here if you need me, and I'm here if you don't."

"Go Normans!" I said.

PART 3

TERRA (not) *FIRMA*

CHAPTER 17

Bonner School celebrated cultural events, including the annual food drive to aid Native American Indians. On this designated day, students arrived with edible donations, and most of the mothers went to tremendous lengths, ensuring their children were laden down with something special.

It became competitive. The items were wrapped in enough ribbon and designer paper to qualify for a Hollywood set. Tables were placed in the playground, and we'd be called individually to present our charitable gifts. Colorful flyers sent to each home provided ample notice and encouragement to give generously.

Meyera's intention was to do precisely that, but each year, she'd lose track until the morning in question and spin around the kitchen in a blind panic, frantically searching for something I could bring. If charity begins at home, sometimes it stays there. Mom didn't want to part with her treasured tins of pate *de foie gras* or smoked oysters any more than I wanted the embarrassment of presenting them.

Meme grabbed a box of chocolate truffles, claiming they were likely to be appreciated and, best of all, they were still in date, which was always a bonus at our place.

"At least it's not Limburger," Meme said, laughing. "Donating that noxious-smelling cheese would be embarrassing."

Cinco de Mayo was commemorated with a pageant, and in a small school, it was a big deal to see which sixth-grade senior would be voted May Queen. Sitting on a flower-decorated throne, presiding over songs, poetry, and a dance of the Maypole wasn't of personal interest until Meyera mentioned how much she'd like me to win. She wanted to choreograph evidence that all was well in California, and nabbing the title was important for this endeavor, but I'd need to play a long con launched well in advance of this goal.

Some class competitors woke up late for the challenge, scrambling to gain time and favor, but found neither available on an urgent basis. Others were strategic in crafting their campaigns and curried support with bags of candy. Playing hopscotch with lower-class students gave me an advantage, and keeping my shoe out would assist with the aim of making me a shoo-in for the vote.

Gail Garnet determined her daughter Sabrina would be queen, but this was unlikely. She had a slight speech impediment, and a bad case of dandruff. Simply stated, she lacked the popularity enjoyed by her attorney father, Jacob Garnet, who was of Mexican descent and fiercely loyal to his roots. He represented California fruit pickers during the 1965 grape strike, and consolidated the workforce while ensuring the terms he hammered out remained as firm as his resolve for even-handed dealing.

Jacob had the trust of union members and was known as a crusader for fair pay, better working conditions, and insurance benefits. John Steinbeck would've been proud of him, but had Jacob Garnet gotten to work earlier, *The Grapes of Wrath* might not have been written.

A hero at work doesn't necessarily make for a hero at home, but his charisma was effective in the field where he spent most of his time. He always kept the best values in mind but occasionally lost track of other bits, and news of his infidelity reached Gail. When it did, he was contrite and wanted to come home to his competitive wife and slightly stigmatized daughter, but Gail insisted upon divorce. Sour grapes were easy to swallow while she waited for the final dissolution of their marriage, and she continued to wait for settlement sums to hit her new separate account before allowing him to return.

They continued living as they'd done previously, with the exception of monthly spousal and child support payments, which formed a new addition to his financial obligations, but he was over a barrel. His wife (now technically ex-wife) had the upper hand and wasn't going to let it go to waste. Gail was a hardline negotiator and as tough as any he'd encountered, if not more demanding.

Gail was aware of Sabrina's social isolation, and she resented the other mothers flaunting their perfectly presented girls. That crown would rest on Sabrina's head by any means necessary in a spirit that was as close to Huey Newton as Gail Garnet would ever get. If donations were needed to secure this prize, so be it.

Mr. Garnet expressed concern but not about the money Gail wanted to give the school, which was fine. His issue was that these sums were earned on the basis of fair play, and to advance cash to buy the title compromised his ethics. He loved Sabrina and wanted her to win, but winning this way didn't seem right. Neither, however, did living alone, and he reluctantly wrote a check, which Gail delivered the next day, along with a veiled offer of further sums should Sabrina become May Queen.

Voting day approached, and a deluge of support hit the administrative office where Mrs. Bonner, Mrs. Jasper and Mr. McPhee acted with decorum in their respective roles as owner, principal, and head teacher. They responded diplomatically to enticements designed to favor this girl or that, and rather than exercise undue influence, they avoided the appearance of impropriety by staying stoic. This enabled the school to accept an influx of gifts while demonstrating a commitment to impartiality, and most parents accepted the legislative process, except for women like Gail, who sought any loophole that might allow her girl to win.

Gail wasn't alone in her efforts, and aggressive campaigns were mounted on behalf of numerous daughters, during which a number of otherwise level-headed mothers seemed to lose it. Financially and emotionally invested to a degree well out of proportion with the event, they became fractious over flower arrangements and catering orders. Some snits were caused by the allocation of parking places, and when it came to designing the May Queen's dress, civilized relations had broken down completely. Mrs. Jasper was forced to pull rank, insisting she make the final selection. Meyera managed to miss the fireworks, but that's easy when you're at home in bed.

Overt compliments gave way to covert criticism, but everyone knew the cause of these clashes was that everyone wanted their daughter to win. Only one category was exempt from this wave of maternal devotion gone wrong, and that shady corner of peace fell naturally enough to those without girls. Those brave women who only bore boys tried to step in and offer support. They pledged practical, psychological, and gender-neutral help but were shunned.

Eligibility to join this ruthless challenge required a daughter, and without one, they were invisible. Unless you had a girl in this race, the shutters were lowered, and the drawbridge raised. Only XX chromosome contenders and May Queen mothers-in-waiting were allowed. It must've been entertaining for anyone unencumbered, especially those whose XY children were refreshingly male.

My father and Jacob Garnet were in regular contact as business associates who became friends. They struggled to make sense of a mutually agreed upon nonsensical world in which one was penalized by an impropriety for which he'd pay forever, and the other grappled to gain information. Gail's maniac maneuver to secure success for Sabrina was mentioned during a business conversation when Jacob asked how much George paid toward my bid.

My father knew nothing about the competition and wouldn't have unless I won. Meyera might've been desperate to bump up the dossier on our irrefutably fantastic life, but she wasn't about to add unwelcome pressure. Although victory wasn't mandatory, the only f-word never allowed in our house was failure.

I overheard Meyera tell our neighbor Lois that victory would assuage her concerns about what George might do next, and while this upped the ante for wanting me to win, she ascribed it to paranoia.

Lois disagreed and said, "Just yesterday, I talked about paranoia with no less than the Head of Psychiatry at the hospital. He called Billing to ask if a patient's insurance provided adequate coverage, and I thought, what are you nuts? Here's another *mashugana putz* who thinks insurance companies will dictate the choice of physician, treatment, and hospital. Can you imagine anything more ridiculous? I told him to stop being paranoid, but he says paranoia is an unjustified fear of persecution. Well-founded concerns constitute an astute assessment, and George is so unpredictable that you've good reason to be worried. This definition is direct from the horse's mouth at Cedars Sinai, so don't think he doesn't know from crazy. He's tasked with making sense of this *farkakte* world."

Meyera considered George crazy, especially when he called after talking with Jacob Garnet. It was late, so Meyera picked up, and I heard only one side of the conversation.

"Hello George, how can I help you this evening?' Meyera said. "Yes, I'd heard something about Jacob and Gail making a donation to Bonner. Of course, I know what May Queen is. This event has been running since the school started, and, no we don't need any money to prepare. I'd like to point out it's a school-sponsored contest and not a commodity you can buy. Money to pay for what? George, you're not listening. May Queen isn't a beauty pageant; that would be cruel to unattractive girls, but I told you it's a popularity vote. How much did you say the Garnets donated? $75,000.00, are you sure? I had a quick cup of coffee with Gail the other day, and she told me they had pledged $25,000.00. I wonder, George, where do you think the rest went?"

Meme came into my room, where we maintained radio silence while my parents continued their discussion.

"No donation in the world would be sufficient for Sabrina," Meyera said. "Expecting so much from that poor creature is callous. I'm sorry to say, but as much as you like Jacob Garnet, his daughter isn't May Queen material."

Meme looked at me and whispered, "How's the competition going?" Her suggestion that I memorize the names of my constituent's pets was a great advantage, but as I was about to confirm this, Meme abruptly leaned forward to listen more attentively and said, "I don't like the sound of this. Gail may be trying to rig the result. She'd beg, bribe, or buy the title if possible. That, or she's found another way to extort even more money from her husband."

"George, why persist in asking questions I've already answered?" Meyera said. "The plain truth is that to become May Queen, you don't write a check. You're missing the point entirely and need to understand this is a culturally wrapped contest. Have I answered all your questions? If so, I've got to go and put dinner on."

Meme waited until the call ended before asking, "Do you need any help from me?"

"Yeah, I do," I said. "If I'm absent, some other girl will steal this. Younger kids grateful for my attention have short memories, and I don't dare miss a day."

"Six to go, and then the vote," Meme said.

Meyera was knocked off her precarious perch by my father's call, remaining under the covers for days.

During her dreadful bout of inebriation, I was dutifully sent off to school each morning by Meme, who said, "Don't worry, I'm here, and everything's going to be fine. You go to class and focus on your studies. With all these parents caught up in May Queen mania, it's about time someone reminded you to think about learning."

My grandmother had an instinct for when to anticipate a spike, particularly social. She knew the lengths to which some women would go to pervert the course of fairness. Sabotage for your daughter in some circles amounts to no sabotage at all.

Meme contacted head teacher Harold McPhee, who wasn't long out of Ireland but adored sharing his sensibilities in Santa Monica. Venturing from Tuam to County Galway, he forgot the N17 in favor of the 405 freeway and was an optimist whom everyone adored. Hoping that he and Meyera might hit it off, I invited him to dinner, and they got along in an utterly appropriate arm's-length way.

Mr. McPhee might've been better than the Blarney Stone, but that didn't mean Meyera would kiss him. Instead, she explained the difficulty with George, describing the legal, emotional, and long-distance arguments. George could go jump, as far as she was concerned, but my becoming May Queen would be a bounty in the retaining custody box.

Although hopeful I'd bag the prize, Meyera was interested in triumph for additional reasons. At school events, she sat alone in those uncomfortable white folding chairs during parents' nights and graduation ceremonies. Her single status felt excruciatingly solo, while others sat smugly as Mr. and Mrs. socially sanctified. Even chronically on/off again couples managed to pull it together a few times a year, and enjoyed a respite from the spiteful rest simply by being part of a two-man team. Despite Meme being by her side, Meyera felt isolated.

"I honestly think the only exercise my ex-husband gets is ducking responsibility, sidestepping obligations and shirking accountability," Meyera explained.

"If he does it fast enough, perhaps we've got a new dance craze?" Mr. McPhee said.

Meme enjoyed meeting my head teacher and was pleased to have direct contact at Bonner, should it be needed. As the May Queen mercury rose toward the top a year later, she felt it necessary to place a call and left a message for Harold McPhee to call Mrs. Elsie Zeiler. A name with little if any association to Buchanan, which was nice and neat. The lady always said it was handy to know how to attract attention and even more useful to recognize when to avoid it. My grandmother wasn't looking to muddy the waters but wanted to ensure equity, and after three o'clock, her phone rang.

"Harold McPhee here," he said. "I'm returning a call received earlier today from a Mrs. Zeiler."

"Hello, Mr. McPhee, it's Elsie," Meme said. "Thank you for your prompt reply. I've got a favor to ask about this May Queen contest, and I'd like to enlist your assistance if it's not inconvenient."

"Mrs. Zeiler, we've not had the pleasure of meeting, but I can assure you every precaution is taken to ensure the highest standard of...," he said before being cut short.

"But Mr. McPhee, we have met," Meme said, interrupting. "Over dinner with my granddaughter and her mother Meyera."

Mr. McPhee stumbled out an apology. He'd had a long day, and the weight of this contest pressed him to the very edge.

"Of course, I remember you," Mr. McPhee said. "The different name threw me, and if I'm not mistaken, aren't you referred to as Meme?"

"Anything other than grandmother will do," Meme said. "I'm interested in the role but not that title. It's this May Queen competition that's led me to contact you."

"Mrs. Zeiler, Elsie or Meme, whatever the name," Mr. McPhee said. "You're the last person from whom I'd have expected to receive a call of this nature."

"I don't see why this is such a surprise?' Meme said. "I'm every bit as concerned about the integrity of this process as you are."

A pause ensued, during which Mr. McPhee realized that Meme wasn't trying to corrupt the voting, and she recognized that he thought she was.

He was the first to respond and said, "Please forgive me. The stress of so many parents making so many offers is clearly taking a toll. How may I help?"

Meme explained that she'd come to know a sizeable check had been donated to Bonner under the guise of a gift, when bribe might be more accurate. How she came to know this was of little consequence and much less important than the local paper article about the school's dire financial situation referencing $75,000.00 needed to sustain it.

Bonner's tenuous grip on the grounds was about to be prized loose by property developers eager to annex the property, and she didn't want that to compromise the voting. Difficult times demand drastic measures, but why wait to cure a situation that can be made safe from the get-go? Meme asked Mr. McPhee to make a fair and square tally before delivering the votes to potentially impressionable board members. Rather than suggest unfairness, she simply underscored the need to maintain vigilance, and he agreed.

Voting day arrived, and a surge of Roman gladiatorial excitement swept through the school. Even the boys seemed edgy, and more than the normal number of bees were incarcerated in empty one-pint milk cartons. With presidential campaigns, the voting public can only take so much before everyone welcomes an end, and that's how I felt about wanting it to be over. No concentration that morning, and none needed.

Our teachers were also distracted. Until the afternoon announcement, everything was off-kilter. The bell to assembly rang, and I was placed in a line of girls sitting on a raised dais, allowing the assembly to watch the exact moment of victory for one and crushing disappointment for the rest. *National Geographic* was available at my more intelligent friends' homes, and flipping through the pages of exotic rites, I couldn't comprehend such ceremony from the cultural distance of LA. Today, however, I felt the same about this competition, which caused me to be on the other side of the lens. It was a hot afternoon, with little to no breeze, and unlike the number of words Eskimos have for snow, we're limited when it comes to describing California weather. It rarely varies from 72 degrees and sunny.

The school was beautifully landscaped and reflected this constant climate, with yellow daisies outside adorned by yellow dress uniforms inside, making it a bright place, except on this day, when twelve girls sat in a line, trembling with anxiety-ridden anticipation.

On my left, two girls theatrically grasped hands, three bowed their heads in silence, and four sat coven-like, looking upwards. The pink brigade was in full bloom to my right as two Barbies came to life, braiding each other's hair while theatrically biting their nails. Mr. McPhee resembled a leprechaun with one eyebrow raised while Mrs. Bonner dithered on about the sanctity of our community, which is when I tuned out.

Remembering Timothy Leary's suggestion that we tune in, I directed the needle of attention to the right frequency, allowing me to hear her announce the winner. It was me, and Mr. McPhee leaped up in a basketball player fashion, mimicking the shoot of a winning hoop. He led a chorus of applause, in stark contrast to the tears of disappointment on either side of me. Ruth Mandal was a combative classmate at the best of times, and after the announcement, she was unhinged.

"How can this be possible?" Ruth screamed. "Look at her," she screeched, pointing at me. "My mother says she's a disgrace to grooming. Her hair parting is lightning bolt style, and she always has one knee-sock around her ankle. This can't be right. My father promised I'd win and somebody needs to call him. Get my daddy on the phone. Isn't anyone listening? I said now!"

Ruth's father was a litigator specializing in personal injury claims. He was an angry ambulance chaser of a man who pursued a level of success alongside his pinched and pouty wife that no sum of damages would adequately achieve. Mr. Mandal was always the last to arrive at parent's night, owing to the fact he dashed all over town to meet and intimidate defense representatives. He was proud of the fact that every case crossing his desk guaranteed a high fee. He screwed either an insurance company or a third party without the good sense to retain his services.

It wasn't Ruth's fault that her father was an ass. It was her mother's, who aimed to go head-to-head with the other attorney wives by complimenting her husband's legal prowess but missed the mark when saying, "Such a shame your husbands work late drafting documents. My husband's practice is going so well, the only time he touches a piece of paper is when it's wrapped around something edible."

Hardly an accolade for those acquainted with more erudite practice, but the Mandal's idea of hosting a get-together was to institute class action proceedings. They weren't like other flashy parents, who took pride in hosting even flashier evenings to benefit the school. Ruth loathed me, and the feeling was more than mutual in that my regard for her was an exact match and, more so because I felt the same way about her parents.

Despite my dislike for Ruth, her mother was right in describing me as a disheveled, tangled mess. They didn't know about the chaotic start to my day. Meyera and I were impervious to the sound of an alarm, which we interpreted as inviting continued slumber. The steady seven tones suggested comforting things such as, 'Don't feel you need to wake up. The world will spin while you sleep. Stay here nice and comfortable. Everything can and will wait. You deserve a good long rest.'

These seven blissful beats were followed by the inevitable shatter of sleep and a swift kick up to consciousness. The father of the most popular boy in school was a decorated naval pilot who served his country in Korea and Vietnam. No matter what war he was fighting, his day started fast asleep on board the aircraft carrier, ready for the alarm.

When it rang, he was dressed and catapulted into the wild blue yonder in under three minutes. Considering how much more lead time we had, he saw no reason why any of us should be late. Placing my uniform out the night before, ready to put on jumpsuit style, did little to improve my timely performance. Meyera usually threw a coat over her night-gown before dashing to the car, where white fluffy slippers controlled the accelerator and brake. It was in this *ensemble* that Meyera often expressed concern about low-level fuel.

"Do you think I'll make it home?" she asked, pointing to the gas gauge. "Or have all the gods forsaken me?"

"Not quite all," I said, indicating the reserve tank, "And not quite yet."

It was raining when Meme drove me to school, and when we passed a drenched herd of sopping wet souls jogging along San Vincente, she laughed and said, "What do you suppose it is they're running from?"

Meme claimed to enjoy the sound of reading at night. Turning pages while turning my back on television was her idea of progress. My grandmother was a proponent of finishing the chapter first, no matter how late, but she wasn't in our apartment for the flip side between eight and nine a.m. This specific hour, out of the twenty-four, terrorized us.

You'd think the repeated stress would've prompted us to rise earlier, but think again. Our school run was a domestic version of the Indianapolis 500 speed challenge, complete with a Le Mans-style start. We ran to our car, fired it up and joined the race, but that didn't leave much primp time before school. Mrs. Mandal was correct in her assessment that I didn't care about my hair. I was too busy trying to skulk into my seat without attracting attention.

Tardiness impacted the way in which I learned things, including the Pledge of Allegiance. We began each day by standing to attention and reciting words I recognized in terms of timekeeping. The last line, 'Indivisible with Liberty and Justice for all,' meant I was inextricably late, while the preceding phrase, 'One Nation Under God,' indicated I was severely behind schedule. 'And to the Republic for which it stands' was a close call but nothing to worry about, while 'To the flag of the United States of America' represented a relief. 'I Pledge Allegiance' marked the start of a new day and a rare fact I made it in time, so God Bless America indeed.

"God bless this mess," Meyera said, whenever we returned home.

Our apartment made Tornado Alley look like Kew Gardens, but thankfully, we had a maid called Willie who regrettably cleaned on an infrequent basis. Humming, 'Bom, Pom, Bom' to let us know when she arrived, I'd rush to greet her and was delirious at the prospect of a clean home.

To tidy my room, she rarely needed more than five minutes, and Willie mentioned that most of her clients tried, without success, to get their kids to clean up after themselves. They didn't know the trick of compelling a child to clean is enforced mess elsewhere. Everything was going to be straightened before a sleepover with two friends I'd invited to my home for the first time.

Leah was a petal of perfection whose family founded a cosmetics empire, and they were elegant, *bijoux* and bonsai. Everything, except their fabulous taste and fortune, was in miniature. Even as a child, I couldn't help but notice that the adults barely reached five feet, but what they lacked in height they more than made up for in attractiveness. A better advertisement for their corporate wares would be hard to find; even the dog was glossy.

A cavalier King Charles spaniel imported from England was first to greet guests, sporting a hand-painted look while given to posing. Leah's home was immaculate and had a Japanese garden with moss-covered rocks surrounding a waterfall. Buddha sculptures were partially concealed by cherry trees, chrysanthemums, and bamboo, bordering tiny pathways fit for a Lilliputian. Camellias, daffodils, and roses were landscaped next to a Koi pond with lotus flowers, creating a scene of serenity.

Rebecca's place was also fantastic and her father's study had a magnetic attraction. The fact it was off-limits made it that much more interesting, and I snuck in by myself to find it was lined with books, photos, and awards. He was a successful writer who spent a lot of time at his typewriter, knocking out scripts about Civil Rights, prostitution, and Jesus.

Meyera promised Willie would clean the apartment before my friends arrived. Thanks to Willie's curative touch, weeks' worth of grime would be gone, the carpet free of filth and surfaces clear. It was a tough job, alright, and I all but genuflected at the thought of her arrival. During recess, we counted down the hours leading up to the weekend, but while counting, something sinister transpired in the name of Peaches.

Willie was active in her local community and aimed to direct wayward girls toward an honest day's work. Our building had numerous tenants requiring cleaning, which was more than Willie could manage by herself, providing ample opportunity for Willie's wards to fill this regular role. Meme was skeptical but agreed to a trial run, allowing the needs of tenants rather than social conscience to control her decision.

My friends and I planned to go swimming first, followed by a taco dinner, film, and pillow fight to see us comfortably through the evening. We smiled at each other as Meyera opened the apartment door, allowing our fantastic Friday kick-off to begin. Rebecca was first to speak, and had her father been present, he'd have been proud, if a trifle surprised, that his twelve-year-old daughter could quote Elizabeth Taylor's opening line from *Who's Afraid of Virginia Woolf?*

"What a dump," Rebecca said.

Leah took a few steps back and recoiled at the prospect of entering. Clearly revolted, she mentioned that the murky Koi pond at her place looked more inviting than my home. I understood Leah's disgust and couldn't work out why Willie let me down. Peaches caused disappointment by stealing a five-dollar bill from the first apartment she cleaned, which made Meme furious and firm in dismissing her. My grandmother wouldn't allow access to other girls in need of gainful employment, but before pronouncing this sentence, an inquisition took place, absorbing the time allocated to clean our apartment.

Rebecca and Leah woke early the next morning to clean the apartment before preparing pancakes in an uncharacteristically clean pan. Meyera discovered this activity when making morning coffee and hit the roof.

Lambasting my pals, she said, "What possessed you to take control of my home, and who do you think you are, insulting my housekeeping? I don't have the luxury of domestic staff as your parents do."

I didn't see much of them after that. What was the point of going to their homes knowing they'd decline a return invitation to mine?

CHAPTER 18

Mrs. Bonner invited me into her office to call Meyera. She was certain my mother would want to be notified immediately about the May Queen result. I called home, but no answer. No surprise and I thanked Mrs. Bonner for the loan of the phone. She smiled in a molded expression redolent of a mannequin's mask while assuming my mother must be out.

Although out cold wouldn't be a likely guess, that was the status quo when I got home. It's satisfying to score a touchdown, even if the game means more to someone else. I ran this race for Meyera. Meme wasn't invested other than for amusement, which she confirmed delivered a full quotient. I left a note on Mom's bedside table, obliquely letting her know I'd won. In large letters, I wrote that our kingdom required a horse to reward the queen, and I added those three powerful words confirming that I loved her. Sometimes, she didn't believe me, and sometimes, I didn't believe it myself.

I went to Meme's apartment, where she was at her desk tapping numbers into an electric adding machine with rapid-fire motion. It was a different rat-a-tat-tat from the one my father laid claim to aboard that fighter ship, absent of a verifiable name. Meme was shrouded in a cloud of blue smoke, and the quality of light was as harsh as the smell emanating from the ashtray. She had one last column to complete and ushered me in with the same hand that indicated silence, replicating a gesture mastered by many a Japanese geisha.

As a bookkeeper, my grandmother was punctilious and saw the back of many an auditor over more decades than most had been alive.

When they advanced, she held her ledgers as a shield, and used numbers as a sword. Meme buried them in so much detail, and secondhand smoke, they virtually had to be carried out on a stretcher.

Meme was to the West Coast what Aunt Louise represented in the East. Both meted out how much, when, and for what. Rather than God, it was in them I placed my trust, and they, effectively, did the same thing, regarding religion as a fulcrum. One sold stocks and shares to the church, while the other had nuns maintain mountains of silver. Meme looked up from her desk and casually asked after my day. Although she refrained from addressing the elephant in the room, everything about her seemed to point upward, including her eyebrows, which surpassed those of our head teacher, Mr. McPhee.

"We did it," I said. "It's in the bag."

"How wonderful," Meme said, walking over to hug me.

The sleeve of her muumuu caught in a tangle of office equipment. Business *accouterments* temporarily placed in a corner nine years ago took root, creating an uneven topography of ancient typewriters that acquired a gravity all their own.

"Do you mind if I call Lois and invite her over?" Meme asked. "She's been in a state of worry all day. Thank goodness it's all decided, and the chickens with their heads cut off can go quiet. Won't that make a welcome change?"

Lois was knocking on Meme's door less than three minutes later, and I couldn't help but think what a prompt fighter pilot she'd have made. Lois couldn't stand the suspense, and her eyebrows rose even higher than Meme's or Mr. McPhee's while insisting on having an answer.

"Will someone tell me?" Lois asked. "Or is it you should want to kill me? Enough already with the waiting. *Bubbeleh,* please tell me what happened and who won?"

The smell of Oscar Meyer bacon woke me the next morning, and Meme was sitting at the kitchen table with a cup of coffee, obviously feeling relaxed. I could tell, without her having to speak, because she still wore her dressing gown. When in a casual mood, she'd traverse the pool area in her robe to reach our apartment, while other occasions involved a more formal muumuu, assuming such a thing existed. Meyera was out of bed and revved up. She practically *pirouetted* around the kitchen while preparing breakfast.

"My daughter won," Meyera said. "Seems the race is to the swift, and I've never been more pleased with any victory. This one really means something to me, and the others can sit back to watch my daughter receive precisely that which they wanted for theirs. Damn it, this feels good, and I feel good. George can kiss my sweet you know what. Is everyone ready for scrambled eggs and bacon?"

I looked at Meme, and one glance was all it took for her to catch my meaning.

"I don't know," Meme said in answer to a question we'd considered countless times.

Neither of us knew what to expect from this euphoria or how long it would last. Meyera was in rare form alright and almost too happy when the phone rang. I picked up and found my father on the line, who'd just finished talking with Jacob Garnet.

"I understand congratulations are in order," George said. "Well done, but I don't suppose you'd do your old man a favor? Try to be a little less ideal when compared with my client's kids?"

Meyera was going to milk this for all it was worth and pulled the receiver from my ear, saying, "Greetings, George, the absent father that you are. You must be proud of our girl, considering everyone else is, and today is about victory. Yes, I know the vote was yesterday. Honestly, George, there's no point in talking with you."

I took the phone from Meyera and said, "Daddy, you should probably know that Sabrina Garnet wants to compete against me at horse shows. No, her father doesn't know about this yet. She's still deciding which thoroughbred to get. Yes, I'm aiming to win; otherwise, what's the point? I understand that you won't be at *Cinco de Mayo*, but I appreciate the call."

Meyera commandeered affairs, as she was born to do, and expressed concern about adequate photographic cover. Worried that the school might skimp on this issue, she wanted to hire a separate individual dedicated to capturing the celebration and, more importantly, my place in it. Meme was sure to nix this idea.

Another example of profligate expenditure, needless squandering, and financial waste. I waited for her choice of words and was stunned when she concurred with Meyera. Correctly taken photographs would stand the test of time, and Meme thought this type of documentation might be useful in ways we'd yet to imagine. Apparently, we had some money set aside, and the arrangements were made.

The day of the pageant was surreal. Our poor photographer was sent high and low, always with the same aim, which was me, but Meyera was so ecstatic I didn't have the heart to stop her. Even when she breached basic propriety by mentioning to more than one parent the difficulty of discerning their child at such a great distance, offering photo opportunities with their kid sitting on the throne. She was feeling generous. The photographer was booked until five, but roped and tied would be more accurate.

While being made to heel, he was a credit to his profession and didn't mind being frog-marched around the campus, but drew the line at climbing up a tree saying, "Mrs. Buchanan, I'm a photographer, not a monkey."

Meyera went to tremendous lengths preparing for the occasion, starting with a massage and facial at Elizabeth Arden. Forsaking the Magic Mirror in Brentwood, she had her hair *coiffed* in Beverly Hills before presenting herself at I. Magnin for the heavy artillery. An Yves Saint Laurent dress, Oscar de la Renta heels, Halston daytime wrap and Gucci handbag, accented by Francois Pinton sunglasses (originally designed for Jackie O), were sourced in no time. When *in toto*, Meyera was a force of nature. She felt cool, she looked cool, and when she strutted into Bonner, heads turned as a waft of Chanel No.5 greeted everyone before she did.

Gail Gordon was a good sport who shrugged off the May Queen stuff, but we drifted from our best friend status of earlier times. I lost her to a bevy of bands, bras, and *Tiger Beat* magazines while she couldn't locate me among the tangle of lunge lines, bridles, and saddles.

We had no animosity and an abundance of history that made us preemptively sentimental for a time we were in the process of kissing goodbye.

"Meyera, it would be a shame to allow that crown wilt," Mrs. Gordon said. "I have a number of treatments that could preserve those flowers, and if you're interested, feel free to contact me."

"Well, what's the worst that can happen?" Meyera said. "Flowers wilt, but photos are forever. The local papers will, of course, cover this event, but do you think it might go national?"

Mr. and Mrs. Mandal were within earshot of this conversation, and it sparked one of their own.

Ruth's mother berated her husband by saying, "What's wrong with you? When you learned how to make money, didn't anyone teach you how to spend it? You made a promise, you failed to deliver, and you will bear the consequences."

Her insults increased in volume, and Mr. Mandal became a cowering dog of a man, diminishing from Great Dane to dachshund right before our eyes. When the event was officially over, Meme was the first to know, and she reached for her belongings in advance of everyone else.

This surprised Meyera, who didn't know about the signal, which was a covert communication designed to attract my grandmother's attention. It also constituted an act of pure plagiarism, and I'm not proud to admit this, but we pinched Carol Burnett's famous ear tug. Given our affection for this comedic icon, Meme characterized our gesture as a mark of respect rather than theft, and suggested our appropriation was akin to a tribute. Things were winding down, and Mr. McPhee asked to have a quiet word with Meme.

"Fair and square, sure needed a helping hand this year," Mr. McPhee said. "I've no idea how you came to alert me, but that first count was necessary."

While not surprised, Meme was interested to hear more. Apparently, Mrs. Bonner received a check from Mr. Mandal for the full $75,000.00 needed to keep the school afloat. Although it was donated to secure the crown for Ruth, we'll never know whether Mrs. Bonner was prepared to accept it. She hadn't bet on one of the grandmothers asking Mr. McPhee to make a first count, ensuring the vote was accurate.

Mrs. Bonner tried to return the check to Mr. Mandal, but his wife insisted the school retain $50,000.00 to penalize her husband for failing to procure the prize. His inability to give $75,000.00 away would be forever memorialized by a $50,000.00 donation. Gail Garnet's check for $25,000.00 was already in Bonner's bank, and when it was added to the $50,000.00 from Mr. Mandal, she achieved the $75,000.00 total.

Meme laughed while suggesting that the real victor was Gail Garnet. The local papers reported a donation confirming the school's $75,000.00 target, but there was no reference to those responsible.

"Jacob Garnet will assume it's entirely his donation," Meme said, "not knowing his wife parted with only a third for the school and kept the rest. Gail Garnet gains $50,000.00, and I imagine she feels good about giving $25,000.00 to Bonner. Mr. Mandal is down by $50,000.00 rather than $75,000.00, and Mrs. Bonner receives the requisite sum needed to sustain the school. I'd call this a fair and square result."

"A rare case of two wrongs making a right," Mr. McPhee observed.

"At least the contest remained uncompromised," Meme added.

"Until the madness begins again next year," Mr. McPhee concluded.

When the school was strapped for cash and fast funds needed, the Palmers could've released the pressure. Belinda was in my class, and her parents were striking. Her father broke ground repeatedly to build the Wilshire Corridor, while his wife was a traffic-stopping icy blonde beauty whose standard for personal maintenance was so stringent she probably looked fantastic when fast asleep.

When Nina Palmer walked into a room, she became everything of interest in it. Alfred Hitchcock would've adored her. She was a steely, blue-eyed, smoldering siren able to go head-to-head with Tippi Hedren, Grace Kelly, or Janet Leigh. None of Hitchcock's blondes had more mysterious sex appeal than Nina, including Kim Novak, Eva Marie Saint, or Ingrid Bergman.

They lived on Rockingham, right around the corner from Gail Gordon, and both homes were stately yet reflected different interior designs. Asia influenced the Gordon house, and the Palmers favored Chanel. Sophisticated aesthetics were rarely noticed at either mansion. Almost everyone used the side kitchen door. Structure and discipline permeated Belinda's house, where fresh flowers, delivered each week, always stood rigidly at attention in all the common rooms.

Belinda's mother was a devotee of clean-living and regarded exercise as superior to religion. Her 'keep-fit to keep him interested' motto might've been the first such slogan. She'd been a slave to daily workouts well before Jane Fonda turned aerobics into a multi-million-dollar industry. Nina was no doubt using a rudimentary version of the Thighmaster long before Suzanne Summers could spell it.

Nina had been married, widowed, and left fearfully alone to face the world with five children to care for. By her own admission, she was scared stiff until a friend, from what she'd later term her first life, fixed her up with then-eligible bachelor Sydney. No one was more amazed by this turn of good luck than Nina, who was delighted to marry a miracle man. She set to work to provide Sydney with two babies of his own, starting with Belinda and concluding after the birth of her younger brother.

Nina commissioned oil portraits of all seven children for exhibition along the grand stairway in display that brought *The Brady Bunch* to mind. Closer examination revealed a more complicated tribe. Nina's grandson is older than her youngest boy by separation of two years, which will forever make the uncle younger than his nephew.

Belinda had a learning disability and a slight speech impediment, neither of which could be cured, but the family remained stalwart in their resolve that she would lead as normal a life as possible. While heaps of money helped make this happen, cash alone can't deliver what they did to such a fantastically loving degree.

Belinda's parents directed all sorts of resources toward their daughter, and sustaining her in a regular environment soon ran as smoothly as silk. Parties at their place were fantastic. Her five elder siblings were on hand to hand us anything we'd need, including towels, at her frequent pool parties.

When Meyera arrived to collect me from such a *soiree*, she noticed a few raspberry-colored clouds in the water and asked if a child had injured themselves.

Nina scowled and said, "Not exactly. I irritated our pool man by insisting he vacuum the base twice in preparation for this event, never dreaming that he'd add a urine indicator dye."

"Is he retaliating?" Meyera asked.

"No, he's Vietnamese," Nina said.

Meyera became friends with Nina, and their place was one of the few Meyera felt comfortable visiting, except for the no-smoking rule, which Nina must've been the first to instigate. Had anyone else made this demand, Meyera would've regarded it as rude, but this social constraint was issued by the lady of the house, so she rolled her eyes and complied.

Nina and Meyera had a ritual greeting reminiscent of puffins, during which Nina would reach over to undo one of Mom's blouse buttons while shaking her head from side to side. Meyera would tut and redo the button, laughing hysterically.

"If you've got it, flaunt it," Nina said. "What's it going to be, Meyera? Will you deal with the world from desire or stay buttoned-up and disappointed instead?"

Belinda's learning difficulties introduced us to the concept of compassion, compelling us to be kind. In class, she replied to a question concerning genetics, defining genes as something we wear and, while others would've been ridiculed, we controlled our laughter. When her parents got to work raising funds for the school, it was no laughing matter either.

Nina withdrew from the May Queen mania and threw her considerable might into elevating Bonner's coffers. The process of enhancing reputation and attracting funds wasn't a million miles away from her activities for Sydney. Life with the Palmers was one round of high-level entertaining after another, and Nina organized a special day at the races to attract interest from potential investors. These stunts were choreographed with one aim in mind, and that was snaring venture capital.

Finance was an essential part of her husband's business and formed the actual foundation underlying his monolithic structures. The name PALMER was emblazed across a dozen skyscraper cranes along Wilshire Boulevard, but masses of money were required to keep it there. Nina's charm was as arresting as her beauty, and at each *soiree,* she'd propose the same toast, 'To Sydney, a man who excels at erections.'

Nina tried to cajole Meyera into joining us at the track and was determined to drag Mom back to the world, saying, "You'll only have one contender for every man's attention, and that's me. Just wait until we walk in together. I almost feel sorry for them."

"I'm not sure about going," Meyera said.

"Don't be ridiculous," Nina noted. "You won't find so many wealthy men in one spot anywhere else in town. I'm not throwing this much effort at paupers. A design critic is as low as I'd go."

"Let me think about it, and I'll get back to you," Meyera said.

"Meyera, I'd rather you get back to you," Nina concluded.

Willie Shoemaker was riding that day, and while I regarded him as a pint-sized portable hero, Meme disagreed. His fondness for being photographed with Jayne Mansfield was something she considered ridiculous and failed to make him a star, on or off, a horse.

Presenting me with two crisp ten-dollar bills, she said, "There's no point going to the races if you can't make it interesting."

Meme instructed me to look after Belinda by keeping a close eye on her all day and counting any change she might be given. Meyera was enthusiastic about the event but not enough to join us, and opted to read a Dick Francis book instead. Mom devoured the large literary legacy left by that tiny powerhouse of a rider, lapping up every word he published. Power was in evidence on and off the track that day. Nina's efforts to turn three private stands into one proved so successful it shamed the Turf Club.

Hiring a string quartet wasn't the best choice. The soothing sounds obscured the tannoy, making it difficult to hear race results, but she swiftly dismissed them after Sydney gave each musician a two-hundred-dollar tip. The local television sportscaster retained to act as an advisor to their guests, proved inspirational, but when Belinda and I presented our flutter, it was spent astonishingly quickly, leaving us with nothing to show. The sportscaster chalked this up to jockey error and made everyone laugh by suggesting our jockeys had to stop for directions.

Livery tailored track assistants ran significant sums of money from our area to the betting booths downstairs, and thanks to a generous flow of tips, they were the most consistent winners throughout the day. Nina confessed the event was a challenge to create. Placing their money with Sydney was so secure she had to think of something else to represent risk. Belinda and I tried to meet Willie The Shoe but were shooed away from the paddock area and hovered near the track exit, hoping he'd sign our programs.

I leaned over the balustrade and mimicked my father at a New York Yankees game by shouting, "Hey, jockey, jockey."

One program accidentally dropped on the turf likely to be trampled, and I identified that as Belinda's, unless a groom picked it up for signing, which meant it was mine. The moment those words escaped my lips, I understood Meme's message and wondered if she had an insight into the darker aspects of my character, prompting her warning. I was caught in the grandmother's trap. She sure knew how to set them.

Nina found us and said, "What are you girls up to?"

I snapped to attention, as would someone seriously suspect, and said, "Just admiring the horses."

"We want a jockey to write his name for us," Belinda added.

"If you want a famous man's autograph, ask for your father's," Nina said. "He's more important than all the flash flesh here. Let's go girls, this is another mission accomplished."

Nina was soon in the spotlight again, acting as hostess to Sydney's recent business associates. This time, the evening was choreographed as a normal formal night at home where everything was perfect. The only slight blight was a quarrel instigated by Sydney when returning home from work in a cross mood. Unhappy about having to entertain, he turned on his wife, who wasn't up for an argument, and rather than rise to the bait, she absented herself from the home to have a quiet shot of Stolichnaya at The Corkscrew on San Vincente.

It was five-thirty when she gunned the engine of her new Mercedes-Benz, and the guests weren't expected until seven. She pulled into a reserved section of the parking lot, thinking the custom paint alone justified this liberty. It was pearlescent white, and few dared touch it, even when reaching for the door handle. Checking her face in the rearview mirror, she found it faithfully flawless and strutted into her favorite haunt where everything stopped, except the jukebox, which continued to play *Back Stabbers* by The O'Jays. Men otherwise engaged snapped to attention when Nina swayed to the funky beat, and two well-dressed bucks at the bar adjourned to a table, hoping she'd join them.

"Why walk all the way over there when we've got a seat for you here?" asked Buck One.

"We'd be honored to buy you a drink," Buck Two added.

She'd planned on having a dram alone but sized up the room in an automatic reflex. While a shot of something strong would settle her nerves, male attention was another preferred substance, and a bit of harmless flirting after her tiff with Sydney might do her a power of good.

"Sure, set me up," Nina said. "I haven't much time. I'm hosting a dreadfully dull dinner party tonight and must get home to fly the company flag. I married a narcissist posing as an industrialist, and worst of all, my husband lacks appreciation for the effort it takes to look like this," she stated, standing up to prove the point.

"You are absolutely stunning," said Buck One.

"It must be exhausting to be so beautiful," Buck Two noted.

Nina was unaccustomed to neat liquor, and the Stoli crept from her toes to her teeth.

Straightening up, she prepared to leave and said, "Duty calls, gentlemen. The dullards await."

Nina and Meyera met for coffee the next day, and that dinner was described in detail.

"It was the most uncomfortable evening I've ever endured," Nina said.

"What went wrong?" Meyera asked.

"The spat with Sydney wasn't the issue," Nina said. "He was conciliatory and apologized when I got home. The real problem occurred when I opened the front door to greet our guests and found the same two bucks from the bar."

"You must've been mortified," Meyera said.

"I wanted the earth to open up and swallow me right there on the spot," Nina admitted. "Mercifully, nothing was said about the pre-dinner drinks we shared."

"Was Sydney aware of anything amiss?" Meyera asked.

"He assumed the awkward atmosphere was caused by our afternoon argument," Nina said.

"That was fortunate," Meyera added.

"Yes, although I remained in agony all evening trying to remember exactly what I'd said and when memory delivered a *verbatim* extract, I visibly flinched," Nina confessed.

"You must've been on a knife-edge," Meyera said.

"Thankfully, discretion really is the better part of valor," Nina observed.

CHAPTER 19

Westlake School for Girls is where I commenced secondary education. Located in Holmby Hills, the campus was situated at affluence ground zero, with Beverly Hills to the east, Beverly Glen to the west, Bel Air to the north and Wilshire Boulevard to the south.

It was a place of academic excellence, wrapped within the embrace of Spanish architecture and manicured grounds. It was also the place where Meyera failed to maintain a minimum grade point average and was asked to leave midway through her first year in seventh grade. Mom's acceptance to Westlake was dicey, to begin with, and in addition to undiagnosed dyslexia, her more obvious impediment was that she was Jewish. Dr. Joe was a personal physician to the school's owner and headmistress, making thorny matters pertaining to admission disappear. I hadn't matriculated, and already, I was fulfilling former hopes while facing fresh ones.

I'd resigned from the swim team, and Meyera was taking it pretty hard. Meme felt the same but had the good sense to stay quiet and see how things played out. There's a point at which parental encouragement gives way to vicarious insistence. Participating as a Palisades Porpoise was fun, but compared with the stable, there was no comparison at all.

My first team competition at the Los Angeles Athletic Club was well attended, with supporters filling the bleachers on both sides of the water. The twenty-five-yard pool seemed small when compared with The Biltmore Santa Barbara, which stretched the Olympic standard of fifty meters plus one foot, which served as a disincentive for swim teams seeking a place to practice. It's a magnificent pool, even in the rain, when the water looks to be falling upwards in reverse.

Prerace energy is hard to contain, but a member of the Malibu Mermaids gave me a tip in an act of surprising generosity, considering the pressure she was under to win the regionals, nationals, a college scholarship and at least one gold at the Olympics. She had to score every time and, when cut, claimed to bleed chlorine. To reduce stress, she used her teeth to pull threads from a towel, which, at a distance, looked like ordinary *futzing*. She suggested that we both pull while focusing.

That's when the towel stuck in my braces, but stuck is too gentle a word. Entrenched, enmeshed, and irrevocably attached would be more accurate. She had to dash and couldn't help me. Her meet was up next. Mine would immediately follow, but I was stranded, starting to panic, and wondering just how kind this Mermaid was after all. The towel was swinging from my braces like a terry cloth frond fanning the tile floor when a mother from the Tarzana Tunas or Studio City Shamus came to my aid. She could see I was struggling and grabbed her glasses to remove the towel.

With less than a minute to spare, I was released and ran to the block just in time for the gun, launch, and race. I hit the water like a lopsided torpedo and moved fast but inaccurately. At the finish, I looked up at Coach, who confirmed I came in second, but he seemed pleased. Finding a swimmer who responds well to competition was more important than winning that race.

I didn't bother collecting the swim meet medal, which wasn't a function of arrogance but disinterest. One whinny was all I needed to turn from the confines of the pool to that of the riding ring. Meyera and Coach conferred to create reasons why I should remain on the team, but Meme suggested I speak directly with him, allowing an informed view to precede my final decision.

Wisdom — there is no substitute, so forget what the people at Porsche say. Coach was scheduled to call just before dinner, and I sat on the long green couch to discuss my athletic future.

He got straight to the point and said, "The important thing to remember is that you've got what it takes to take this all the way. Training and effort are the building blocks, but winners must want to win. You want to win, don't you?"

"Yes, I want to win," I said, "preferably at horse shows rather than swim meets. I'll only be half the equestrian that I am a swimmer. Swimming is in my blood, but my heart is with horses and not the pool. What would you do? Choose something you love, or something you're good at?"

This precise question dogs many of us throughout life, and it certainly dogged me. Which to follow, aptitude or interest? An uncomfortable pause followed, during which Coach was considering his words. I could picture him lowering his shoulders and raising his chin before saying, "What I'd choose is what I'm best at. Aptitude rather than adoration delivers results. Having made that choice, I'd anticipate interest would follow."

I was anxious about Westlake, and shopping for the new uniform at Bullocks Wilshire brought home what a big change this would be. Meyera was also suffering from nerves caused by the California Real Estate Exam, the preparation for which was knocking the stuffing right out of her. Calculators and practice tests infiltrated our lives, accompanied by emotional outbursts.

Mom got so caught up in swotting up she forgot to hem my uniform before the first day of school, and I spent the better part of that day rolling the waist up by hand. This was effective for brief periods of time, but the damn thing kept falling below my knees, which kept me busy and distracted from orientation. I struggled to find my feet but never managed anything approaching solid ground. Academically, I was adrift, and athletically too. Our PE teacher admonished, "Winning isn't everything, but losing is absolutely nothing.'

Greek Mythology and *To Kill a Mockingbird* were the only pockets of educational warmth I could find, but Atticus Finch alone was worth the price of admission. A literary character representing an ideal, he led me to consider what it would've been like to have been born black.

Late at night in bed, I held up my hand pretending to be black but immediately recognized my folly. I was so cloistered that I might as well have raised the other pretending to be royalty. *Dandelion Wine* formed part of our seventh-grade syllabus, and the author, Ray Bradbury, addressed our school assembly. His topic concerned the continuing coming-of-age that takes us by surprise, and was candid in his description of a recent timeline collision startling him.

The circumstances involved one of his four daughters and her suitor, who asked for permission to propose. When it was granted, Ray wanted to cry but held his tears back for later that night in the shower. That's what he wanted to recommend: crying in the shower. He suggested we all try this as soon as possible because the catharsis of adding tears to cascading water was resplendent.

Westlake's mascot was a wolverine, which should've tipped me off. I wasn't like senior class sisters Sharron and Shelia Aztec, who typified the student profile. To mark the occasion of their first period, they were presented with diamond rings and, at age sixteen, received matching her's & her's Jaguars. The Aztecs had it all — and then some — with horses, holidays, and homes everywhere. Cash for college and careers was on hand, in addition to money for mistakes if needed.

Concerning what maketh the man, opinion widely varies, and at Oxford, its manners, while Francis Bacon felt it was reading. Shakespeare favored clothing, but Mr. Aztec had it down as money, and he made a lot. They were untouchable and insufferable. They knew it and didn't care.

The ceaseless demands of that year continued on a dreary Monday morning when I encountered my first period. This betrayal by my formerly friendly body wasn't unexpected. I attended a single-sex school and spent most of my time with women who made mention of this traitorous order.

Period ills seemed as infinite in variety as the tackle needed to cope, and they toted special aspirin with which to combat cramps while banishing the blues. I assumed this musical genre was inspired by lonesome stragglers, but perhaps it derived from menstruation. Dealing with this new menace wasn't attractive, and neither was its regular occurrence. Once a year was doable, and once a quarter maybe, but once every single solitary month was a tall order. Someone's having a laugh at the expense of women worldwide, and I decided to seek a definitive solution.

Meyera had undergone a hysterectomy, which meant no more monthly management and no menopause either. To me, these represented immediate and long-term goals. I asked Dr. Lothar if I could avail myself of the same procedure, but my request was denied. Despite decades of inconvenience ahead, there was no getting away from it unless I'd been manufactured by Mattel, but he described hormones as friends of the type worth holding onto.

My cousin Sandy provided support, and having traversed Liberia before transporting my pony, she was accustomed to making things better on a local, if not global, basis. At Christmas, she risked electrocution when installing my Easy-Bake Oven, graciously dismissing the shocks repeatedly encountered.

It took hours to make one cupcake, but Sandy said, "What do you expect when creating confectionary by fairy light alone?"

Getting your period was something even Sandy couldn't fix, but she drew our attention to the list of activities on the Tampax box. Tennis and golf might be worth adding. Anything was preferable to self-pity.

When I mentioned menopause, she laughed and said, "That's intensely delayed gratification."

I shared sighs of resignation with a girl in the stall next to mine when we emerged from our Westlake water closet cubicles in confusion. Tampons aren't the easiest to maneuver. The directions are anything but instructive, involving complicated diagrams suited to a third-year medical student. In dealing with these demands, we should be treated as Jill, rather than Jack, on top of his year at Johns Hopkins and headed for the Mayo Clinic.

The girl looked at me in the bathroom mirror and said, "At least you're a WASP. I'm Jewish, so guess what happened when I told my mom? She slapped me. Can you believe it? I'm trying to come to terms with what I figure is a life sentence, and what does my mother do? She smacks me in what's called the *Mazel Tov* slap."

"In my family, we aim to avoid adding insult to injury," I said. "Yours is the first injury to insult I've heard."

My first period impelled me to ask Meme about my birth mother. I wanted to know more precisely who she was and what she did with her life. Although detailed information was scant, Meme was given to understand that my natural *mater* was a legal secretary who would've been a lawyer had times been different, and women welcomed to those hallowed halls of higher academic learning. She was swift to suggest that more accurate facts could be obtained from the Department of Social Services and promised to investigate it on my behalf.

To take my mind off the new monthly demand imposed by menstruation, Meyera and I went to see Roy Roger's trusty steed, Trigger. This exceptional palomino had a credit list rivaling many top stars and branded merchandise spanning so many items he can correctly be called the grandfather of ancillary rights. Trigger's team kept him in the headlines, and he made well-publicized visits to children's hospitals, scaling several flights of stairs to reach children in need of cheer. Ensuring the public recognized Trigger's commitment was easy, considering his ceaseless efforts to work even on his day off.

Meyera and I drove along Route 66 into the San Bernardino High Desert to see Trigger at the Roy Rogers/Dale Evans Museum. During the ride, we sang the signature tune, *Happy Trails,* followed by Meme's favorites: *Ma! (He's Making Eyes at Me)* and *Roll Me Over in the Clover.* The moment we arrived at our destination, I ran from the car shouting, "See you at Trigger."

Dashing from the air-conditioned car into the sweltering hot sun was a shock, but nothing compared with the trauma of stepping into the museum. Trigger was there alright, accompanied by an automatic whinny and galloping hoof track that kicked into gear every time the door opened. Although tacky, I had no issue with that, but I took exception to the fact Trigger was taxidermized and displayed in an undignified rearing position. I was speechless while waiting for Meyera to finish a cigarette outside in what must've been a welcome spate of quiet. I hope she enjoyed that brief rest. She'd soon encounter a distraught daughter ready to fire off some serious questions.

"How could they do this to Trigger?" I asked. "Will Rogers would never have allowed Bootlegger or Soapsuds to be stuffed. And Wilbur wouldn't permit this for Mister Ed. Misty might've been a mess, but at least she was alive."

While directing my comments toward Meyera I stared indignantly at the museum docent, who was now in something of a state herself.

Clearly flustered, she looked at Meyera while addressing me and said, "Aren't you glad we have preserved Trigger? We've got footage featuring him in his heyday."

"What about Silver?" I said. "Do you think The Lone Ranger would approve of this?"

The docent tried to mollify me by mentioning that a warning would be added to the museum's promotional material, alerting visitors to Trigger's current condition. While Meyera nodded, I wondered if the docent expected Trigger to recover and, if so, we were dealing with a crazy person.

The docent pulled a pen from her pocket and placed it in the palm of her outstretched hand, intending to lure me toward it as if coaxing a deer toward pellets. I approached with doe-like caution while she tipped it one way to have Roy Rogers and Dale Evans float to the top before sending them back down. When the docent asked if I'd like to keep the pen as a reminder of my day at the museum, I knew she was crazy alright.

Looking again at Trigger, I declined her offer on the basis that I was unlikely to forget the experience and headed out the door. Meyera accepted the pen, no doubt dreading the long drive home. Having to contend with a sulky kid wasn't the outing she'd planned, and desperate to salvage something from our ill-fated adventure, Meyera suggested we have a Mexican meal. A dismissive shake of my head indicated staunch resistance, and we drove in silence until a large, empty parking lot caught Mom's attention.

She slowed down and said, "I know what we should do."

Her tone was lighter than I judged appropriate, and she was suspiciously confident about this sudden inspiration.

Although willing to bite the bait, I adjusted to perfect pout-pitch before asking, "What do you have in mind?"

"How's about I teach you to drive?" Meyera suggested.

I was only twelve, but my legs were long enough to reach the accelerator. Meyera preferred I go for the brake and wished for one on the passenger side during our first lesson. Sitting behind the wheel of Mom's Mercury Cougar was invigorating, and learning to drive five years ahead of schedule was a treat. I even came to terms with the pen when struggling to shut a desk drawer in my late 20s, and found it jammed at the back. It seems we do meet again.

Meyera encountered the same phenomena when standing in line at the bank. His name was Jim Myers, and, once upon a time, Mom loved him. She must've done. Had they married, she'd have become Meyera Myers. Jim and Meyera met in their early twenties when her friend Jill Southern brought him to Dr. Joe and Elsie's party celebrating National Potato Day. Their chef, Marvin, was accustomed to their 'any excuse for a party' ethos and set to work preparing this simple dish with a stylish twist, allowing only scalloped, duchess and *dauphinoise* on display. He did the same for National Pancake Day by creating fresh fruit accompaniments that Carmen Miranda would admire. When Jill walked in with Jim, all the air left the room, and Meyera fell head over heels in love.

Jim wasn't a born blue blood but he was a determined newcomer, ready to make his mark on the world working in television. Although camera-ready, Jim would never consider a career as on-screen talent. He agreed with Meyera's crowd that such figures were no more than talking props. As a television executive, Jim's role was to source inexpensive programming, so he secured exclusive broadcast rights for boxing matches and roller derby races, propelling him to success.

Jim was fiercely ambitious and drop-dead gorgeous. When Meyera spotted him standing alone by the pool table, she was tempted to ask if he'd had a misspent youth, but she moved toward Jill in the first instance, asking to have a quiet word in the kitchen. Following polite rules of engagement, the 'all's fair in love and war' adage wasn't something she subscribed to.

"Who on earth is that, and where did he come from?" Meyera gasped. "Your date is gorgeous. Are you serious about him?"

Jill was a debutante, but not just any debutante. She was Las Madrinas, which is arguably the most prestigious in LA. Jill was actively raising funds for Children's Hospital, which is how she came to know Jim. He was acting as a stand-in for her new *beau* that night, but, thanks to

Jim, a major broadcast company contributed a substantial sum to her charity, and she was keen to pass the hat his way again. If Meyera fancied him, all the better, and Jill couldn't wait to introduce them. She wasn't the only one.

Meyera was partial to candy, both chocolate and that which appeals to the eye. She stayed sweet on Jim and had a high romance, leading to hopes of matrimony, but Jim feared he couldn't afford her. Meyera was too much ermine and mink, which was a characterization that preceded his fond farewell.

Losing love to economic disparity broke Meyera's heart and, at twenty-two, formed the only financial hardship she'd encountered. Ironic, considering it was a chance encounter at Bank of America that brought them together again when standing in line behind Rod Serling, creator of *The Twilight Zone*. Picture, if you will, seventeen years later.

The second time around gave them both a boost, providing an opportunity to rekindle what they'd lost previously. The usual preamble to coupling was in full throttle, especially now they had more in common.

Jim's divorce was as distant as Meyera's, and they each had one daughter. A circuit of dinners and playdates jogged along at a comfortable pace, allowing time for Jim's daughter Meredith and I to become friends. Meredith Myers had dark curly hair, deep-blue eyes, and a blinding smile, just like her father's. She was older by a year or two and ideally placed to lead the way toward her every whim. Meredith adored crafts and, at the time of the meeting, tie-dyeing was her top favorite, so we utilized this method to redecorate virtually everything we could lay our hands on.

By expanding our definition of loose material, what started with shoelaces advanced to pillowcases and towels while we took everything from pristine white to a deep purple. Fortunately, when parental units are in love, a multitude of transgressions can be dismissed with little consequence and large doses of humor.

Meyera was sitting at the vanity table preparing for a date with Jim when our neighbor Lois stopped by. Plonking herself down on Mom's bed, we watched Meyera apply makeup with the precision of an Italian

Renaissance painter. When reaching for the hairspray, Mom's robe slipped, exposing La Perla lingerie, which Lois complimented, prompting my curiosity.

"Why have you bought that?" I asked. "It's not as if he's going to see your underwear, so why bother with fancy stuff?" I said while Lois and Meyera exchanged a sly smile.

"With new lingerie on, you feel better," Lois explained. "You know it's there even when others don't."

This comment lodged in my mind, remaining dormant until my adult years when surfacing on the rare occasion I purchased lingerie. Lois was right about donning silk, satin, and lace. You really do feel better, but there's another aspect to this elevated garb that should be printed on the label. Some sort of warning is needed, alerting us about the association each piece will have with the one who enjoys the bounty of unwrapping it.

Purchase these items with John, Jim or Jack in mind, and good luck wearing them a second time for Sam, Sebastian, or Scott. There's an indelible connection between the garment, the guy and you, forming a mental *ménage a trois* that's hard to shake off, no matter how silky the fabric. Second showings involve risk, unwittingly inviting three to bed.

All indications pointed to a long stretch of green lights along the runway while our craft headed gently toward an upbeat future for Meyera, Jim, Meredith, and me. This confused Meyera when sitting down with a cup of Yuban coffee, intending to relax while reading the paper. She lit a cigarette and turned to the Sunday social supplement, but rather than stumble across the article, she smashed straight into a flashy spread detailing an even splashier marriage between Jim and a woman we'd never heard of. How did this happen, and who was she? These questions came crashing down in a cruel way to learn about the end of a relationship.

While we weren't necessarily ready to commit, Jim obviously was, and Meyera climbed into the tomb of her bed, remaining there for days. I was distressed but empathetic and aware of the cause driving Mom's suffering. I refrained from the usual search-and-destroy mission to remove spirits from her reach. My well-worn *reconnoiter* left large bottles of scotch, vodka, and gin accessible in all the usual places. I was no stranger to this version of hide-and-seek. I checked under the kitchen and bathroom sinks, but serious trouble such as this was sure to involve the laundry room as well.

There was a prepositional element to this endeavor, and rather than think of precise places, I conceived of general areas such as behind the long green couch, curtains and living room stereo. Top also occupied a special place, and not just the obvious locations as a kitchen cupboard, fridge, and bookcase, which were easy, but serious sleuthing required a stepladder to the top of our stationary and linen cabinet.

Bottom was popular, as in laundry hampers, ironing baskets, kibble bags, trash bins and closets, while boots delivered significant yield whether riding, rain, or dress. Each pair contained spirits on the left side only, because Meyera was a southpaw.

Inside served as a location in which to stash contraband, with no end of intoxicants concealed within the barbeque, dishwasher, freezer, vegetable bin, double boiler, hatbox, and silver cabinet. Smaller fifth-size bottles were secreted inside the Asian wok, toaster oven, and Cuisinart. The most well-stocked local was under Meyera's bedframe mattress, and after the breakup with Jim, I was thankful we didn't live in a larger apartment.

Meyera's remand to a private hell lasted ten days, during which I encouraged her to throw something of substance into the caldron of boiling alcohol to absorb the fuel of her free fall descent. Rather than gourmet meals, I offered light sustenance such as egg on toast.

Our deal about me keeping my head down to study limited my culinary skills and focused attention on cleanup, which I've come to regard as more attractive than actually cooking. Show me a filthy kitchen, a pair of marigold gloves and some cleaning products, and I'd know what to do.

The subtle, and not so subtle, pressure to get to the stable finally got Mom out of bed, which was best for us both. Meyera occasionally exercised a sixteen-hand bay called El Cid owned by actress Stefanie Powers, who, even before her *Hart to Hart* television series, was acknowledged as a sweetheart, both professionally and personally.

Meyera never met the woman whose horse she hacked, but was familiar with her co-star, RJ Wagner, from early days at Lake Arrowhead. Despite having regarded RJ with slightly less disdain than she did Elizabeth Taylor, it's unlikely that he'd remember Meyera, considering that Natalie Wood married him twice.

"I'm glad you're getting some fresh air," I said to Meyera. "Riding will do you good, and eventually, you'll get over Jim."

"You're probably right," Meyera said. "But right now eventually feels like forever. Let's face it, Dorothy Parker was right on the money when she said, 'Time may be a great healer, but it's a lousy beautician.'"

CHAPTER 20

Erika looked after my pony while New York had me tethered for the summer. My perfectly situated pal was a pixie come to life, with short blonde hair and a huge smile showing symmetrical teeth obtained without braces. She favored a hackamore bridle when riding bareback balanced by her long legs, and, in my absence, April needed exercise. *Ergo*, I needed Erika.

At horse shows, we were friends first, competitors second and cruel kids third. Sitting in the bleachers at the Flintridge Classic, we learned about discretion, which was a lesson that remained with me, be it on a plane, train or in line at the grocery store. Nudging me in the ribs, she suggested I check out the braids on the next entry, and after I confirmed the need for emergency haircare concerning horse and rider, she confessed to wondering how they'd get around the course, considering they looked unfit to ride in a boxcar.

I was surprised that the warm-up ring was still standing. The tip of her boots pointed so far out she could take the railing right down. We laughed and slapped each other on the back like a couple of post-kill jackals.

Our hilarity subsided long enough for me to mention the girl's hunt coat, which had a nice trim and wasn't half bad, but then the all bad happened when a woman sitting in front of us turned around and said, "My daughter made that hunt coat herself, and I'll be sure to pass on your kind words."

Mortification is a remarkably swift emotion, but I suppose they all are. Erika and I earned high place ribbons that day, along with low-down humility. Embarrassment was in evidence again when we returned from riding on the trail, thirsty to the point of parched, and ran to the clubhouse fridge for a blast of blissfully cold air. No doubt the same would be delivered by a bottle of High C chilled to icy-cold perfection.

We saw it at the same time and reached for it at the same time, having noticed the limited amount of liquid left in the container at the same time. The only thing we didn't do simultaneously was consume it.

Without thinking, I downed the paltry contents in a fraction of a second, and Erika said, "Why not leave some for someone else? Shouldn't you give me a second thought?"

An only child isn't always aware of selfish acts because we're rarely called upon to sharpen our sharing skills, and many of us would rather part with the title than grant a license. I was shamed a second time when consuming High C and humble pie. The winds of change were blowing, and the 60s gave way to the next decade.

Bob Dylan claimed we didn't need a weatherman, but some form of guidance wouldn't have gone amiss as it was a turbulent transition. The 70s bit back at the previous period by embracing that which had been rejected, and corruption crept into the narrative, impacting everything from ideals to fashion. This happened more gradually at our apartment building, but it happened alright. Before I'd witness these changes, another visit to New York was on track.

Ready to greet Laurel, I placed *The Arrival of the Queen of Sheba* on the turntable with the volume up to a full blast, as Handel would've wanted. She came through the door, and we hugged while Laurel asked what was on the summertime menu, suggesting we add a little tennis.

Swinging us side to side while deciding the order of things, I said, "Let's start with the stable in the morning, swim in the afternoon and tennis in the evening."

"The riddle posed by the Sphinx is now answered by the pampered," George said, "and puts an erudite end to that country club conundrum."

Laurel and Alex picked up precisely where they'd left off, which was in love. If correctly harnessed, the energy generated by their attraction could heat the enormous club pool, where we'd be stationed on our sun loungers by one o'clock every day. Maintaining a beauty regime is serious business, despite the fact it looks relaxing to the untrained eye.

Experienced participants appreciate what a complicated endeavor this is, and we'd whip up a special concoction of hair conditioner with fresh lemon juice. Fresh is essential to this concept. It required refreshing on the hour. Supplemental skin care involved a trip to the grocery store to buy mayonnaise, egg whites, honey and cucumber. Moisturizing is a must, demanding many varieties.

While others practiced safe sex, we practiced safe sun by topping up with Bain de Soleil and turning our loungers every twenty minutes in tightly controlled increments, approximating a human sundial. Given our commitment to sun-kissed skin, we kept fairly accurate time and achieved comprehensive color by stretching in a variety of poses to reach hard to get areas such as under the arm, back of the neck and bottom of our feet. Sides are also tricky, but mostly a matter of balance. Laurel was vigilant about maintaining consistent tan lines and constantly adjusted our bathing suits to obtain uniformity.

"Anyone who says that getting a tan doesn't require work," Laurel said, "doesn't know what they're tanning about."

Unlike the panoply of poolside fashionistas, we weren't mani-pedi people and weren't interested in pink, allowing us to take pride in the fact we were built for speed rather than comfort. The chlorine in the club pool was significantly more stringent than that used in LA, causing Laurel to call it sheep dip. As one bathing suit after another became chemically annihilated, she shook her head disapprovingly but said that given a choice of maintaining personal shape or that of a swimsuit, it was a small sacrifice. Our skin took a hit when submerged in sodium bromine, but the lingering scent was worn with a certain satisfaction.

Returning home to walk Charlie, I put my hand inside the wrist portion of the leash, lasso style, affording greater control when strolling the streets of Manhattan. Although technically a poodle, he wasn't the type of dog to pick a fight with, and he demonstrated this fact during an afternoon spin around the block of our East 64th Street apartment building.

We were enjoying the smell of summer and the sense of being in the heart of heat as steam poured from Midtown streets, the back of restaurants and the subway below. Three Archie Bunker look-alikes were loitering outside a subterranean garage wearing undershirts that, in varying degrees, had once been white but were suggestive of stained briefs.

"Hey girly, quite a dog you've got there," said the stained man. "Don't walk away when I want to show you something," he added to raucous chuckles from his friends.

Reaching into his pocket for a handful of quarters, he said, "I'll give you this money if you give me that dog."

"No, thank you,' I said, repeatedly pressing the crosswalk button, willing the signal to change.

Crossing the street seemed like a good idea, but traffic was heavy, and pedestrians were at a disadvantage, delaying our escape. By slight rearrangement, the stained man attractively displayed the coins in his palm and lumbered toward us, like a Clydesdale with a list to its gate. Balancing his heavy cargo caused him to labor for breath, but he advanced toward us as if wading through treacle.

Charlie didn't have the Doberman instinct to quell first and chomp second, but presumably, poodles are more proactive. When only three steps separated the stained man from where we stood, the dog burst forth with a roar. Place a canine in charge of a charge, and potential peril disappears. The noise even a poodle can make is downright deafening.

I was impressed by how a halting sound inspired action, and never have I seen anyone galvanized into retreat so fast. Although threatening to any eye, the stained man reversed direction with much greater speed. Sound is solid and able to act as a wall. Not for nothing is Phil Spector's genius described this way. Considering the stained man's amplitude, it was amusing, as are all things threatening when safely tucked away in retrospect.

Charlie distinguished himself as a dog ready to repel danger, which is always good to know and almost impossible to ascertain unless trained or tested. Before acquitting himself with proven *chivalry*, Charlie's bravado had been a source of speculation, and faced with a critical moment; we wondered would he or wouldn't he defend.

More often a moribund issue, it's the owners who'd rush to a beloved pet's aid should a dangerous situation arise. Ever mindful to keep him on the leash, I took Charlie to a baseball game, and after finding a vacant bench near the diamond, I sat down to watch the game while Charlie took his seat on the ground, making us eye level.

The game was well sponsored, with promotional banners and smart team uniforms decorating both sides. Picnic tables were flanked by a carpet of blankets on which heaps of sandwiches competed for space against platters of salads. Everything edible was huddled under foil wrap, wilting in the sun as hot as the coffee consumed by families who first annexed then spread like a fan across the grassy space. With so many people parading around the park it resembled a green beach.

I was paying attention to nothing in particular, but Charlie remained focused when we moved from vertical to a prone position while traversing first and second base. The lasso leash grip kept Charlie and I tethered, but thankfully, someone's dad stepped in to stop the dog's fast pursuit of the ball. Had he not intervened, I'd have rounded third.

For me, the experience was analogous to water-skiing without the benefit of liquid, but for the baseball players, it was one of intense irritation, which I found churlish considering I was covered in grass marks, unlike their pristine uniforms. At twelve years of age, the only thing I had in common with these teams was the phrase 'pony league.'

There's a certain creed among parents who watch kids play sports, which allows nurturing care to assume a community property aspect when administering treatment to the injured. Two families jostled for position, wanting to coddle me, and guided by equity, I allowed one to confirm I was fine while the other dispensed my first, but not last, slice of cold pizza.

A toddler moved toward me as would a sumo wrestler, and after a series of swaddled yet bold baby steps, he stopped while pointing to my skirt. The adoring audience astride his family atoll laughed while reaching for a camera, explaining he sympathized with my situation. The stains were the color of Kermit and he knew *It's Not Easy Being Green*.

Laurel and Alex's choice of song continued to be a significant issue that we affectionately called Play it again, Alex. Once resolved, it left something of a gap, but nothing that diminished the impact of the final selection. They picked a track impervious to time in the way of all nostalgia.

Music contains a distinctive intimacy that's both immediate and long-term, forming the soundtrack of our lives. This is the playlist that transports us to a particular place in a vivid and emotive way, often more visceral than a millisecond of time trapped in the shutter of a camera. Chicago's *Make Me Smile* was first in the frame, only to be supplanted by Badfinger's *No Matter What*. This song made sense since their relationship was stable, but stability was interrupted when we went to visit a third Marock sibling in Maine.

Aunt Louise was the eldest, and Maude was the youngest, which placed Uncle George Marock smack dab in the middle, just like when he left Manhattan for Maine in the middle of the night. Sketchy details concerning the reason behind his sudden departure point to a series of business deals, social register status and alcohol use all going south. The same things that found alignment further north where he and his wife, Lucille, lived in a place so dense with life, most of it is concealed most of the time.

Their landscape was no mere rich tapestry. It was an iron curtain, with blackberries basking in rare summer rays protected by powerful thorns, forming an impenetrable screen guarding their privacy. This enclave was carved out with their own hands, including the house, which was constructed with smoothbark beech, officially recorded as extinct.

When Uncle George first laid eyes on the place, it was dilapidated, but an affordable deed was available. He was strong, and his wife was willing to become a survivalist to a degree, often mistaken for antisocial. Although a long way from Lucille's native Boston, she lent a hand by making do with what was to hand. When my father, Laurel and I drove up, they were outside, ready to welcome us with actual affection.

Laurel took this brief separation from Alex fairly well, considering it took ten days away from their time together. Rather than moody, Laurel was a little moony. High-energy cheerleader routines gave way to somber songs performed with sincere teenage longing. We'd lie in our separate feather beds buried under the weight of Aunt Lucille's patch-work quilts, listening as a horned owl in the barn hooted to a barred owl likely located directly above us.

Uncle George was convinced each wanted the other to disappear and believed in the adage 'good fences make good neighbors' but took it further, regarding a good neighbor as one whose fence you can't see. Aunt Lucille had a different storyline in which the owls want to know *Hoo* each other are, but since neither can answer the question, their conversation continues Aesop style.

Breakfast in Maine comprised of fresh muffins and homemade blackberry jam, along with roast coffee for the adults, and hot chocolate for me, which was a treat, even without marshmallows.

Uncle George begrudgingly offered to get some in stock but said, "I don't see the sense in messing up a perfectly fine beverage with such a fancy waste of time."

"It's the little things that create a large impression, and small details amplify the bigger image," Aunt Lucille explained. "The important bits may be as tiny as an eyelash, but it all gets tucked into memory, and marshmallows are now a reminder of this visit. Anything left in the pack will provide comfort after the girls have gone. A reminder that just might tug at your heartstrings too."

He departed for the car and twenty minutes later returned with a huge bag of this malleable treat, saying, "Here you go, Mrs. Marock, plenty of marshmallows to consume and mourn."

Aunt Lucille loved to sing, prompting Uncle George to claim she shampooed more men from her hair than populated the entire state. He wasn't a fan of musicals *per se* or *South Pacific* in particular, but he always tapped his foot when she burst into song. He did when she launched into a number from *Annie Get Your Gun* while Laurel and I followed to the best of our Ethel Merman ability.

We had the sun and moon, but I suggested that since Aunt Lucille and Aunt Louise both loved to sing, why not get together? A silence descended, destroying breakfast, and what had been a spirited morning was now on life support. The prognosis wasn't good, but I would've continued to breathe life into that lost moment until Laurel's look prevented me. She had me so well trained I could've passed for a Crufts champion.

Aunt Lucille revived our formerly energized spirits by suggesting it was time to go outside, but before departure, I sought clarification concerning the distance to which porcupines could shoot their quills. Uncle George laughed, and everyone was relieved to have moved on to a less combustible subject. The ten days passed quickly, and while leaving, I promised to be perennial like the plants in their garden.

After our return from Maine, George became distant, canceling numerous dinners in the city dwarfed by a number of no-shows at the club. His last-minute absence allowed a more relaxed atmosphere when Laurel and I dined *a deux* on Daddy's dime, but he'd occasionally join us on Sunday nights for low-key meals at a local Italian restaurant. Distracted and wanting to hunker down at home, he'd return to his study, making calls to his friends with the same greeting, "Hello Tiger, what's the good news?"

For George, the study was a place of refuge where he'd disappear to play backgammon, drink scotch, and chain-smoke while watching high-volume television in the same tormenting blast that Meyera tuned in while shuffling her cards for Solitaire. Mechanical squawk boxes at both ends produced a foul form of noise pollution, and despite their different locations, they represented the same insult to tranquility.

Meyera's harsh fanning of each card made a punishing horsewhip sound when hitting the glass coffee table, infiltrating otherwise quiet rooms. George retired from a featured role to walk-on extra and, if needed for continuity, he'd be on hand, but anything more made him fade from view. Communication was conducted by notes attached to the refrigerator door where hastily composed missives, written in George's exquisite handwriting, greeted us most mornings. Expressing hope that we'd have fun in his absence, my father used minimal ink and even less space to express these thoughts. Monks seeking to retain *chi* look profligate by comparison, but this was as close to Buddhism as my father would ever come.

At seventeen-minutes-past-three in the morning, Laurel and I heard a whooshing sound outside. I can confirm the exact time thanks to a transitional object relationship I maintained with the digital alarm. Learning to read the clockface eluded me for longer than I care to admit. Looking into the garden, we saw George standing with Charlie under the sprinkler, which covered both man and dog in artificial rain, but the next morning, I caught the end of a conversation between my father and the maintenance man who lived next door.

His name was Clayton, and he had the warmest, most welcoming laugh I've heard to date. Clayton was adept at anything a house, stable or landscape needed, and epitomized the concept of able-bodied by reminding me of a black Paul Bunyan. He's the guy you want to be standing next to in the event of an emergency, and he was also the man who gently coaxed an inebriated George back inside before turning off that nocturnal shower. Always ready to lend a hand or, in my father's case, a towel when needed, there was something about him that brought Boo Radley to mind. Both figures revealed humanity with humility.

I couldn't find our dog Charlie and was frantic. He wasn't in the kitchen, living room or trespassing on his favorite couch in George's study. Running to the backyard, I called his name, and Clayton answered, allowing me to find them both in the neighbor's storage barn stacking a cord of wood while two radios broadcasted different baseball games.

Clayton explained that they keep each other company while ensuring the measurements are exactly four-feet-high, four-feet-wide, and eight-feet-long with enough wood to keep everyone as warm as toast all winter, but when it came to baseball, they both had it bad, as neither could decide on just one game.

Separation anxiety was getting a firm grip on us all, and we were not at our best. Short-tempered and tempted to tears would be more accurate. There weren't many days left before the calendar countdown sent us into meltdown. Laurel and I were leaving the city later than expected after George missed my informal swim meet at the New York Athletic Club.

I was hoping he'd make a brief appearance and, to assist this hope, lingered in the shower while Laurel was concerned about traffic interfering with the time needed to return for her date with Alex. They were going ice-skating, which was something I loathed, and had they gone bowling, there'd have been hell to pay.

Although furious with George, I vented my frustration on Laurel, accusing her of tolerating my father's inconsiderate behavior, which I found unbecoming to them both. Laurel looked directly at the road but remained silent, which irritated me further. She clenched her jaw and abruptly pulled to the curb, asking me to get out, allowing her a minute to calm down. I also needed a breather, whether I knew it or not, and she'd drive once around the block, returning in five minutes.

We were in front of my father's apartment building, but as she pulled away, Laurel said something about where to meet, which sounded like the corner. The doorman saw me, and running away from what I thought was trouble caused real trouble when George was told I'd been seen without Laurel. Spotted alone on a New York City Street amounted to trouble, no matter how exclusive the Lennox Hill address was, and should Meyera find out, it might threaten visitation rights.

Furious with Laurel, he asked, "What was I paying you for? What have you done with my trust? When will you be ready for a final flight home?"

Laurel ran up to her room, and I wanted to join her, but George cordoned off access while pointing to a prepacked weekend bag I'd take to join Trudy in Central Park East. Dante described nine rings of hell but destination Trudy sounded like a tenth. I arrived at the Lien residence, as would an asylum seeker who's rescued by the wrong side, and in less than thirty-seconds, Trudy asked if I still stank of horseshit. Popping his head around the door while brandishing a camera, Mr. Lien wanted to take the traditional photo of us girls back together, so we posed in a tastefully decorated room with William Morris wallpaper and linen from Liberty's in London.

Everything was plumped, buffed and shiny, reflecting a demand for perfection that permeated the place. Crossing into their world required surrender to a higher authority, requiring an A-game from all entrants.

Upmarket staging for the most elegant Manhattan properties paled in comparison with this magnificent home, where Mrs. Lien rarely spent time claiming to have none for herself. There wasn't a minute to relax when rushing to the trainer, tennis, beauty salon, and analyst. Strict sanctions pertained to all her properties, and anything able to crumble wasn't allowed outside the kitchen unless entertaining. A series of servants maintained her commandments in a way that made God's ten look like footnotes.

Mr. Lien was holding not one camera but two when George came to collect me. Our dads enjoyed amassing an archive chronicling an ostensible friendship spanning several leatherbound albums. These were the same embossed books from which Susan's image had been removed, including a series at the boat pond in Central Park when she was heavily pregnant and I rambunctious.

Although hard to stand still long enough to take pictures, the camera's satisfying snap made a fun moment last. Little did I know that Kodak can guarantee good images, but what happens after that is on the consumer's back.

Preparing to depart Trudy's beautiful but bookless room, I packed everything except an awkward apparatus required for orthodontia involving a wire running around the circumference of one's head. It's hard to misplace, but my hideous hardware was nowhere in sight, and George grew impatient while theatrically checking his watch. In times of crisis, he could be relied upon to provide criticism rather than comfort, and discharged complaints like a machine gun with bullets of blame coming so quickly I couldn't dodge them.

Trudy pulled the cistern top from the toilet and held my headgear up as if it were a dead rodent while asking, "Is this what you're looking for?"

CHAPTER 21

Laurel and I weren't the only ones to fly West from New York at the end of summer. Clayton from next door came to live at the apartment building indefinitely. He wanted to see California, where living among friendly natives in nondemanding weather appealed to him. Everyone understood this, including the family he worked for, who wished him well while silently cursing George for poaching their most valued treasure.

Meyera and Meme would have dedicated on-site support at an attractive rate, made possible by slight exploitation and subsidized housing, as Clayton could occupy whatever apartment might be available at any given time. This arrangement made sense to all concerned, commencing with his arrival at LAX.

As passengers were disembarking, I spotted Clayton and enthusiastically leaped into his arm. Only one was needed to raise me high-up above his shoulders. Releasing that warm laugh, he seemed pleased to see a familiar face, no matter how young.

"I see my fan club of one has announced me, Mrs. Buchanan, and thank you for meeting my plane."

Meyera extended a firm handshake and apologized for the hot weather, which, even by California standards, was unusually warm for January.

"Welcome, and please call me Meyera," she said, but he never did.

Most tenants referred to my mother as Meyera, reflecting a new demographic shifting to the left. Some tenants left for reasons of marriage, while others moved due to promotion or the purchase of property, but it all led to relocation. We lived not far from the ocean, where the tidal flow seemed to reach into the building, claiming outgoing tenants into obscurity while depositing fresh ones.

Clayton's timing should've been perfect. The antipathy between New York and Los Angeles was largely confined to humor, but the day-to-day differences proved difficult, making him feel trapped by having to conform to a work schedule, not of his own design. Back East, he was accustomed to autonomy and knew what had to be done, including the preferred order in which to do it, but Meme had different plans and liked to map out Clayton's entire day despite constantly changing her mind. The quality of his work was impeccable, and painting, carpeting, or shifting anything was never a problem. It wasn't the work but a clash of cultures that became problematic.

A new resident named Heather arrived just before Valentine's Day. She was the youngest I'd seen, but she signed the lease on her eighteenth birthday after passing a credit check in record time. Her fair skin hadn't seen much sun, making her cornflower-blue eyes more dramatic, and a cascade of waist-length, straight, blonde hair was parted, as we all did that decade, straight down the middle. She was a trustafarian with recent access to a fortune so vast it was difficult to ascertain its actual amount.

With nothing but money and time, she'd come to California from the East to idle in neutral while deciding the course of her future. Surveying the landscape — both poolside and personal — there was an air of secrecy about her, but when Clayton was around, she managed to unwind. Going from total strangers to fully ripe familiarity virtually on contact, they spent most evenings together.

The fizzy buzz at Heather's place hadn't begun to settle when another apartment became occupied by the trendiest tenant to date called Don, who worked for a record label. His on-again, off-again relationship with a woman called Carol was confusing. Their fluid status made it difficult to tell if she was officially in residence or a frequent sleepover friend.

They'd saunter down the hallway with Carol in tight jeans and Don wearing corduroy flares, placing them dead center of contemporary fashion. These people weren't just on the vanguard, they were cutting edge, forging a fast association with Clayton and Heather, whose first-floor apartment was in front of the pool, as was Don's and, possibly, Carol's. Clayton removed the screens from their front windows, enabling everyone to step straight out rather than walk through the hallway. I thought this was ingenious, but Meme didn't like it. She also didn't care for their music, which changed the mood throughout the building, making everything modern 'in' while everyone over thirty was 'out.'

Meme asked me to grab her cigarettes, which she'd left by the pool, and as I was heading back in, Heather's window slid open while Clayton gave her a goodnight kiss. She was in the nude, and when closing the curtain, Clayton noticed me and placed his finger in front of his lips, indicating silence with the same gesture used to reassure George last summer.

I repeated the same signal so he'd know the message was received, silently promising, in the way of mimes, not to breathe a word to a soul. The same spirit of cooperation was lacking in other residents. It wasn't just loud music but sex in the air, accompanied by pot, and copious quantities of incense. The proliferation of candles didn't help matters either, and an uncomfortable urgency crept in, particularly when Heather's parents came to call.

They were a conservative couple who demanded access to their daughter's apartment, but, as landlord, Meyera's hands were legally tied. Escorting them to Heather's front door was the best she could do, but Heather's father was livid, and his hands shook to such an extent his wife had to write a note informing their daughter that they were waiting in the manager's apartment.

Heather's mother said it was a relief to know their daughter was safe, but her husband looked as if he'd explode. Everyone was lost in their own thoughts. The mood shifted from distraught to relieved, and then angry. Judging by the look Heather's mother shot her husband, it moved again to depression when she played with her strand of pearls, in the same distracted way she listened to him describe the difficulty when too much money is provided too soon and it's too late to stop it.

Bored with her pearls, she twisted her engagement ring, which was so big and bright that I wondered if it might be battery-operated. Meyera apologized for the fact that California Law was so strict. Heather's dad appreciated Meyera's position, but Meme came in, and took a deep drag of her cigarette before asking when the lease was signed. Meyera checked the top right corner, confirming it was dated February nine, which Meme said cured the situation.

Everyone looked confused by her statement, and I had to admit that my grandmother sounded like a befuddled elder, but Heather's mother wanted to hear more. Her understanding was that California Law prevented them from gaining access to their daughter's apartment, but Meme suggested they were considering the wrong law by focusing on those pertaining to tenants rather than the rights of minors, who don't have many. Heather's father repeated the fact his daughter was eighteen and a legal adult, which clearly eluded my grandmother's understanding.

Meme wasn't in the mood to accept insults, and allowed an awkward silence to remain while stubbing out her cigarette in a way Bette Davis couldn't improve upon before mentioning that the age of majority was recently reduced from twenty-one to eighteen, effective from the fourth of March. Heather, however, signed her lease in February, a month before California considered her a legal adult, sending her swiftly from major to minor.

Meme now had everyone's attention, and agreed to withhold formal eviction proceedings should they remove a technically illegal tenant from her property. The matter of the security deposit was yet to be determined, but Meme thought they shouldn't hold their breath on that. Heather voluntarily moved, if a frog-march be said to be elective, and was remanded to confinement under her parent's roof with the term of incarceration yet to be determined.

When they left the building, Heather's mother berated her by asking, "What in the world were you thinking spending all day by the pool listening to rock music, smoking pot, and sleeping with a black man?"

"When you put it that way, I wish I had done it sooner," Heather said.

Clayton was inconsolable without Heather, and it wasn't long before he moved back home. There was a cruel symmetry that year when Laurel was expelled from New York, and Clayton refused California. LA wasn't enough of what he was expecting, and too much of what he wasn't.

A new building, breaking ground next to ours, obliterated the view from Victor's apartment, and he decided to find alternative accommodation. Before this momentous move, we went to San Francisco, where Victor was part of the Nob Hill social elite, so we stayed at the Fairmont Hotel. While Victor's son Keith and I traversed the hairpin turns of Lombard Street, cavorted in Chinatown, and fed sea lions off Fisherman's Wharf, Meyera was falling in love. Seems San Francisco really is where many hearts are left.

Meyera was standing with a group of Victor's friends at a cocktail party in the Venetian Room where Tony Bennett first sang, *I Left My Heart in San Francisco*. Well-dressed conservative natives were sharing a reverence for the track's inaugural location, but Meyera wanted to talk about *Bullet* and that incomparable car chase with Steve McQueen.

The superiority that San Francisco lords over Los Angeles was growing tiresome, and she listened to a debate about which city was more sophisticated. Struggling to stifle a yawn, she noticed a good-looking gentleman making his way over to her by the name of Bernard Bennett, who thankfully, was no relation to Tony.

Bernard worked in Washington, D.C. as a high-ranking member of the Air Force, and Meyera wasn't the only woman to wrestle her eyes off him. She was in great spirits, looked stunning, and they hit it off immediately. Dating aggressively, they were available for press photos snapped on several occasions, confirming they were a handsome, if not golden, couple who met at the Golden Gate. San Francisco is a city of romance, sparking a serious relationship enabling robust Yang to settle in with Mom, while Yin accompanied my father.

Meyera's good fortune continued a winning streak, and she passed the California Real Estate Exam. To celebrate, we sold the apartment building and bought a house on Old Ranch Road, which was so spectacular, that three words don't do it justice. Mom's first paid commission shored up her confidence, validating the struggle she'd braved to get there, and living in Sullivan Canyon was to reside in a seventh heaven located off Sunset Boulevard. Rustic corrals and hiking trails characterized the canyon, enhanced by swimming pools, tennis courts and a smattering of movie stars.

Cliff May's California Ranch-style architecture wasn't to everyone's taste or financial reach, and there's a caveat to canyon living requiring a love of horses, dogs, children, and dust. Joni Mitchell wrote *Ladies of the Canyon* a few miles away, and while listening to her distinctive album, we became the children of ours.

1780 Old Ranch Road was a three-bedroom home with a generous living room and patio space, creating a secluded *bijou* sanctuary. Last in and first out of the moving van was that long green couch, which remained under a beamed ceiling by the living room fireplace for the next twenty-one years. Sliding glass doors, stretching full-length toward the patio, visually invited the outdoors in, where a second fireplace in the dining room made the most mundane meal more appetizing.

The property had ample room to build a corral, but my pony, April was in Malibu, so we left the avocado, peach, and lemon trees in that portion of land undisturbed. River Ridge Riding Stable also represented refuge, which wasn't surprising since it was overlooked by Serra Retreat. Run by Franciscan friars with fantastic taste, this ecumenical haven could pass for heaven, defined by any denomination seeking utopia. Opposite the river, separating our stable from private property, I noticed a familiar looking man flying a kite with whom I presumed was his grandson.

Without thinking, I said, "Atticus, Atticus Finch?"

While reeling in a grounded kite, he smiled and said, "So I've been called in screen credit."

I was starstruck, and not just by Gregory Peck, but that would've been enough. Talking with a literary hero come to life was a treat, and I kept a close eye on that location yet never saw Mr. Peck there again. I never saw him anywhere else, for that matter. Meme didn't see many people when we moved to the canyon and missed having casual chats as she'd done at the building.

When in need of conversation, she'd simply open the garage door before inviting passersby to look at her impromptu garage sale. Our mailman regularly participated out of a sense of duty, but everyone else engaged in shopping while having a pleasant chat and, as far as Meme was concerned, the more the merrier. This was an excellent solution to her occasional lonely blues until Meyera discovered several significant items of furniture, artwork and books missing, thanks to Meme's bargain basement price.

An awkward crossover in clientele made matters worse when Mom's first real estate assignment was to find a home for actress Bea Arthur, famous for playing irascible roles in popular sitcoms including *Maude* and *The Golden Girls*. Meyera was having a tough time coping with the demands of an exacting buyer and complained about working with a typecast character, given endless questions about whose dumb idea it was to put this near that.

The list of grievances generated on each showing made Meyera's heart sink, but even sink became a sensitive word because her client didn't care for any she'd seen. Meyera hadn't the foggiest notion of what she was supposed to do other than call each architect, asking what motivated a particular design. Her feet ached, her head hurt, and her feelings registered anger. This wasn't a toe in the water start; it was a fire hose pointed directly at her.

Meyera was virtually weeping with exhaustion when, finally, they found a home that Bea was willing to buy without putting Cliff May through the rigors of her theories on design. Meme was delighted but looked sheepish while quietly taking me aside to confess there may be a problem. Never a good start to any conversation, but it seems my grandmother had another bout of those damn blues and held a brief garage sale in a bid to cure it when a woman she recognized from television burst in demanding to buy a large Venetian mirror with two matching lamps.

Meme had no idea who this woman was, and only later realized it was Bea Arthur. She asked what I thought we should do, segueing from her problem to we who must solve it, as per the code between us. We shared a solidarity that no entity could break, and any union would be proud of. I suggested that Mom needn't be appraised that Bea Arthur purchased her things, and Bea would be unlikely to guess that Meyera was the source of her new Italian treasures. With enough dust sheets to cover what's left, Mom might not notice anything at all.

Meme's spontaneous sales attracted a lot of attention, and by employing this slightly skewed method of introducing herself, she became acquainted with most of our neighbors. She enjoyed great popularity at the annual Canyon Christmas party when people of radically different ages would sit next to her seeking a chat.

Conversation soon turned to consultation when she'd field questions ranging from early Los Angeles history to more personal topics concerning marriage. Famous for her candor, and flattered by the attention, she'd take a long drag from her Tareyton 100 cigarette before dispensing advice such as sleep adequately, avoid sugar, and spend less than you make. Adults were reminded to treat their spouses with the same level of courtesy extended to a common stranger.

A member of Motown's Rare Earth lived up the road, and when *Get Ready* went platinum, a gold Corvette coupe roared in the canyon, rivaling Cliff May's tan Continental. Both were driven like bats out of hell, sending kids on horses scrambling for cover. At seventeen, Cece was a canyon siren who appeared partially naked even when dressed. She catered to clients at the Trancas Canyon Beach Salon, booked appointments and attended aftercare in ways that attracted women from Zuma to Ventura.

They came for a cut and color, but returned more frequently than necessary to see the weed wielding receptionist at the door. Procuring pot to a mature customer base was profitable, and patrons were able to relax with something other than a margarita.

Cece made an obscene amount of money working only on Saturday, and her mother turned a blind eye to this venture but refused to allow the sale of pot in the canyon. Throwing a tantrum, Cece bravely addressed her mother as Woman, and I could hardly wait for the next *contretemps* with Meyera allowing me to use this generic term, but when I did, Meyera asked if I'd gone stark raving mad. So much for the poetic idiom pervading the music industry's kids.

The diversity of homeowner occupation dissolved under the canyon's unifying atmosphere, and sharing an exceptional place provided a powerful element that can't be ascribed to blind advantage alone. This backdrop shaped our lives, and, as with epic films, the sense of location influenced and embraced us.

Several psychiatrists, psychologists, and therapists living in the canyon noticed this phenomenon. Inspiring years of speculation from all quarters of that profession, including their adolescent progeny, who wondered just how many times we'd been cited in professional papers. Whether a particular parent's practice was Analytic, Gestalt or even Bioenergetics, they all agreed we appeared on every page of their adolescent development books. To a man (but mostly women), they were fascinated by the concept that this place eased puberty.

While the professionals wrote about their offspring, I walked through adolescence with a selection of kids and parents alike. It didn't take long to join this circle, and the process was reminiscent of playing jump rope with three. You need to watch the motion, the swing, and the selection of when to leap into the beat. Social Darwinism to start, and robust infusion at the end made Sullivan Canyon a fantastic place to be.

CHAPTER 22

My friends in LA were affluent but didn't possess the arrogance normally associated with piles of money. Most attended private school, but a few went to public, where they were unencumbered by hours of homework, papers to write, or a plethora of teachers to please. This sounded attractive, and I attended Paul Revere Junior High, which was a short walk ending in a huge leap from academic study.

I transferred my way from a C to an A but unwittingly went into a modified war zone. Busing wasn't a word I'd heard before stepping into tuition-free territory. The concept of shifting kids from lesser LA Unified City School Districts to better ones was a new one for me. A legally sanctioned way of saying a long overdue sorry for unforgivable oppression, benign discrimination is a good idea, but integration wasn't working, as described in *Black & White* by Three Dog Night. If we'd followed the lyrics to the letter, things might've been different. Starting out together rather than navigating puberty would've stood us a better chance of assimilation. After hours of riding on a bus, asking teenagers to blend was as effective as adding colors to an emulsion mixer, expecting to find plaid paint.

I was assigned a shared locker, which was something of a novelty considering the solo accommodation I was accustomed to in private school, and at the barn. Small cards were issued in homeroom detailing the number, combination, and name of the girl with whom I'd act as locker-partner, but turning the dial right, left, and right, I might as well have set it to 6-6-6.

Although a few dicey items, such as scissors and a Swiss Army Knife could be found in my tack box, it was a surprise to find my partner's supply which went beyond the stationary counter, approximating a vault the Crips or Bloods would envy. Most of the weaponry was disguised as hair grooming equipment, and she stashed enough to survive a siege, if not mount one.

My locker-mate deserved some space she could call her own, and shutting the door on this arsenal, I said, "It's all yours Yahna."

Fiona Maxim lived in Venice Beach, and when visiting, I was impressed by the level of affection Mrs. Maxim felt toward her husband. It was impossible not to notice the way his wife leaped to the phone when he called in from business trips. She retrieved the ringing sound with a smile in her voice, connoting joyous enthusiasm. For an investment banker with a large office on Franklin Avenue, he made a lot of out-of-town house calls, but Fiona's mother worshiped him, so he must've been quite a guy.

Fiona's parents met in high school, and Mrs. Maxim (nee whatever maiden name) was enchanted from the get-go. Aiming to look up his schedule, she took a student job in the administration office and transferred herself into most of the classes he was enrolled in. Debate, advanced calculus, and drama, she braved them all — except woodshop and football. Her plan worked.

After graduation, they wed, bought a modest house, and had Fiona, representing everything a couple could want. Only hitch was Mr. Maxim wanted a bit on the side as well. Mrs. Maxim harbored suspicions but tried to keep dangerous thoughts to herself. As did her daughter, who said nothing despite feeling that something sinister was afoot. This didn't soften the blow when the doorbell rang, and two detectives asked to be allowed in, but before they'd sat down, Fiona knew the reason for their visit.

Mrs. Maxim had been informed of her husband's infidelity by two well-wishing friends and was unable to sleep after that. Nighttime was the worst. The cineplex in her mind was designed by devils, conjuring torturous thoughts more hellish than Hades. The image of her husband in bed with another woman cut her to the quick, and she retained a private investigator, hoping for proof of the rumor's inaccuracy.

The identity and address of her rival were soon obtained, but impassioned attempts to reconcile with her husband failed. She remonstrated, begged, and pleaded with him to stay, but her efforts were in vain; he wasn't willing to come home. Mr. Maxim was lost forever, and coming to that conclusion caused Mrs. Maxim to lose her mind.

Cleaning the house to its customary varnished perfection, she attended to the laundry in the same way, taking her time to carefully fold and iron. She applied fresh makeup and *coiffed* her hair before driving to Benedict Canyon, pulling up in front of the house belonging to her husband's mistress. Observing the restricted parking rules, she was pleased to have arrived after ticketing hours and knocked on the door.

When it opened, Mrs. Maxim confirmed the identity of the woman standing in front of her, needing to be certain it was she who stole her husband, life, and soul. Placing a Walther PPK pistol to her temple and pulling the trigger, it only took one bullet for Mrs. Maxim to kill herself, destroying everyone else around her.

Meyera's troubles were of a more mundane nature, and working in real estate claimed much of her time, requiring a solution to the six day a week stable run, which would've been seven, but our trainer insisted we give the horses a day off. Brittany and her elder sister Naomi were long-standing clients at River Ridge. Stunning, and socially gifted, they exemplified what California can do when creating creatures of exceptional beauty.

Naomi was six years my senior, and Brittany was ahead by four, but their reputation as the beautiful Shay sisters paved the way for almost anything, such as the discretionary withholding of speeding tickets, which were dismissed after a single smile. Should they add a light laugh, everyone concerned considered it a well-deserved tip. Naomi's peaches and cream complexion was accented by rich red hair surrounding large blue-eyes, while Brittany's darker skin, deep brown-eyes and incredibly white smile reflected a certain light.

Both siblings illuminated whatever they looked at, and the only being impervious to their gaze was a Saint Bernard called Snowball, who presided over the air-conditioner in their kitchen, depriving the room of relief. He was a pleasant and jolly fellow deep down, but the high-temperature had him on the ropes, where long strings of saliva gathered at his jowls before descending bungee-style down to the ground. It wouldn't take much to move them, but to move at all was too much for him to consider. Not when stationed dead center of a draft, shady spot, or wet puddle.

Snowball struggled to cope and, while heroically applying himself to the task, no one could bear to budge him. California was a challenge for the poor chap, and even with Snowball's aspirational name, the air-con did little to dispel his discomfort.

Naomi drove us to the stable before Brittany turned sixteen and obtained her license, but Naomi's mind was transitioning away from the stable toward higher education. On the day of a horse show, Naomi was under the covers, coping with her first heartbreak, making it difficult to rouse her for the drive to Bell Canyon, where we'd ride her horse Smidge in different classes. This was an audition to see if Smidge and I got along and, if so, Naomi might allow me to buy him.

Calling her a third time, I said, "It's time to get up, pick me up, and go."

Twenty minutes later, her passenger door swung open to receive me on a rainy day that soaked us all the way down to our boots under a solid grey sky. It was raining inside the car as well. Naomi was inconsolable while filling the silence on my passenger side with tears. Carole King's *Tapestry* underscored her lament about losing Robbie, but as far as I could tell, he wasn't all that great, not if he could do this. I'd never seen emotional damage done to a friend before, and hitting the freeway, we went from carpool, to car flood.

Naomi asked me to dig out her wallet with his photos in it, and I found one she was referring to, in addition to one of them kissing, with Robbie's hand flying the bird when the image was snapped. Snapped and now broken is how I'd describe Naomi, but I was at a disadvantage not knowing how to provide comfort.

Being on the precipice of puberty but not quite at the teenage border made my council ineffective, and while my heart went out to her, I was too young to understand romance gone wrong. The best I could deliver from the passenger seat was sympathetic silence, punctuated by the sounds made on the end of a telephone line. Embellishing my indistinct mumbles with words would be a disaster when asked, "Why had he slept with someone else, and what was she going to do?"

Never have I wanted questions to be rhetorical more than those, and Naomi sobbed while signaling to change freeway lanes. The only thing I had to offer was physical presence in lieu of substance, and without knowing Robbie, I disliked him intensely. Even when absent, he remained a powerful presence that morphed into the first emotionally painful event I witnessed befall a friend. As with other significant occurrences, this took root on a recognizable timeline, becoming personally historic, and although confined to memory, it still retains some punch.

Brittany's love life was a complete contrast to her sister's. She was fully in control, in demand, and in the limelight wherever she went. After receiving her driver's license, she took charge of transport to the stable, and I'd wait for her outside Pali High, where she couldn't have been easier to spot. Tall, lean, and laughing, she had a trail of guys behind her in a male parade. It wasn't just her blinding beauty, but her charm that made everyone laugh, as she did while waving her entourage away.

We jumped into her brand-new sports car, which was another example of her stratospheric luck. Brittany dated liberally, freely, and spontaneously but rarely allowed return engagements, other than an association with the boy down the block, which continued steadily.

His father ran the Mazda dealership for all Southern California, and even he couldn't believe his son's good fortune in scoring Brittany. For her sixteenth birthday, he procured a limited edition Mazda, fully loaded with five forward gears, a sunroof, and a quadraphonic stereo. Known for rotary engines, this piston model was one of less than a hundred manufactured under special license from Japan, with custom metallic light-blue paint adorned on delivery by a massive red bow.

Driving like the wind along PCH, we listened to *Let It Bleed*, which goes well with the end of a continent. Finding the right track on Brittany's Blaupunkt was easy with her breakneck speed up, and the sunroof down. The ocean made an ideal accompaniment to tracks such as

You Can't Always Get What You Want, yet we seemed to do exactly that when local police warned us about speed traps by indicating with their hands that we should slow down.

Radar enforced areas of ticketing change frequently, but thanks to Brittany's smile, we remained one step ahead. Describing her dates from the night before, she felt it important that I know a few things in advance of expressing interest in boys. While I wondered whether my pony April should wear the red or blue halter, Brittany told me about blowjobs and sex.

"Making love is much more fun with the lights on," she said. "Turning them off is a big turn off; take it from me. Going down on a guy is an act of generosity that's always appreciated, so no need to be stingy on that front. *Fellatio* is a fabulous way to show that you care and, in time, you'll perfect this practice. Adding a personal touch to individual technique takes a while, so don't worry about awkward first attempts. Remember, most guys regard even a mediocre blowjob as magnificent. Don't be afraid to laugh in bed since it's supposed to be exhilarating and, with the right guy, it's the most fun imaginable. You've got a lot to look forward to."

Brittany's sexual seminars were a long way from Laurel and Alex's sedate summers, but a damn sight more interesting. Arriving at the barn at warp speed, I resembled the guy in Maxell's advertisement, who was blown back by the g-force sound, but I loved that Mazda.

Our trainer looked at Brittany and said, "This year, she wants your sister's horse, and now she has her eye on your car. Better be careful, or she'll nab all your boyfriends too."

When Brittney dropped me off at home, I opened the mailbox and found the airline ticket for my departure to New York the following week. My heart didn't just sink; it felt as if it had been rubbed against a cheese grater. This journey would be made during a night flight. I wanted to arrive fresh for the inevitable challenges on the East Coast, and after unpacking, I intended to luxuriate in a long hot bath, but my father was anxious to hit the shops in Manhattan.

George and I made it to the seventh floor, but there are twelve in total, with a pool on the roof. Madison Avenue is famous for advertising agencies, but it's not all 'mad men' and boasts a world-class emporium at 45th Street. The urban location contrasts with the wares on display, and everything needed to track, trap, tame or obliterate is here.

Since 1892, Abercrombie & Fitch have set the sporting goods standard and are to wilderness equipment what FAO Schwarz is to toys. This is where President Roosevelt, Charles Lindbergh, Amelia Earhart, and Ernest Hemmingway bought their hunting, shooting, camping, and fishing gear. My father continues this tradition under the glassy-gaze of gazelle and moose heads mounted on the walls with the same vacant look as Trigger. Stepping around elephant foot umbrella stands is suggestive of safari, and the same could be said of my father's big game retailing assistants, one of whom struggles under the volume of our gear while the other squires us to the gun section. This is my father's mecca, if not mother ship, and I asked if he'd regret pointing a rifle at Rudolph or going bang-bang to Bambi.

George was caressing a Remington, and laughed before saying, "Are you kidding? After two or three days tracking the damn deer, if you haven't shot one, you're ready to drop a bomb on them."

It was a slow summit to the eighth floor. Prizing himself away from the cornucopia of contraband on the seventh wasn't easy. It stirred separation anxiety, but the array of fly-fishing tackle upstairs made for a soft transition. With over eighteen thousand lures and forty-eight thousand flies, the comprehensive stock was ready to be dispensed in accordance with the gentlemen's choice, guided by experts with encyclopedic knowledge. This is where fine-tuning happens, and anglers align location with lure to land the right result.

The rooftop pool was used for casting lessons, designed to enhance fishing technique, rather than work out what actor should play which role, so I returned to the cash register where our stack stretched full-length across the counter. Customers stared at us, and I couldn't decipher if this was because we commandeered the place or wiped out most of the merchandise. With each purchase, the cash register rang in a symphony of spending.

A turbocharged barbeque, open-fire copper kettle and cool box awaiting monogram were followed by a collapsible mahogany table with twelve folding chairs and limited edition antler cutlery. Spode bone china, in settings of the same number, featured the game we wished to place on those plates. When I suggested we use plastic, George was appalled. Had I asked Julia Child to prepare instant macaroni or offered da Vinci a ballpoint pen, his expression would've been just as aghast. China is what we had at home, on the boat, and what we'd use in the wilderness.

When asked if Aunt Louise and Maude would join us, George said, "There won't be any Ferragamo heels around the fire."

A can of snake repellent and an even bigger bottle of spray discouraging bears were added to our haul. We had everything, from balms for bites to more serious medical supplies required for intensive surgery in a third-world nation.

George asked, "Why the worried look when you know scorpions and spiders prefer to be left alone? A vacation in the wild doesn't include embroidered toilet paper."

Aunt Louise and Maude invited us for dinner at the Rainbow Room, where two men at the table next to ours swapped jokes like seasoned tennis partners. Pretending to focus my attention elsewhere enabled me to hear several knee-slappers without detection until I laughed at one joke, which went as follows: *Nixon, Eisenhower and Kennedy are on the Titanic as it's sinking. Eisenhower points to the lifeboat and says, 'Women and children first,' but Nixon climbs in, saying, 'Screw the women,' to which Kennedy replies, 'Do you think we have time?'*

Maude asked about our shopping expedition, and George mentioned how pleased he was with the new tent chandelier. The band played *My Funny Valentine* before segueing to Charlie Chaplin's composition *Smile,* which was punctuated by Louise in soprano. I wasn't a barometer of talent, but I didn't need to be when recognizing she didn't possess the level required of a professional singer.

Circumstances quashed her dream before she'd had a chance to test aptitude, and it was the same with her painting. All her canvasses were filled with bright, happy colors and bungled representational images, leaving no doubt that her pursuit of the arts should be confined to pleasure. She'd never know that the source of her bliss was both blind and tone-deaf because the muse wasn't evaluated; therefore, it would never desert her. Nor would the rapture she derived from singing as an amateur devoted to an avocation for fun.

The concept of blissful ignorance made sense, especially if the alternative involves a harsh confrontation with absent skill. No *forte* to accompany *Furia Divina*? No one wants that. Providence watered down what couldn't have been into what might, enabling her to duck disappointment without knowing it. Some heroes are better left unsung. Stephen Sondheim's *Send In the Clowns* took sentimentalists into a spiral among patrons and servers alike.

I laughed and said, "By all means, send in some clowns as quickly as possible."

CHAPTER 23

Clayton met the Abercrombie & Fitch delivery van. He was tasked with packing our car.

Shaking his head while surveying the lot, he said, "You sure did buy a bundle, and I believe Armageddon could be survived with half the amount."

Fly-fishing equipment was loaded as a top-priority over more mundane items such as suitcases, and I was instructed to ensure mine had a selection of dresses. When I asked if they'd be needed at a campsite, my father gave me a lecture about well-brought-up young ladies dressing appropriately at all times.

After several adjustments, the car was packed, and George peeled out of the driveway but came to a sudden stop, tooting the horn three times before saluting Clayton, who returned the gesture as we hit the road. George needn't have worried about the surprise aspect of our destination. I slept for most of the ten-hour journey. It was easy to doze during George's telling of the longest joke in history involving a haunted house. If Jesus thought his father's house had many mansions, he'd no idea how many George could come up with. This tale rivaled the length of Homer's. Granted, it was a long drive, and neither of us were particularly interested in show tunes.

Arriving at what looked like a Norman chateau in Canada, a smart squadron of luggage attendants came streaming out from underneath turrets and towers crowning an enormous high-pitched copper roof. Le Manoir Richelieu is located on a cliff overlooking the St. Lawrence River, with stupendous views in all directions.

George smiled and said, "We won't be roughing it. No sleeping, lounging, or dining surrounded by anything other than Louis Fifteenthinspired furnishings. Rather than tarps and tents, we'll have silk tapestries, but the fly-fishing gear will be used. Absolutely all of it, which is what the trip to Abercrombie & Fitch was actually for. The rest was window dressing to shore up the joke and throw you off-track. All this equipment made the ruse seem real, and your expression, when convinced that dresses were needed for camping, was well worth the investment."

Looking at the mountain of gear, he cursed not having a camera to hand, but the gag remained one of his favorites. He said that a wealthy man would be attracted to this world-class hotel while a wealthy fisherman is drawn to the lake, but we'd enjoy both. Wild Atlantic salmon was among the finds my father wanted on the end of his line, and first thing in the morning, we'd hire a guide.

Le Manoir was plush, reflecting Cardinal Richelieu's reign, and his presence was felt in every nook, cranny, and recessed fireplace. When wandering off looking at the art, George panicked, having no idea in what direction I'd gone, and quickly calculated that the building extends 425 feet, which was ample room to roam, if not conduct, a cattle drive. Calling my name in a cadence, all parents recognize as controlled hysteria, he walked so fast as to constitute a controlled run, allowing anxiety to increase under the Cardinal's watchful eye. The Richelieu crest and coat of arms were everywhere that I wasn't, but a bellboy emerged from underneath a French wrought iron fixture offering to help.

George snapped and said, "This is serious. My daughter's missing, and I insist on speaking with an adult. Find someone who didn't travel to work by skateboard."

George couldn't abide skateboards and sawed the light-blue one given to me by a tenant in half, making me reluctant to introduce him to my pony. The concierge found me gazing at a portrait and escorted me back to my father, asking if we'd like some refreshments. I opted for a Shirly Temple, and my father requested something stronger than a Roy Rogers.

Each day, our first port of call was the Bait & Tackle shop, which listed business hours as open mostly before noon. I mistook George's mention of maggots, worms, and flies for another ill-fated attempt at humor, but the joke was on me. The flies from Abercrombie & Fitch represented angling artistry in the form of aquatic origami designed to attract and kill, but those carefully crafted imposters weren't alive. To disguise the fish fact from falsehood required both real and synthetic lures, so we purchased live bait. Any relationship between my rod and a fish would be a matter for my father or the guide. All I had to do was cast and catch, which wasn't a problem if I studiously avoided the business end of fishing. By tacit agreement, the creepy crawlies that captured their imagination would remain anonymous to me.

The guide put unspeakable things in his mouth before hooking them on the line. This might've been a ritual to appease the mountain gods, believed by locals to disapprove of those who work on Sunday, but it was Wednesday, so why put a maggot in your mouth? Fishing in Charlevoix is a favored spot for those seeking rainbow trout and Chinook salmon.

The deep water of this glacial-fed lake can sustain these species, which appear in the shallows early morning and late afternoon when the temperature drops. Brown trout is popular, occupying the lower depths, and with so many varieties at various levels, I regarded the lake as a liquid lasagna.

A Perspex box in the bait shop contained the skeleton of a Northern pike with treacherous teeth badly in need of orthodontia, and the thought of those extended jaws swimming at the depth of the lake made me nervous. I determined to stay in the boat. No matter how many we caught, there'd be fewer out, than in, the water.

The bait shop had the air of an abattoir tailored to fishing. Rows of tubs, tanks, and barrels filled the place, containing critters thought by fish to be extremely fetching. Whatever you wanted on your line, plate or perhaps even your wall, they had the bait to attract it. While peering into a vast vat, I noticed a boy looking at monsters of a more amphibious nature.

Tripping over kids my age was always a benefit, and I asked what he was looking at. He didn't reply and, assuming he was shy, I leaned over to see for myself and then shrieked at the sight of frog and lizard creatures.

George was at the back of the shop, where customers weren't allowed to go, and hollered, "Stop screaming. There's no point in speaking English to the locals, they won't understand you."

No wonder the boy ran away. Approaching him a second time, I trotted out my rudimentary Spanish and said, "*Hola! Como estas?*"

Despite my humming *Oye Como Va*, he marched determinedly out the door, and watching his retreat, I decided to give it a try in French, which isn't my strongest language, but I can fake it for short periods of time. It was my last attempt at establishing contact, considering he'd be unlikely to know Yiddish.

"*Salut!*" I said, with feeling. "*Como Sava?*" I added, with what I regarded as considerable *suave*.

There was no response, but had he replied in French, I'd have been in trouble. I'm brave to begin, but a coward at the end of each non-English sentence. When it comes to foreign languages, I'm a premature communicator. At least I'd tried to observe the kid code of being friendly when out on the road, but he waltzed over to where his father and their guide were packing a boat just like ours.

Staring at him, I knew it would be a matter of minutes before he felt compelled to look back. This globally effective trick is unencumbered by language barriers, and eventually, he looked in my direction. I stuck my tongue out, prompting him to tug at his father's sleeve while pointing toward me. By the time his dad looked up, I was looking intently at our boat, and when his father returned to the task at hand, I fanned my hands from either side of my head in a pejorative gesture. Tapping his father on the shoulder, he said something that visibly irritated his dad, who glanced over to where I was standing focused on wiping my sunglasses. This game was shaping up to be more fun than friendship.

Angry Monkey was a facial expression I'd been perfecting for years. It's instinctive and presumably derived from primates but remarkably effective when employed by humans. In the absence of words or the luxury of time, Angry Monkey can be used to express a range of emotions, from disappointment to aggression.

No subtitles are needed to understand the message. This caustic grimace is internationally recognizable, but not to the boy's father, thanks to my split-second timing. Pulling at his dad's belt, the boy lodged a third complaint, causing his father to slowly but deliberately stand up before thwacking him hard on the head. It was the only sound clearly heard from where I stood, and the boy ran to hide behind the landing.

Leaving him undisturbed, as you would a wounded animal, I was mortified while wondering to whom I should apologize first, assuming I could find a way to do so. The most elaborate and extended game of charades would be insufficient to express my culpability, but time to rectify the situation evaporated when I was called to our craft.

It was a small boat, requiring me to stay as still and quiet as the lake surrounding us. Fresh air, clear water, and a huge sky created a calm such as I'd never known. Anglers don't talk while fishing for reasons more soothing than not frightening the prey, but serenity surrenders at the sound of a strike. The battle commenced between my father and a huge brown trout. Both ends of the rod remained determined.

"That's right, let it play," the guide said. "Not too much line and not too fast."

George maneuvered the fish away from the rocks, instigating a struggle with nature. First is the hook, followed by a splash, turning to terror before the chase. The fish floundered for a few seconds while the water returned to still, in a process that was repeated as we came close to the final catch. Zigzagging fiercely left and abruptly right, the fish resisted, making everyone's behavior dramatic.

George was wound more tightly than the line connecting him to the trout when he hollered for the landing net. He caught it, and a mighty beast wrested from the water was flailing furiously in the woven trap held by the guide. The bait bucket spilled toward me, and although not happy about this, I would normally have let it slide, but siding toward me was something abnormal. Webbed feet on a wet surface sail incredibly swiftly, and although our guide reached for the salamander, he missed it, enabling this prehistoric predator to surf the bottom of our boat in a direct line for me.

My father handed me the net to free his hands for the immediate task of bait capture, and his aim was steady if a little long, to calculate. Not dissimilar to the trout, our renegade salamander moved manically left and right, with each shift mirrored by my more substantial leanings, causing our boat to rock. George had the newt in hand and handed it to the guide before handing his free hand to me, which was to receive the net, but he remained empty-handed. I dropped it and didn't even realize I'd done so until after it was gone.

Silence of a different nature followed, of a type that usually accompanies bereavement. Fishing is a three-act play, and on this day, it was a tragedy. That salamander became a symbol of international friendship gone wrong, and I deserved some form of retribution but didn't expect it to arrive in the form of an amphibian.

Dinner helped mollify miffed spirits. Bear goulash and wild boar took the edge off disappointment. Scarfing down a savage supper soothed our bruised, angling appetite, and George achieved closure by applying Kubler-Ross's five stages of grief to fly-fishing. We dined well while waiting for our lake expeditions to prove more successful, and we didn't wait long.

It was either blind luck, proficiency, or the fact we weren't fishing on a Sunday that attracted the blessing of the gods. Whatever force was at work enabled us to catch forty-seven rainbow trout in the space of five hours. I'd cast my line, and before it dropped, at least three fish would rise volleyball style, all calling, "Mine."

Our catch egregiously exceeded the number allowed by permit, but Manoir Richelieu's contacts ensured blind eyes were turned, enabling our considerable success to become chef's special that night. Perfect timing. We were heading home the next day, and George was melancholy about leaving the lake. Returning to the rigors of New York would be demanding, but I tried to lift his spirits *Casablanca* style by mentioning we'd always have the Kodak Colorama, where Eastman delivered what nature could not, sixty-feet-wide by eighteen-feet-tall.

Laughing at my reference to the world's largest transparency, George said, "I bring you to Quebec, and you pine for Central Terminal."

When we returned to Manhattan, I called Meyera, who was flustered and rushed to get off the phone. She was happy to hear from me but busy packing for a weekend with Bernard Bennet in Georgetown, where he'd like her to meet various people during several dinners ranging from casual to formal. In high spirits, enjoying the process of selecting which outfits to bring, her preparations weren't confined to clothes and included a bikini wax treatment so painful she offered to pay the beautician double the amount to stop. When asked if she'd like Aloe Vera lotion, Meyera requested a fire extinguisher instead. Mom was so immersed in her travel plans that she momentarily forgot to ask how things were on my end.

"Did you enjoy fishing in Canada?" Mom asked. "Hang on, I've dropped a cigarette and can't find it. It's burning, and I can smell it. Give me a second, will you? Damn, I just found another one already lit in the ashtray. What's it doing there? Okay, here it is; I found it. The first one is right by my foot under the bed. That's better. Are you looking forward to Maine? I always had a soft spot for George and Lucille. They were a great help, or at least tried to be when your father and I started to breakup. Do give them my love, but I've got to go. Haven't even begun to pack, so big kiss and bye for now."

I had the sneaking suspicion that the storyline in California had moved on a pace, and similar to a soap opera junkie, I felt the jangled twist of separation from my series. There was a more serious playing for keeps attitude about them lately, but the butterfly hadn't quite emerged from the chrysalis, and until it did, Meyera was likely to remain skittish.

"Okay Mom, have fun," I said. "Take care, and don't flirt with any bikers," I cautioned, referring to our Northern California drive.

It had been a little over a year since Meyera met Bernard in San Francisco, where she'd been elated from the start. Her optimism influenced everything she touched, spilled, or stained with sugared up black coffee. Our road map was covered almost entirely by overlapping circles of cups past. It resembled a caffeine version of the Olympic rings but was legible enough to lead us from California State Route 1 to 17 Mile Drive, along a breathtaking coastal road running through Carmel and Monterey. Our journey became even more hair-raising when a gang of Hells Angels spontaneously escorted us.

Riding in the back of our Mercury Comet station wagon, I was the first to see them. Two or three bikers was no cause for concern, but twenty-five to thirty is a different matter. Although Fontana is credited as the organization's birthplace, Monterey is a significant location, often regarded as Hells Angels' head office, and this was unquestionably their patch. I waved at them, and they looked lasciviously at Meyera while gunning their engines.

They circled, spiraled, and squired our car without her consent, but Mom masked her fear by saying, "I don't know what all the fuss is about. You're too young, and I'm too old."

Launching into *Born to Be Wild,* I followed with *Motorcycle Mama,* adapting it to Meyera as circumstances dictated, but Mom maintained single-minded concentration on the road. Driving steadily, she allowed nothing to interrupt her eyeline in an unblinking stare kept on the highway. The entire entourage of motorcyclists could've been riding naked with their hair on fire, and she'd have ignored them.

Meyera wasn't going to dignify their presence and asked, "Please stop singing songs from what I presume might be from their initiation ceremony when I'm trying to concentrate."

The bandanas, engineer boots, and leather jackets were as impressive as patches indicating seniority, enabling me to play a Harley Davidson version of car bingo while spotting full and associate club members. Although better than identifying out-of-state plates, Meyera remained unimpressed by the parade of skull motifs and didn't want to engage in a discussion about beards. She didn't find it at all amazing that their hair didn't get tangled in the spokes or the fact several riders' fingernails rivaled Struwwelpeter's.

"To hell with this, I've had enough," Meyera announced. "Having been to Pamplona's bull run, this is the first time I've been made to feel like a bovine. How's about we buy some fresh strawberries and real honeycomb at the next stand?"

The produce in this part of the world is out of this world, and to call it superb would be an insult. The fruit tastes as if injected with sugar. It was a relief to pull over, off and away from the road, but it took ages for chaos to rush past, given their large number. The first to be seen doubled back theatrically, blowing a kiss before roaring down the highway. I had a road of my own to contend with, as driving to Maine with Maude would be a challenge.

George and I (accompanied by our dog Charlie) collected my grandmother. We traveled on banked roads, past birch trees bordering buildings built over a hundred years ago, by intrepid souls who tamed this beautiful but inhospitable land where everything had to be earned or conquered. Frugality was observed while achieving commodious living, but compared with these people, the Amish were positively bling.

George drove. Leaving Maude behind the wheel was tantamount to having Mr. Magoo control the car, and when we arrived, the atmosphere between Maude and Uncle George was frosty. I immediately began unpacking the kibble, grooming brushes, and dog bed for Charlie while my father confirmed his appreciation for allowing me to stay. George reiterated the fact that in New York, Charlie wasn't allowed to sleep on my bed, but Aunt Lucille winked at me, indicating that things might be different in Maine.

Glancing at his Breguet watch, George feigned surprise at the late hour, claiming they had to set off for the return drive. Wearing the same timepiece chosen by Napoleon, Victor Hugo, and Stendhal impressed my *pater*, who was pleased to employ it for staging an exit, enabling everyone to relax.

Uncle George asked if Louise still had a sign on her desk that advised clients to get the bastards before they get you, and I confirmed that she did. It was, however, placed in a drawer when the archdiocese came to call for investment advice. Uncle George conceded that for Lou to build from nothing was a grand achievement. One that could never be taken away. However, he took exception to those who relish riches when take is all they do.

"When it comes to deceit, they've fooled the best," Uncle George said. "Most notably themselves. Wealth should be relegated to bank balance and not be allowed to become a state of mind."

The problem between Uncle George and Aunt Louise started a long time ago when she advised on modest investments, but the money that was made quickly fell away. Having tasted the crumbs that fell from her table increased his hunger for a seat, and Uncle George wanted to dine with the big boys, having developed an appetite for greed.

"I bullied my way in when I should've walked out," Uncle George said. "But I stayed too long and got fleeced."

It wasn't a free ride he'd been looking for, but a helping hand to hear Uncle George tell it. Something was needed to get them back on their feet, but did Louise extend that lifeline of credit?

"Did she hell," Uncle George said. "With eyes averted, she lifted her skirt while stepping over the carnage. She's got a calculator for a heart that tabulates rather than beats. I've repaid all my debts with interest while keeping everything of real value. When you get right down to it, everything's on loan. Louise destroys the important things that, by definition, can't show up on a balance sheet, and her myopia is the most pernicious kind. Money doesn't strip us of manners. That's something she relinquished voluntarily. Enough about Louise. Maude's the one you need to keep a close eye on."

Uncle George had a few secrets, including a false foot prosthesis that remained hidden under his overalls. It would've escaped my attention had he not mentioned it, claiming the injury was caused by snakebite. A mighty viper, lurking in the brush, attacked him in the blink of an eye, and I tried to evict this image from my mind when Aunt Lucille placed a plastic carton on a string around my neck to hold the blackberries our dog Charlie and I were setting out to gather.

The screen door was still open, and we were halfway out when Uncle George said, "Watch out for snakes and have a good time."

We returned in record time with a full carton of fruit but were exhausted from our fast-forward mission. Aunt Lucille felt guilty about our pace, having been quickened by fear, and gently admonished Uncle George about the danger of fiction masquerading as truth. Taking me aside, she quietly confessed his false foot wasn't the result of a snakebite but was caused by something far more frightening, and that was his motorcycle, ridden in the rain under the influence of alcohol after an argument with Louise. A terrible trilogy that took his appendage and turned him forever abstentious, never touching grape or grain again. They were respected figures in the community, albeit one dedicated to the proposition that such a concept is superfluous.

Aunt Lucille drew water from a pump in the kitchen and placed it on the stove to heat. When ready, she filled a cast-iron tub with claw-and-ball feet and submerged me in luxurious bubbles. After soaking until the water turned tepid, I emerged like a newly minted penny.

Departing for New York the next day would be difficult, and Georgia O'Keeffe might've felt this way when Alfred Stieglitz inveigled her from Taos to the City. My father arrived, and Uncle George gave me a three-twirl spin after Aunt Lucille's bear-hug goodbye. As we drove away, they were standing in a pose that brought *American Gothic* to mind, had Grant Wood's figures been Rubenesque and happily waving.

CHAPTER 24

In LA, the topic for discussion concerned moving back East to Washington, and I could tell that Bernard Bennett had been to visit because Meyera's Steuben silver was out. The more streamlined pattern was polished to a blinding sheen and not by nuns at this time of year. Rather than read tea leaves, I discerned events based on place settings, making it easy to recognize that things were getting serious.

Accordingly, I paid a bit more attention to the relationship, although my interest was directed toward what impact this would have on my pony, April. Bernard Bennett was ascending the Air Force ladder, requiring him to remain in Georgetown, but he was handsome, polite, and successful. The fact he was divorced, without children, and interested in creating a ready-made family made him ideal.

I liked him for himself, his interest in me, and how impossibly happy he made Mom. Although nothing was written in stone, plans were beginning to take shape, and I expressed willingness to have a new home, school, and friends if furnished with a guarantee that our animal entourage would accompany us.

"Since Bernard's a decorated pilot," I said to Meyera, "does this mean we no longer fly commercially? Will the Air Force transport April, or do Flying Tigers have a Pegasus division?"

Wondering about sedation for April, I asked if FAA regulations would allow me to accompany her in the aircraft and, should that not be the case, perhaps train travel might be worth investigating. Throughout this conversation, I looked over at Meme, who was sitting on the long green couch, smoking with an air of detachment.

The ash from her Tareyton 100 cigarette was in a precarious but momentarily perfect arc that threatened to fall at any moment. Phlegmatic about cigarette hygiene at the best of times, her cavalier attitude didn't seem out of place; it was her absence of attention that caught mine.

"Does this mean you'll live at the Georgian?" I asked my grandmother.

The question referred to an Art Deco hotel on Ocean Avenue at the end of Route 66, home to one of LA's first speakeasies favored by Al Capone and Bugsy Seigel. It was where Clark Gable and Carole Lombard met for what they thought were private trysts, and where Charlie Chaplin and Humphrey Bogart propped up the bar during the day. This was also the place where Meme threatened to move when seriously displeased, making it clear she was unhappy.

As a provisional refuge, she had outstanding taste, and with recent developments, I wondered if this would comprise her safety net. Meme continued to smoke and gaze at the geraniums on the patio, bringing that cigarette all the way down to the bottom without breaking the bend in the ash. My grandmother was to smoking what our friend Lois achieved when peeling an orange. Both reached completion in one deft maneuver.

This formed the only unattractive aspect of my grandmother's attendance at the annual Canyon Christmas Party, where hosts delighted in her tales of lore but were quick to supply an ashtray. Many a Moroccan rug were billed as resilient, but no one wanted to put that warranty to the test, not in LA.

Meme said something vague about the future being a hard thing to get hold of. So many things shift before they take place, but she had a few ideas to mull over and would let us know. In point of fact, it was Lois who let us know, when she called early on Sunday morning asking to come over.

Lois arrived anxious but masked it by brandishing a bag of bagels. Oil stains on a second package promised Danish pastries I hoped survived the crushing weight of newspapers clutched against her chest.

Meme was still asleep, and Lois went into Meyera's room to talk in private, asking me to give it an hour or so before disturbing them.

She confirmed coffee was taken care of and hoisted two Styrofoam cups to prove it before disappearing into Mom's room. Ten minutes later, I heard wailing to rival the wall in Jerusalem. Lightening isn't supposed to strike twice, but perhaps there are no universal laws apportioning the pain we encounter. It's said a sword only cuts once, while the written word lacerates endlessly, and cut to ribbons was how Meyera felt after reading about Bernard Bennett's marriage to a Virginia socialite.

The society page called it a spontaneous gesture of love everlasting, but it was an impromptu move that just about killed Meyera. This devastating blow was made even more excruciating by its resemblance to her break with Jim Meyers. With Jim, we didn't know the reason for his flight into matrimony elsewhere, but with Bernard Bennett, we did. At least everyone did but Meyera.

During Meme's weekly conversation with her sister-in-law Betty, my grandmother mentioned she sent Bernard packing and confirmed we'd remain at home in Sullivan Canyon. If Meyera had to make a sacrifice, that was tough luck. Meme wasn't prepared to watch a man walk away with it all.

"I had a few seconds alone with Bernard when everyone was out of earshot," Meme said. "All I had to do was ask if he was looking forward to living with me as well?"

Betty was justifiably horrified and said, "Children aren't chattel. Stealing from your offspring is a particularly heinous form of theft. Especially when it involves the concerted annellation of their happiness to preserve a self-serving status quo. What you did should never be done. It may not be the eleventh hour, but it's well past nine Meyera time, and if she gets another shot at a solid future, I trust you won't interfere again."

The wedding announcement destroyed Meyera's matrimonial aspirations, placing her hopes of happiness out on the street during a critical make-or-break time. My grandmother didn't need more than a moment or two to destroy her daughter's future, and should there have been a level playing field, Meyera would've crossed the finish line but was spiked by *mal-intent* instead.

It takes time to create a relationship but only a second to destroy it. Meme pulled me aside, confirming we had the money to buy Naomi's thoroughbred Smidge, in addition to cash with which to build a corral for April in our backyard. Since we were staying put, she suggested we create a nice design around the avocado, peach, and lemon trees. April would become a home pet, and I'd have a new horse in Malibu.

"What do you say?" Meme asked. "Turn your pony into a Suzuki and start showing seriously?"

Having turned down the apple at Belmont Park racetrack, I accepted the orange in LA, and April moved to Old Ranch Road, where everyone bedded down, including Meyera, who elected to do so during an open house showing. Nerves had gotten the better of her when she had more flies through the door than prospective buyers, and toward the end of viewing hours, she helped herself to a nip, then a nap, followed by a rude awakening.

A stringent call from the real estate office insisted we remove her from the premises immediately, leaving no trace of this unprofessional mess. Meme was an outstanding navigator, which was a big help considering I've little to no sense of direction and was behind the wheel illegally, but we formed our own emotional economy run, struggling to stay on track while mitigating damage. Our talents were complementary, as we followed the same compass, moral and otherwise, leading to the open house where Meyera was waiting on a hardwood chair like a disciplined child.

Once in the car, Meme directed us to an address so far downtown I asked if we needed to swing back and get our passports. This detox center was new to us, and I suppose that was the point.

The last time we took Meyera to a recovery facility, she was asked, "What on earth is the almighty Meyera Zeiler doing here?"

A familiar scent greeted us when walking into that recovery center. It took a moment to realize the head of catering was wearing L'Heure Bleue by Guerlain from a more recent bottle that was given to her at the Zeiler residence in Freemont Place. Once renewed acquaintance was made, she couldn't stop laughing about the Zeiler's cook, Marvin, and how she came to fill his high-heeled shoes.

Ten days later, Mom came home, struggling to sweep up the scraps of her self-confidence, starting with the now imperceptible shards of a smashed and shattered start with Bernard Bennett. Sorrowful regret would be useless in the aim of reassembling herself, but she wanted to create a fresh new image to present to the world. Only trouble was she couldn't stop crying and, had we a swimming pool, she'd have filled it with tears. Finding another real estate office to work from was fairly easy, but choreographing the courage to continue proved more challenging.

Walking into Mom's bedroom, I watched as she greeted her reflection in the mirror while saying, "I'm Meyera and may I show you the house?"

April's move from Malibu allowed her to enjoy a brief period of stardom at Sullivan Canyon before infamy. She was crafty and learned to escape the confines of her corral Houdini-style, aiming for the grain shed across the street. One pony's bliss is a barn owner's rage, and this neighbor was a surgeon who flew into a rant when discovering April's Bacchanalian brawl. His face was incandescent when he threatened, "Get that pony off my property, or I'll shoot it dead."

I was tugging at April's halter with all my might, but the mare was overweight and, even if trim, more than capable of pulling three times her size.

It would take a while to prize her mouth from the alfalfa molasses bin, and to buy that time, I asked, "How do you reconcile saving lives all day with threatening to kill my pony?"

The surgeon living to our left was tolerant and forgave our dog for availing himself of their pool, which formed an irresistible destination for an English springer spaniel born to do the backstroke. I'd frequently receive a measured phone call informing me that, once again, Flush was refusing to depart the water despite knowing perfectly well where the steps were located.

Apologizing for the inconvenience, he'd ask me to either collect the pet or provide consent for the hose to be turned on him. At least the cat kept pretty much to himself, and we never had one word of complaint about Netter-boo. April redeemed herself by getting me out of a jam in junior high school.

Paul Revere is where students learned many things, including how to smoke, which was a function of peer pressure rather than a formal tutorial. When handed a lit cigarette in the girls' bathroom, I accepted, but was immediately apprehended, requiring me to meet with the principal. After admitting I was in possession of this incendiary item, my failure to actually smoke it wasn't a useful defense. The rules governing schoolground behavior forbade cigarettes and were controlling. Considering such hard data, I suggested amends be made by featuring April in a photo with students from the school-sponsored magazine drive.

"What's the point of Paul Revere without his faithful steed?" I said.

A flashy Up and Over photo in *The Los Angeles Times* featuring me riding Smidge at the Santa Barbara National had come to his attention. Snapped at the Earl Warren Showgrounds, he asked if I knew that's where the Warren Commission got its name. I didn't but confirmed that the Chief Justice married my mom and dad. The principal shot me a disbelieving glance until I explained that my father's Episcopal side of the family wouldn't accept a rabbi, and my mother's Jewish heritage refused a priest, so they went the legal route with then-Governor Warren instead. It was my grandmother's idea, on the maternal side, who taught me how to enhance events, making them more attractive to the press.

The principal probably imagined an otherwise ordinary school picture made magnificent by my top-of-the-line thoroughbred, and I didn't mention that the one I had in mind for the photo was suggestive of Thelwell's work. We hadn't hammered out terms, so why disillusion him with a shaggy pony?

The conversation turned toward appropriate sanctions such as detention, and I agreed that, in ordinary circumstances, this might be a good idea, but this raised humanitarian concerns about my mother, who was struggling with a new career, fresh heartbreak, and financial difficulty. To add further worry would be an act of cruelty, and who among us had the heart? Better to allow my indiscretion to pass and regard the incident as leading to a fabulous photo opportunity with April in front of the school sign on the appointed day. The principal agreed and excused me from a full day's class to act as April's wrangler, which he suggested was a Tom Sawyer type of punishment.

At River Ridge, the lesson began, with horses evenly spaced around the ring. We have the weight in our heels, and hands are light, in a good recipe for life as well as riding. The other mothers are cozied up in the small spectator stand at the side of the ring, where their clearly defined roles are reflected in each other's admiring eyes. They are devoted wives to indulgent husbands, efficient captains to armies of household staff, and attentive *maters* to the needs of their precious progeny. Their clan pressed, starched, and ferried kids to school, the stable and social functions, while always remaining immaculate. Sitting elbow to elbow under the wooden canopy, they gossiped in rain or shine.

Somehow, Meyera heard the call because she certainly answered it, which was unusual since she preferred to remain sheltered from social discourse, reading a book in the car. Hidden under the shade of a eucalyptus tree is where Meyera could be found, but today, she emerged at an angle before walking unsteadily to join the others in tenuous movements, suggestive of a spider venturing cautiously from its web.

The other mothers no longer share a sense of *bon ami* but watch the lesson in silence. Their conspicuous quiet adds to the sound of hooves beating in a steady one, two, one, two rhythm to which we trot.

Everything feels edgy when our trainer says, "Arch your back and heads up, please."

The ring is large, and at this pace, it takes time to complete each rotation. As I ride past the huddled mass of mothers, only a few seconds are available to listen for clues, but I can see them from any point in the ring, no longer smiling or *kibitzing*. The air of breezy patter has turned sour.

Meyera's presence disturbs the comforting predictability of a regular routine. Her appearance in the cramped spectator shed is so rare as to be unique, and Meyera is talking, but they're not listening. She's smiling, and hoping to attract the same in response, but is studiously ignored.

Another rotation of the ring reveals she's met with disapproving looks, and despite being lit herself, can't seem to manage the same in relation to her cigarette. Miscalculated attempts call more attention to her stupor, and our lesson ends ahead of time.

Several offers to drive us home are parried when my considerable experience behind the wheel is made known, and I safely squired us back to base, where Meyera woke the next morning feeling guilty. She tried to elevate the mood by asking if her sackcloth was back from the dry cleaners, and confirmed she had plenty of ash to work with. While dreadfully sorry, she hoped I still loved her.

"I love you less, but I still love you," I said.

The female furies who passed judgment that day felt differently, but as pampered women, they considered themselves victors in a world crafted around security. Sitting imperiously on their perch by the ring, they were downright smug, but immunity will do that.

The one on the right was J. Crew through and through, with crew neck collars, crew cut hair, and a small face from which a high-pitched voice flew, causing her to chirp rather than converse. Her light-blue eyes matched the light-blue tint of her milky-white skin, giving her a homogenized one percent look. She wore a Cartier watch on the left wrist, with a Cartier diamond tennis bracelet on the right, and preferred brands needing no boost for recognition. An extensive collection of Hermes scarves adorned her ever-present Burberry trench coat, probably purchased in the children's department given her diminutive size.

When she laughed, there was a fluttering noise embellished by a vague motion of her tiny hands, with teeny fingernails painted in the light pink and white French style preferred by her husband. He was an accountant who worked hard, and did well, before being instructed to work harder and deliver more. Rarely did we see him, as he seldom left the office.

The mother on the left was curvaceous, raucous, and low-cut. Her beehive hair, full pouty lips, and lacquered nails featured flashy red. Gesturing animatedly, her polished digits caught the light, resembling the bloodstained talons of a successful hunting hawk. She favored fur coats, but faux or real, who knew? Leopard and zebra prints were always in pole position adorned by a diamond ring so ostentatious, she claimed it was difficult to lift her hand unaided. Her husband joked about needing a crane to lift the Cracker Jack box it came in, but loved the fact that his wife attracted attention.

He was in plumbing, at the ground level of a groundswell in property development when residential, commercial, and municipal buildings needed his wares. His wife joked about his financial rise corresponding with a lapse from grace turning him away from the Father, Son, and Holy Ghost toward a more personal trilogy of install, maintain, and invoice.

Secretly, he snubbed the other guys with their graduate degrees and, having found gold below ground, let the professionals knock themselves out while he enjoyed plenty of free time, and even more money to go with it. When other dads arrived at horse shows in a boring bevy of BMWs and Mercedes, he noted there was no tow bar on his Ferrari, which was flaming red, just like his wife.

Roaring up at shows around midday, he'd unpack gourmet delights from Harrods while passing Moet & Chandon to any and all takers. Flirting with the mothers, he'd hand bottles of Fuller's London Pride to the men, but the concept of giving was subordinate to the real work of creating a world-class impression. In place of academic qualifications, he opted for ancestry, tracing his family back to Scotland starting in 1745. Although delighted with the ancestral crest, he found the clan colors disappointing, but the shop in Edenborough was swift to suggest a different authentic tartan of his own design. Male immunity is another slice of the same affliction.

Mom's attempt to connect, even if briefly, with a brigade that dismissed her in the space of an arched eyebrow will always be remembered. Should the women who passed judgment that day encounter a real problem, God help them.

CHAPTER 25

"How does a week on a Dude ranch sound?" George asked. "There's one in Montana, and if you like, I'll make a reservation."

I couldn't imagine anything more fun, even if Charlie wouldn't be joining us. George explained the dog hadn't been well, and our vet felt the trip was unsuitable, but we'd have fun riding on trails. Although my father was comfortable with mechanized engines and weaponry, he couldn't make the same claim about horses, and decided to reacquaint himself with the art of riding by signing up for a series of six lessons at our local stable. He then took the uncharacteristic step of taking them but found his equestrian ability wasn't what he'd remembered, and the idea of riding all day was losing its luster.

A further complication was that he'd nixed his shot at continuing with the lessons after making an unwanted advance toward the instructor at the conclusion of lesson number five. His good intentions fell by the wayside when placing his hands on her shoulders while going in for a kiss, but she stepped back, ready to say something polite but firm, when he moved in again with his tongue. She immediately took "no thanks" to mean "no way" when the barn owner appeared asking George, in no uncertain terms, to refrain from returning.

As to whether this injunction applied in equal measure to me, we'll never know. I only found out about the incident from neighboring Clayton, who was always up to date with developments at the barn.

Uncomfortable about appraising me of this incident, he said, "As a rule of thumb, men in their forties should steer clear of women not yet twenty. It only causes upset, and if your father were ten years younger, he'd still be ten years too old."

As with his tarnished riding skills, my father's looks were far from what they had been, yet he regarded his appearance as unaltered. His reflection in shop windows, revolving doors, and highly polished brass plaques at the side of elevators provided a reliable level of comfort. Close examination, during his daily scrutiny in front of the bathroom mirror, delivered delusional results, confirming his level of attraction hadn't changed. At least not in his mind's eye, where the airbrush artist of memory provided nips and tucks where needed.

What nostalgia didn't cover, optimistic imagination did, but the George who groped was far from gorgeous. Like many middle-aged men, my father regarded himself as something still spectacular and was surprised when a woman, younger by decades, wouldn't want him. He considered his overture an act of generosity and, if nothing else, was looking to be generous with himself.

George thought Lake Placid with Maude might make an acceptable alternative to riding in Montana, and we three rode together for five hours, from Rye through the Adirondacks, accompanied by Charlie. Our dog refused to go exploring, and I couldn't tell if this was a function of his not feeling well or remembering all too well the time he got skunked. The noxious sulfuric scent that burned his nose was lethal, and seemed to reactivate whenever he got wet. Charlie wanted to stay home. This was a challenge with Maude moving like a storm cloud through the cabin, with the same lack of levity Lurch demonstrated on *The Addams Family*.

Looking to avoid her, I asked for a quarter to buy an *Archie* comic, but she denied this request, and directed me to the club library. A copy of the 1928 club yearbook caught my attention, and it chronicled a checkered past of exclusivity policies that remained in full force, as did the rule forbidding pessimists, faultfinders, or annoying penny-pinching applicants. Women were forbidden to smoke, and men mustn't prefer alcohol over nature, with an addendum denying club access to negros and Hebrews. Little wonder George and Maude felt at home here. They were among the like-minded.

Discussing this over dinner with George wasn't my best choice of topic. He didn't know or care about the club's policy on admission. He regarded it as irrelevant, and I should've left it there, but didn't. While my father was chewing his medium-rare roast beef and reaching for the wine, I asked if he knew about the club's founder, Mr. Dewey, who created the decimal system, which was a great help to library-going girls across America.

George nodded approvingly, and took another bite while I continued to share my recently acquired knowledge by mentioning that Mr. Dewey remained firm on the issue of discrimination. George helped himself to the fresh asparagus while I explained that, rather than renounce racist views, Mr. Dewey resigned as New York State Librarian, which surprised me because I thought borrowing books was for everyone.

George slammed his knife against the side of the plate before moving toward the center of the table, saying, "I don't want to discuss restrictive rules, and none of this has anything to do with you."

Selecting a rule that had to do with him, I said, "If anyone asks whether you like scotch more than the lake, make sure you answer lake over alcohol, or you risk suspension."

My father was furious and said, "I don't know where you're going with this, but allow me to explain. Unlike the delusional view espoused by rock music, the world won't become one, and we won't all get together to love, let alone like, each other. If we're lucky, we'll tolerate one another, and if not, we'll retreat to lakeside locations such as this."

After dinner, we stopped at the sundries shop, where my name was added to the account for an unlimited comic book charge. While this wasn't my intention, I took full advantage until the end of our trip when George informed me that I was to visit Trudy, who was down in the dumps and sulking in the Hamptons. Enlisting my support for her was less of a request and more of a demand, but I agreed to try lifting Trudy's spirits.

"Go away, I'm not in the mood," Trudy said. "If you're hungry, take from the pantry fridge and not the two in the kitchen. Mom volunteered to help cater some tennis events, and Esperanza's been cooking for days."

Trudy's greeting, while not welcoming, had an element of honesty that I found refreshing. I wasn't in the mood either, and more than happy to grant her request to go away. She had a forcefield of anger around her, and after a twelve-month absence, seeing Trudy for the first time was a shock. She'd developed an hourglass figure, in addition to breasts, and while we were both fourteen, I was an ironing board by comparison.

Her perfect complexion was as visible as the piercing heartbreak she suffered, thanks to a jerk called Topher. Even though I was luke-warm where Trudy was concerned, it was hard to see a contemporary in agony, so I tried to inveigle her toward the light, starting with the suggestion she step outside. What I'd have done with her after that, I'd no idea, and never needed to, as she staunchly refused to leave the confines of her admittedly vast bed. She claimed that invitations to whale watching, clambakes, and lobster dinners left her as cold as the crustaceans involved.

While her Pinot Grigio-guzzling parents sat in refined, if not restrained, relaxation, wondering if their daughter would join them, Trudy retained a stiff stance against the world from a supine position.

With all this rigid posturing, the family curved away from each other, mirroring the hardwood banisters and Windsor chairs in their home. Examine them individually, and you'll find activity, but when together, they seemed to halt while occupying the same space located worlds apart.

I became a stand-in for Trudy, seated where she'd have been during meals and presenting myself, along with her apologies, at various events, including a concert she promised to attend with her father.

He was disappointed she couldn't muster enthusiasm, and I put my shoulder to the wheel, saying, "Since you've not seen the light of day, why not try the night? Your dad got the tickets for the two of you, and this is Dionne Warwick we're talking about. She's a legendary talent, and you'll love the performance if you get up, take a shower, and go."

Glaring at me from under the bedspread, Trudy fixed her narrowed eyes on my forehead, as would an assassin before taking aim, and said, "Nothing and no one can compel me to go. I agreed to accompany Dad, but that was before I met Topher, and now, I can't face it. The thought of getting up makes me sick. I want to stay flat on my back, but to do that, I need you to get Dad off mine. You'll have to go in my place. It's the only solution."

I served as Trudy's substitute, and the show was spectacular. Warwick delivered one of the best performances I've ever seen. It inadvertently gave rise to the first real laugh shared with Trudy when she waved me into her room late that night, asking about the concert. If I wasn't mistaken, she seemed genuinely interested to know, and I reported that *Walk On By*, *I Say a Little Prayer* and *What the World Needs Now Is Love* were terrific, but breakup songs *Make It Easy on Yourself* and *I'll Never Fall in Love Again* might've been hard for her to hear. Especially with Mr. Lien shouting, "This groovy music is right on."

Trudy laughed and asked if I was crushed with embarrassment. She laughed even harder when told how hard I tried to pretend I didn't know her father, but he kept dancing in my direction, saying, "Cool man."

She was creased with hysterics, and muffled the sound with a pillow while beating the bed with an almost dead teddy bear.

Coming up for air, Trudy said, "I had no idea he'd pull a stunt like that. You must've been humiliated. Last time I took him shopping in the city was the last time, for sure. The only thing he claimed to understand were the price tags."

Trudy couldn't understand why her parents didn't know how tragic they were, and she planned to be radically different from them both. Topher hadn't taken to them either, but it wasn't a clash of personality rather than attitude toward contraception that caused the problem.

When Topher asked what she used for birth control, Trudy laughed and said, "My parents."

There's something contagious about a sulky teenager that spreads self-pitying sadness like an emotional flu. Under par is how I'd describe the temperature of those two weeks, which I spent wondering what I was doing in constrained circumstances rather than having untold fun in California. Even without Trudy's *gravitas*, I was a bit blue on the East Coast, and in her current condition, she felt the same, irrespective of where I might be. What crushed her at present wouldn't be fatal, and on that cruel aspect of heartbreak, we agreed.

Without either of us noticing, a truce was formed, but it snuck up rather than knocked at the door and, to our mutual surprise, was welcomed in by us both. After that, we didn't talk all that much, but didn't feel the need. Trudy remained ensconced between the covers of her duvet and F. Scott Fitzgerald compendium, reading for research rather than enjoyment while turning each page looking for clues to better her game in the romance arena. I'd lumber up to her bedroom door bearing a tray of tantalizing snacks with which to tempt her, but she sniffed at the sustenance on offer while mumbling an anemic word of thanks before returning to reading.

Only once did she laugh when I said, "Come on, Trude, you've got to eat, or the next guy will be hugging a skeleton."

Esperanza was a film buff, and we'd watch *The 4:30 Movie* together while consuming copious quantities of crab legs and blueberry pie. Seared scallops served to restore Trudy's reluctant appetite, allowing her self-styled hunger strike to be broken by portions of chocolate mousse crossing the emotional picket line. Participants in the last days of the Roman Empire probably dined the same way, but we had more time and, by the look of it, greater resources.

Esperanza understood the difficulty with Trudy in particular and the family in general. Having worked in service to the Lien's for a long time, she had no illusions about who they were when most themselves at home and described them as, 'People with everything to hand and nothing to hold onto.'

They had a family car, which remained in East Hampton. No one could face traffic on the Long Island Expressway. Esperanza gunned the engine in a way that reflected her style of cooking which was quick, confident, and commanding. Delivering us to Sag Harbor, we had a sneak peek past John Steinbeck's house, which was off-limits to the public, but we'd watched *East of Eden* and wanted a glimpse of his secluded hideaway.

I envied him the freedom to travel with his dog Charlie and couldn't wait to be reunited with mine. Esperanza claimed that classic movies improved her English, and new vocabulary words were easy to spot since she tried to pronounce them with a mid-Atlantic accent. When separating egg whites from the yoke or corn from its husk, she'd say, "Darling, I can't bear to be parted."

Esperanza and I exchanged the only hug on my departure. Trudy, however, surprised me with a high-five before I left and said, "Keep it together and thanks for trying to get me that way."

Returning to Manhattan, my arrival was celebrated at Luchow's, which was surrounded by Tiffany glass, marble, and mahogany.

Maude indicated toward the Diamond Jim Brady room, claiming it was named after an infamous hood, but Aunt Louise said, "Had Brady been a gangster, he'd have been a damn sight better at it than most I've met."

Recommending the Wiener schnitzel, Aunt Louise felt it superior to the venison once preferred by Roosevelt. She insisted I try the pumpernickel bread, trumping anything available in Germany. Maude was mumbling to the waiter while declining an offer of Pilsner, and Aunt Louise suggested I look at the art, which reflected her fondness for Flemish masters. Should I wish to count the number of deer heads mounted on the walls, I'd be eligible to enter the beer stein competition, and if I won, George could claim his Gaffel Kolsch on the house, which they'd both find refreshing.

Maude mentioned that it was a shame my father couldn't join us, but Marlene Dietrich's *Lili Marlene* could be heard, and Aunt Louise hummed along, putting some effort into Edith Piaf's *La Vie en rose,* which followed. Pointing to the building across the street, Louise said it was occupied by Luchow's partner, who was big in pianos and went by the name of Steinway. She thought it was a stroke of genius to open musical showrooms next to the best Viennese Sacher torte this side of Austria, but Maude said that not everything is sweet.

Without sugarcoating it, my grandmother confirmed that our dog Charlie was dead. Aunt Louise agreed it was a loss and asked Maude to hand me a handkerchief. Anyone could see that I was crying.

Maude rustled around her handbag and retrieved a mangled tissue while saying, "Charlie was ill and didn't have long for this world. You wouldn't want the dog to suffer, would you?"

No, I did not. I wanted my grandmother to suffer and, knowing she detested tears, released a torrential downfall while sobbing, "Poor Charlie, I'm going to miss him."

"Oh dear," Aunt Louise said. "I knew it was a mistake to tell her in a public place. Why not go to the ladies' room and wash your face with cold water to regain composure? When you get back, we'll have the check and go."

The idea of counting mounted heads initially struck me as absurd, but with news of Charlie's demise, recording dead deer seemed appropriate. It gave me a chance to collect myself while processing the loss, but Aunt Louise was transported by Edith Piaf's *Non, je ne regrette rien*, as we left the restaurant.

My father was contrite about missing the lunch and said that Charlie was a magnificent dog who'd always be remembered in our hearts. To take our minds off our troubles, he suggested we have dinner at Benihana the following night. George knew how to eat his way out of a crisis, and I readily agreed to showstopping entertainment at the teppanyaki bar on West 56th Street.

Clayton from next door was stacking wood out back the next morning, and I ran to see him, but before I said a word, he guessed I knew about the dog.

Frowning while shrugging his shoulders, Clayton said, "I know you and that hound were close. He'll be missed, but I'll try to last as long as possible so you'll always know there's someone around. Don't worry. One way or another, I'll make sure everything's okay."

During dinner at Benihana, I mentioned the loss of our dog, but George's demeanor dropped from sympathetic to observational, then all the way down to critical. He mentioned the father/daughter dance at the club, scheduled for the following weekend, thinking it a good idea for us to attend.

Maude was scheduled to take me for a makeover, which I resisted, but my father said, "You need to take an interest in makeup, nylons, and bras. Start visiting a reputable hairdresser, and stop biting your nails. Some significant changes are necessary if you're to look halfway decent for the end of summer *soirée*."

Shopping for this equipment was unappealing, and Maude's suggestion of heels was repulsive. *Why not bind my feet along with free will*, I wondered, but with summer coming to an end, acquiescence was the only strategic move. Following Maude's lead, my hair was cut into a sensible bob with high-maintenance bangs before being dyed brassy blonde. A pair of pumps complimented a new push-up bra, and mascara foisted upon me. Nylon stockings proved a bridge too far, being a torment to put on and a pleasure to take off, which I did in the ladies' room after the second dance.

While swaying to the sounds of *My Heart Belongs to Daddy*, I'd yet to learn that something is needed between foot and leather, making my dogs bark as I limped with blisters for days afterward. The event itself went off without a hitch, except for my eye-rolling, which was a constant problem. Other than that, our farewell to summer *soiree* was a successful note to end on.

Meyera was waiting at LAX and looked into the middle distance while cleaning her glasses. Smiling in a general way, she observed the crowd of disembarking passengers parading past in a steady stream of stale air breathing jet-lagged souls. When she saw me, her smile grew larger. Enthusiastically waving, she noticed my hair and screamed, right there in the middle of the airport where two ground attendants came over to check on us. The moment we walked through our front door, she went straight to the phone, and dialed George's number with trembling hands. When he answered, she was so angry that he could've heard her shouting from LA.

"What in the hell got hold of you?" Meyera asked. "I allow visitation rights assuming you'll use good judgement, and what happens? You send her back looking like a Park Avenue prostitute, and my daughter isn't going to look like a high-class hooker."

Less concerned about my appearance, I considered the prostitute aspect of Meyera's criticism, having had no idea there were women of the evening strutting along Park Avenue, where Joan Barker lived.

As I looked at a mirror on my dresser, Meme said, "It doesn't look all that bad, and you'll have a new style in no time."

Meme was right about the hair, and, at age fourteen, I'd yet to be ensnared in the net of vanity, remaining a *bona fide* tomboy. Although I had little to no concern about personal appearance, Meyera accused George of ruining it. Rather than usher in attractive change, she said he was the conduit of catastrophe.

He must've disagreed because Meyera said, "I don't give a good God damn what you think."

While I considered the distinction between a good God damn and one of less merit, Meme laughed and said, "Your parents mistook a luxurious life for one of freedom, but money only buys freedom from one worry, and that's about money."

She handed me a manila envelope bearing the Department of Social Services insignia and said it contained information about my birth parents, which she'd briefly perused. Sketchy details concerning my father proved inconclusive, but my birth mother's background was spelled out in detail, and Meme suggested I take my time rather than rush to read the file.

Knowing I'd been delivered by cesarean section, leaving the natural mother with a scar, every year on my birthday, I wondered about a woman who was, likely, wondering about me. Speculation as to who she was and what her circumstances were remained a mystery until this pack was delivered, and I grasped the envelope as if it were a key to universal understanding.

Never had I smelled a piece of stationary, but on this occasion, I did, hoping it might contain a sliver of my biological mother's scent. Would I find out what her laugh sounded like or what she looked like when dancing? Having researched the top ten radio hits surrounding the time of my birth, I longed to see a predecessor, of precisely me, singing the same songs I had access to.

What I desperately wanted most was a phone number that would connect me with my birth mother, Becky, so that I could whisper a deep, heartfelt thanks for loving me enough to let me go. Aladdin's cave was about to open, and I was first surprised, then stunned, by the results of this search.

Both Meyera and Becky were thirty when I arrived, but that's the end of any similarity between them. The document revealed that the actual end of my birth mother's life happened when I was five and flying coast-to-coast, unknowingly looking down on her as I traversed Utah. This flat, alkaline state housed a double-wide trailer in which Becky resided, along with an accompaniment of similarly smack-addicted pals, who she managed to shake during my gestation in La Jolla, California. I doubt she made it home from the hospital in quite the same level of comfort I did when departing on our private plane.

Although my birth *mater* was a heroin addict, Meme characterized her as a heroine for allowing me to join their tribe. Dodging a hailstorm of bullets provides the impetus to forgive even the most negligent for absolutely everything, but this shocking revelation still wasn't enough to make me kowtow back East.

George called the next day demanding I spend Christmas in New York and, when I declined, he presented me with an ultimatum of visit or be banned.

Hoping to find some middle ground, I suggested we say *a bientot* rather than *adieu,* but my father was an all-or-nothing kind of a guy who said, "It's my way or the highway."

Weighing the impact of my answer, I concluded that tendering my resignation wasn't an attractive alternative, yet I felt compelled to elect one side or the other. Someone had to cut something adrift, or we'd all perish in this unwinnable war. I'd had my fill of saber-rattling and was sick to the back teeth of sweeping changes. If this meant financial hardship, I'd rather cope on my own than cower in questionable company. Hard graft and grapple would form the balance of my bank account going forward. Character, rather than cash, would have to carry the day. As anyone who's quit a demeaning job will understand, there's a short-lived high derived from driving away, before issues of who pays for the gas are raised.

Taking all this into consideration, I said, "Now that I've landed with Meyera, I'll stay home."

In which direction I'd venture next was yet to be determined, but George was adamant about cutting me adrift should I fail to toe the line.

"I mean it," my father said, "If you refuse to return for the holidays, this is the very last time we will ever speak."

Empty threats weren't part of George's repertoire, and as a consequence, I never heard his voice again. We did, however, meet again, after a fashion, when I attended his funeral seventeen years later. Flying out at short notice, it was with trepidation that I entered the mortuary chapel, where the assembled guests were strangers to me, although my identity was known to them.

Tears are *de rigueur* on such occasions yet mine refused to fall. Taking refuge in the ladies' room, I retrieved a small sheet of paper and pen from my purse, with which I wrote a note expressing sadness that the rift between us had remained unrepaired. When no one was looking, I covertly dropped it into the open casket and said a prayer by way of a final goodbye.

Once the memorial service was over, I noticed a young woman sitting by herself in a quiet corner.

Closer scrutiny revealed that it must be my stepmother, and charging toward her, I said, "Susan, how I've missed you. It's understandable why you left George, but how could you forget about me? All these years, I've wondered where you went, how you were doing and what became of you. Main thing is that you're here, and despite the sad circumstances, so am I."

Nodding her head sympathetically while waiting for me to finish speaking, she straightened her posture and said, "I'm so sorry to tell you that Susan died three years ago. I'm not your stepmother, but I am your sister."

Real tears of both loss and joy fell with abandon. Cynthia and I instantly assumed the role of siblings more naturally than if we'd been raised together without skipping a beat. Reuniting with my sister was the happy Hollywood ending I longed for, but the best bit, was that we had a future to share.

ACKNOWLEDGMENTS

I owe a tremendous debt of gratitude to the following people whose support contributed in large measure toward bringing this book to fruition:

James Maw, made a difficult journey downright fun, and as a writing mentor, managed to blend efficiency with patience.

Early readers Nicolaus Mills, Janet Kerr, and Kaya Axelsson combined candor with compassion to provide invaluable feedback.

Nadia Joseph, the most talented editor imaginable, kept the narrative (and author) on track.

Zoe Gray, Barbara Bryant, David Gluckman, and Jan Martin applied punctilious attention (let alone tolerance) needed to correct innumerable spelling mistakes.

Legendary media lawyer, James Harman, cast his expert eye over contractual matters continuing a tradition of hand-holding that extends over more decades than either of us care to count.

Deep appreciation goes to Woodbridge Publishers in general, and my dream team in particular: Scarlett Mcardle, Ilaria Licari, Alex Griffin, Megan White, Issac Taylor, Ted Morris, and Amber Mason.

My sister, CJ Grace, generously gave unconditional consent concerning my intention to write about our family with unflinching honesty and supported the process by acting as Chief Technology Officer during countless drafts.

Profound recognition goes to Sandy Van Zandt. More than just a cousin, she is a beloved sherpa, showing me the way every day of my life.

I respect, salute, and adore each of you more than any combination of words could ever express.

ABOUT THE AUTHOR

Cat Buchanan is a media lawyer, television producer, and nonfiction writer. After graduating from Sarah Lawrence College, Pepperdine University School of Law, and London School of Economics and Political Science, she worked as in-house lawyer for Granada Television. Moving to the independent sector, Cat created highly successful rock 'n' roll documentaries. A long-standing resident of London, she has swapped swimming in Malibu for hiking on Hampstead Heath. *Girl in Flight* is her first memoir.

24032563R00157